LOOKING BACK

MESOPOTAMIA AND THE NEAR EAST

FROM 10,000 BC TO 539 BC

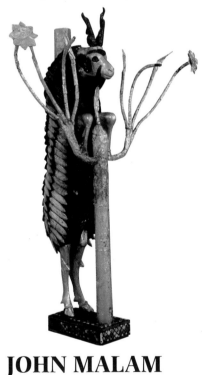

JOHN MALAM

EVANS BROTHERS LIMITED

Evans Brothers Limited
2A Portman Mansions
Chiltern Street
London W1M 1LE

© Evans Brothers Limited 1999
First published 1999

British Library Cataloguing in Publication Data

Malam, John
  Mesopotamia and the ancient near east : from 10,000 BC to 539 BC. - (Looking Back)
  1.Iraq - Civilization - To 634 - Juvenile literature
  2.Iraq - History - To 634 - Juvenile literature
  3.Middle East - History - To 622 - Juvenile literature
  I.Title
  935
  ISBN 0237518856

Editor: Nicola Barber
Designer: Neil Sayer
Picture research: Victoria Brooker
Maps: Nick Hawken
Production: Jenny Mulvanny

Consultant: Dr Alasdair Livingstone, Reader in Assyriology, Department of Ancient History and Archaeology, The University of Birmingham

Printed in Spain by GRAFO, S.A. - Bilbao

Title page: A golden ram, c. 2600 BC, from the Great Death Pit at Ur. It is one of a pair which may have been used as furniture supports.

Note about dates
There are still many problems with dating the past in Mesopotamia. The earliest periods lack documentary evidence, for which archaeologists rely on scientific dating techniques such as radiocarbon. The margin of error within these dates increases with the age of the date, and in this book a mid-point date has been used. For the historical period, problems with dates occur due to the Mesopotamian calendar. The dates of kings' reigns and periods of civilisation given are those generally accepted by today's scholars.

Acknowledgements

cover (background image) British Museum/Bridgeman Art Library (main image) Louvre, Paris/Bridgeman Art Library **title page** British Museum **page 6** Ancient Art and Architecture **page 9** Philip Wayre/NHPA **page 12** Daniel O'Leary/Panos Pictures **page 13** David Heath/Life File **page 14** Trip/H Rogers **page 16** Louvre, Paris/Bridgeman Art Library **page 17** British Museum/Bridgeman Art Library **page 19** Louvre, Paris/Bridgeman Art Library **page 20** Ancient Art and Architecture **page 21** Louvre, Paris/Bridgeman Art Library **page 23** British Museum **page 24** British Museum/Bridgeman Art Library **page 25** Kunsthistorisches Museum, Vienna/Bridgeman Art Library **page 27** Bagdad Museum **page 29** Louvre, Paris/Lauros-Giraudon/Bridgeman Art Library **page 30** British Museum **page 31** AKG Photo **page 32** Ancient Art and Architecture **page 33** British Museum/Bridgeman Art Library **page 34** Werner Forman **page 35** British Museum **page 36** AKG **page 37** British Museum **page 38** Werner Forman **page 40** British Museum/Bridgeman Art Library **page 41** Louvre, Paris/Lauros-Giraudon/Bridgeman Art Library **page 42** Christine Osborne Pictures **page 43** Private Collection/Bridgeman Art Library **page 44** (top) British Museum/Bridgeman Art Library (bottom) Louvre, Paris/Bridgeman Art Library **page 45** (top) British Museum (bottom) British Museum/Bridgeman Art Library **page 46** Louvre, Paris/Bridgeman Art Library **page 47** British Museum/Bridgeman Art Library **page 48** British Museum/Bridgeman Art Library **page 49** British Museum **page 51** Werner Forman **page 52** Iraq Museum, Baghdad/Bridgeman Art Library **page 53** British Museum **page 54** British Museum/Bridgeman Art Library **page 55** British Museum **page 56** Ancient Art and Architecture **page 57** British Museum/Bridgeman Art Library **page 58** Trip/B Vikander **page 59** S Kay/Life File

CONTENTS

INTRODUCTION

This book is about an ancient region of the Near East. The name we use for the area is 'Mesopotamia'. The book covers about 9500 years of history, from 10,000 BC to 539 BC.

It was the Ancient Greeks who first called the region Mesopotamia. This was their name for the strip of land that lay between the rivers Euphrates and Tigris, in what is now the modern country of Iraq. Today, however, when historians and archaeologists talk about Mesopotamia they are actually referring to a much wider area covering the whole of Iraq, together with south-eastern Turkey and eastern Syria. In ancient times this huge area was home to many different civilisations.

A TALE OF TWO RIVERS

Much of Mesopotamia today is a wide, flat floodplain that lies between the region's two great rivers – the Euphrates, and its faster-flowing neighbour, the Tigris. As they flow southeast through Iraq, the Euphrates and the Tigris join together to form a single river, the Shatt al-Arab, which empties into the Persian Gulf.

Today, the ruins of the city of Ur lie in the middle of an arid floodplain. In ancient times, Ur stood on the banks of the River Euphrates.

The Tigris and Euphrates flood twice each year. The main flood is in April and May, when the rivers are swelled by water from melting winter snow in the northern highlands, and by spring rains. When the rivers are in flood, vast quantities of sediment are washed

INTRODUCTION

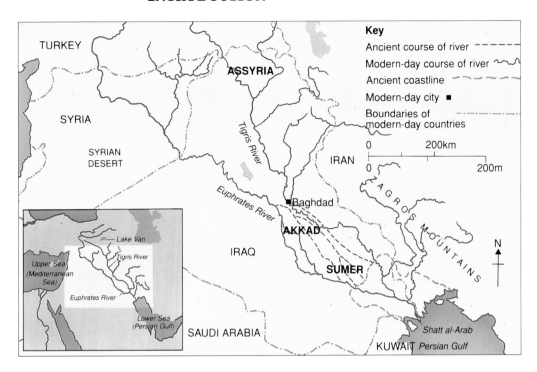

This map shows both the ancient and present-day courses of the Euphrates and Tigris rivers.

downstream. The sediment is dumped at the head of the Persian Gulf.

The landscape the Mesopotamians knew looked very different from today. It is important to examine these changes in landscape to understand the story of Mesopotamia. Both the Euphrates and the Tigris flowed along different routes, much closer together (see map). The River Euphrates was divided into branches, and many towns were built along its banks. However, the Euphrates now flows further west than it did in Mesopotamian times, and the Tigris has moved further to the east.

Another reason why the landscape has changed is because of the sediment deposited at the head of the Persian Gulf by the two rivers. In Mesopotamian times the coastline of the Persian Gulf reached further north, and the Euphrates and Tigris flowed straight to the sea. However, over the past 5000 years the rivers have dropped so much sediment

A CLOSER LOOK

Between the Euphrates and Tigris rivers lies the floodplain. It has a hot and arid climate. Ruins of ancient towns and cities stand isolated on the floodplain – but in Mesopotamian times many of these settlements were on the banks of the Euphrates, linked together by this great river. As the course of the river changed, the old towns of Mesopotamia became stranded on the floodplain, far from the river's life-giving water.

into the Persian Gulf that it has become silted up, and the coastline has been pushed south. The open sea is now about 250 kilometres further away from the ancient cities of southern Mesopotamia than it was in Mesopotamian times.

Mesopotamia is often called 'the cradle of civilisation'. Western civilisation traces its very beginnings to Mesopotamia, and to the people who lived there. This was where some of the world's first experiments in agriculture and irrigation were carried out, where writing was invented, where the wheel was first used, where mathematics was born, and where the world's first cities were built.

ANCIENT PEOPLES OF MESOPOTAMIA

People	Where they lived	When they lived	Main town
Hunter-gatherers and first farmers	Along the Euphrates and Tigris rivers	10,000-3700 BC	—
First town dwellers	Southern Mesopotamia	3700-2900 BC	Uruk
Sumerians	In Sumer (southern Mesopotamia)	2900-2330 BC	Ur
Akkadians	In Akkad (northern Mesopotamia)	2334-2193 BC	Akkad
Third Dynasty of Ur	Sumer and Akkad	2112-2004 BC	Ur
Amorites	Sumer	2004-1792 BC	—
Babylonians	In Babylonia (the area that used to be Akkad)	1792-1595 BC	Babylon
Kassites	In Babylonia	1595-1365 BC	Babylon
Assyrians	In Assyria (northern Iraq and southern Turkey)	1365-629 BC	Nimrud, then Nineveh
Chaldeans	In Chaldea (southern Iraq and Kuwait)	625-539 BC	Babylon

Although other peoples lived in Mesopotamia in the period covered by this book, it is only those in this list who are looked at in detail.

FROM HUNTERS TO FARMERS

In the 1950s, American archaeologists, led by Ralph Solecki, discovered a group of nine skeletons buried deep inside a huge cave at Shanidar, in northern Iraq. This was a cemetery of prehistoric people known as Neanderthals (so-called after a place in Germany where remains of this particular type of early human were first found). The bones were about 45,000 years old. They proved that Neanderthals were the first humans in the Near East, and that they lived there during the Ice Age.

A good starting point for the story of Mesopotamia is with the ending of the last Ice Age, which scientists usually date to about 12,000 years ago. At this time in the Near East the climate began to warm up and rainfall increased. Trees of the forest, such as cedar, juniper, oak and pine, liked the warmer, moister conditions and began to colonise the high ground. The lowland area, through which the Euphrates and Tigris rivers flowed, consisted of treeless grassland (steppe) in the north and desert in the south.

The region was home to many species of animals. Herds of gazelle, fallow deer, asses and aurochs

The Asiatic mouflon is the ancestor of the domesticated sheep.

(wild cattle) grazed the grasslands. Deer, Asiatic mouflon (wild sheep) and Bezoar goats lived in the mountains, and boars in the marsh country. These animals were preyed on by carnivores such as jackals, wolves, bears, lynxes, hyenas, cheetahs, leopards, tigers and lions. There were also smaller animals including foxes, hares, hedgehogs, tortoises, snakes, lizards and frogs. Fish and shellfish lived in lakes and in the Persian Gulf. Ostriches, partridges, ducks and geese were just some of the region's many birds.

It was into this environment that small bands of wandering hunter-gatherers came, attracted by the area's plentiful supplies of edible plants and animals, and good sources of fresh water to drink.

The hunter-gatherers

The hunter-gatherers of the Near East led a nomadic lifestyle. They were wanderers who drifted across the landscape from one temporary campsite to the next. They moved about in small groups, which were probably based around family units, hunting animals and gathering plants.

Evidence for prehistoric hunter-gatherers in the Near East is hard to find. The very nature of their unsettled, wandering lifestyles means they have left few recognisable marks on the landscape. What we can say about them is based on studying hunter-gatherer communities of recent times.

No doubt the hunter-gatherers of the ancient Near East had a great understanding of the animals and plants around them. Perhaps they chose to hunt only mature, male animals, leaving young animals to grow and females to bear young. They would have observed which wild grasses produced the best seed heads. Perhaps each group returned at the same time each year to a particular area on the grassy plain that they regarded as 'their patch', keen to gather its abundant grass seeds. Perhaps one year there was a bumper crop, so they stayed weeks or months instead of the usual few days, enjoying nature's harvest. And maybe this was the moment of change – one of the greatest turning-points in the history of humankind – when hunter-gatherers in the Near East realised that nature could be controlled. As they began to domesticate plants and animals they slowly gave up their nomadic lifestyle, settling in villages and working on the land as farmers.

DOMESTICATING PLANTS

Among the many different kinds of wild grass that grew in the Near East were einkorn and emmer wheat. They played an important role in the development of early farming.

Einkorn and emmer produced large seed heads, packed with good-sized grains. The first farmers gathered the grains of these two plants in the wild, in preference to plants that produced fewer seeds. However, both einkorn and emmer suffered from brittle ears that snapped easily, and both shed their grains quickly. Neither was particularly good for growing as a crop. Then, at some point, wild emmer wheat cross-bred with wild goat grass. The resulting mixture, known as a hybrid, was a plant with tough ears that held on to its grains. When the first farmers realised the advantages of the hybrid plant, they chose it as their main crop.

With each year that passed, the hybrid emmer crop produced more

This arc-shaped area is known as the Fertile Crescent.

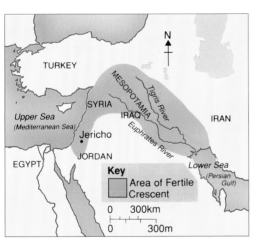

A CLOSER LOOK
In 1916, the American archaeologist, James Breasted, coined the term 'Fertile Crescent'. He noticed that a crescent-shaped area of land extended along the valley of the Euphrates and Tigris rivers, west to the shores of the Mediterranean Sea, then south to Egypt. It was an area characterised by dry summers and rainy winters, where the wild ancestors of wheat and barley grew, and where wild sheep and goats lived. It was here, within this broad arc of land, that the right conditions existed for the first experiments in food production to take place, some time around 9000 BC.

People gather the wheat harvest along the banks of the Euphrates today – a scene little changed in thousands of years.

and better grains of wheat. By weeding out the weakest plants and leaving only the strongest to grow, farmers turned a wild plant into a domesticated one. They gained control of nature and were able to produce more food.

Other plants domesticated by farmers in the Near East were barley, peas, lentils, carrots, turnips and leeks. The cultivation of all these plants began to happen from about 9000 BC onwards.

DOMESTICATING ANIMALS

At about the same time that the first farmers of the Near East were domesticating plants, the long process of taming wild animals to work for humankind had begun.

Young animals were taken from the wild and were raised to provide a guaranteed supply of meat and milk. As they produced their young, their numbers increased. The next step in the process of domesticating animals was when people realised that large numbers of animals could be kept together in flocks and herds. Large, aggressive animals were killed off before they became too dangerous and before they could breed. By doing this over a long period of time, wild animals evolved into domesticated breeds which were smaller and more docile than their wild ancestors.

Probably the world's first domesticated animal was the dog. It was descended from the wolf, and was chosen to live and work with humans because of its suitability for hunting other animals. By around 7000 BC, other Near Eastern animals had evolved from their wild ancestors into domesticated breeds: the goat from the wild Bezoar goat, the sheep from the Asiatic mouflon (a wild sheep with curved horns

From Hunters to Farmers

and a woolly coat), the pig from the wild boar, the cow from the aurochs (a large wild ox with horns), and the cat from the wild cat. By about 2000 BC the donkey and the horse were domesticated, too.

The first villages

Humankind had taken two great steps along the path to civilisation. People in the Near East had learned how to grow crops and how to keep animals. The conditions were now right for an even greater step to be taken. Instead of living in temporary campsites, people began to build permanent places in which to live. These places were the world's first villages, the most ancient of which is about 11,000 years old.

Sheep are an important part of people's livelihoods in the Near East today, just as they were 9000 years ago.

As people settled in villages, the population began to increase. New tools were invented to help farmers with their crops, such as sickles for reaping wheat and barley, and ploughs to till the fields. People discovered how to build ovens in which to bake bread, and from this invention came the idea of baking clay to make pottery.

People learned how to extract linen thread from the flax plant. They spun flax and wool, weaving them into cloth for clothes, bedding and sails. They found out that beer could be made from barley, and wine from grapes. Since there was no longer any need for people to move from campsite to campsite, as they had done before they lived in villages, they began to acquire possessions, such as furniture.

Another key stage in the development of civilisation is the concept of trading goods over a wide area. As villagers produced more grain than they could use themselves, or made more pots than they needed, they traded the surplus for goods that they could not produce themselves, These goods included shells and semi-precious stones which were used to make necklaces, and obsidian, a black volcanic glass, which was used to make sharp cutting tools. Obsidian came from the area around Lake Van, in present-day Turkey but it was widely traded among the first farming villages of the Near East. We know this because cutting tools made from . obsidian have been found throughout the Near East – some more than 1000 kilometres from Lake Van.

This skull comes from the town of Jericho in Jordan, one the world's earliest farming communities, c. 9000 BC. The inhabitants of Jericho worshipped their ancestors, decorating their skulls with painted clay and shells.

FROM VILLAGES TO EMPIRES

The first villages in Mesopotamia were built in areas where there was enough rainfall for crops to grow and enough pasture for farm animals to graze. At first, villages were confined to the grassy northern part of Mesopotamia where there was frequent rainfall. But from about 6500 BC onwards, villages began to appear in southern Mesopotamia. They stood on the fertile floodplain between the Euphrates and Tigris rivers – an area of low rainfall where it was essential for farmers to dig irrigation canals to take water to their crops.

The villages of this early period, whether they were built in the north or in the south of Mesopotamia, existed in the prehistoric period – the time before the invention of writing. Because of this we do not know what the people called themselves.

THE UBAID CULTURE

Ubaid is the name used by archaeologists for a culture which flourished for about 2800 years, from

A CLOSER LOOK

Archaeologists have invented names for the groups of people (called cultures) who lived in Mesopotamia before the invention of writing. Each group of people had a distinctive style of pottery, which is how archaeologists tell them apart:

Culture	Flourished	Built their villages in
Hassuna	6500-6000 BC	Northern Mesopotamia
Samarra	6200-5700 BC	Northern Mesopotamia
Halaf	6000-5100 BC	Northern Mesopotamia
Ubaid	6500-3700 BC	Southern Mesopotamia
Uruk	3700-2900 BC	Southern Mesopotamia

CHAPTER THREE

6500 BC to 3700 BC. The name comes from Tell el-Ubaid, the modern name of an ancient village. The Ubaid people built their villages in the south of Mesopotamia, in the marshes at the head of the Persian Gulf. Their houses were made from bricks of mud, baked hard by the sun. Farmers irrigated their wheat and barley crops by building canals which channelled water from the Euphrates, especially when the river was swelled with floodwater in the spring. Farmers also kept sheep, goats and pigs. Fishermen fished in the marshes and at sea. Ubaid potters made white pots painted with bold patterns, as well as pottery figurines.

Farmers of the Ubaid villages mastered the food production process, and were able to supply enough food to sustain an increasing population. Their craftworkers perfected the use of clay, copper, and stone. Their merchants traded goods with other villages. Religion played a growing part in everyday life, and no doubt each village had someone who was seen as its leader. Under these circumstances the right conditions existed for the world's first towns to emerge.

URUK – AN EARLY TOWN

Uruk is in southern Mesopotamia. In ancient times it was on the banks of the Euphrates. Uruk is

This pottery figure of a bull was made by people of the Ubaid culture, c. 4000 BC.

important because it was one of the first towns in Mesopotamia, with a sizeable population of up to 50,000 people.

There were three main reasons why Uruk grew so big: it controlled a vast amount of agricultural land; it was close to trade routes and it occupied a good position close to the Euphrates. For all these reasons, people were attracted to Uruk. As more people settled in the town, so it spread out across the plain until it covered 500 hectares of land – bigger than Rome under the Roman emperors.

Not only was Uruk one of the first towns, but it was here that Mesopotamian culture began to emerge from its prehistoric period. Archaeologists have found more than 5000 clay tablets at Uruk on which pictures of animals and wheat are marked. Next to the pictures are signs that represent numbers. This shows that the people of Uruk had discovered a method of recording numbers of animals and amounts of crops (see page 46).

The decorated box known as the 'Royal Standard of Ur' was probably the sounding box of a musical instrument, such as a lyre. On this side are scenes from everyday Sumerian life. On the reverse are scenes of war (see page 45).

SUMER AND THE SUMERIANS

From about 3000 BC onwards, the changes that had transformed Uruk into a town were copied throughout southern Mesopotamia. Villages became towns, and towns became cities. This southern region was called Sumer, and its dark-haired, fair-skinned inhabitants were the Sumerians.

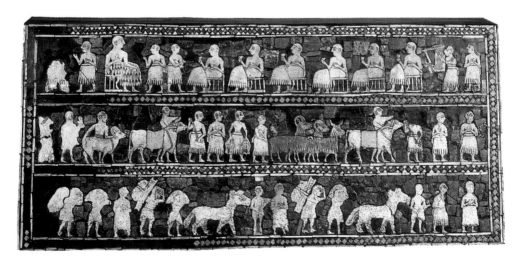

As the Sumerian cities grew, so a system of government developed (see page 26). Each city was ruled by a king and controlled the land immediately around it. Sumer became divided into a patchwork of small city-states, the most important of which was the city of Ur (see page 32). Palaces and temples were built in the towns, and high walls were put around them for protection from flooding and attack. Most significantly of all, the Sumerians invented writing (see page 46).

AKKAD AND THE AKKADIANS

This map shows the lands of Sumer and Akkad and their major cities. The capital city of the Akkadian Empire, itself called Akkad, may lie close to Baghdad, the modern capital of Iraq.

While Sumerian cities flourished in the south, the northern part of Mesopotamia became home to a group of people called the Akkadians. They came from the west, possibly from what is now Arabia. Like their Sumerian neighbours, the Akkadians built cities.

The Akkadians, led by Sargon the Great (see page 27), conquered Sumer. Under Sargon the two regions were united and, for the first time in its history, Mesopotamia was ruled as a single country.

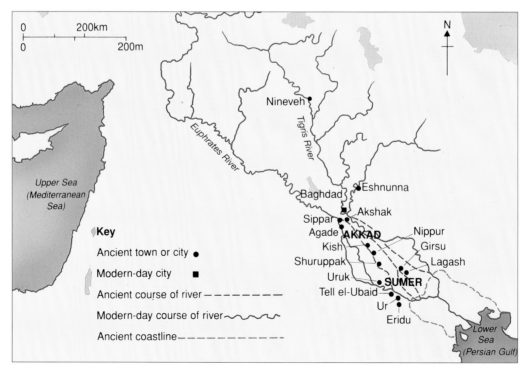

FROM VILLAGES TO EMPIRES

A statue of Gudea, the Sumerian king whose name meant 'the Chosen One'

Akkadian became the official language for written documents and it spread throughout Sumer, replacing the Sumerians' own language which was eventually forgotten. The Akkadians adopted the Sumerian system of writing to write down their own language. They standardised weights and measures across the whole region. They also took over some of the Sumerians' ideas about government (see page 26), and some of their gods and goddesses see page 38).

The Akkadian Empire expanded across a large part of the Near East, covering much of present-day Iran and Syria. At its greatest extent it stretched from the Upper Sea (the Mediterranean Sea) in the north, to the Lower Sea (the Persian Gulf) in the south. But the Akkadians found it difficult to control their vast empire. There were constant uprisings among the people they ruled. Eventually, the Akkadians lost all their lands except for their capital city of Akkad.

SUMER AND THE THIRD DYNASTY OF UR

The end of the Akkadian Empire meant that the Sumerian cities in southern Mesopotamia were set free from foreign control, regaining their independence. For a short time the Sumerian culture flourished once more. Powerful new kings emerged to rule the old Sumerian cities. One of the first of these new rulers was Gudea, king of the Sumerian city of Lagash. He gained

19

The ziggurat at Ur, now partly restored, was dedicated to the moon god Nanna. It was originally about 25 metres tall, with three platforms.

control over other cities in Sumer, revived old trade routes and restored old temples.

Ur-Nammu was even more powerful than Gudea. He founded a dynasty (family) of rulers at the old Sumerian city of Ur, known as the Third Dynasty of Ur (2112-2004 BC). Ur-Nammu was proclaimed the 'King of Sumer and Akkad'. He restored temples and began to build tall towers with steps, known as ziggurats, beside them (see page 32). When Shulgi, Ur-Nammu's son, became king of Ur, he decided that the city should be the centre of a great empire. His army conquered the peoples who lived to the north of Sumer, and others who lived to the east. The empire of Ur became as large as the old empire of the Akkadians. But like the Akkadians before them, the Sumerian kings of Ur found it difficult to control their empire. One by one, the conquered cities broke free. Ur's power decreased and, in 2004 BC, the city was invaded. Ibbi-Sin, the last Sumerian king, was led away in captivity, never to return. The great days of Ur were over.

FROM VILLAGES TO EMPIRES

THE AMORITE KINGDOMS

As the Third Dynasty of Ur collapsed, Mesopotamia and the Near East entered a period of unrest. Groups of people moved across the region in search of safe places to live. The Amorites made up one of these groups. They came from somewhere west of Mesopotamia, perhaps from an area which now belongs to Syria.

The Amorites settled in Mesopotamia and took control of the Sumerian cities. Under the Amorites each city was ruled by a king. Mesopotamia was no longer part of a large empire: it was broken down into small kingdoms which were often in conflict with each other.

Hammurabi, king of Babylon. He is wearing a royal headdress.

THE RISE AND FALL OF BABYLON

Babylon began as a small town in central Mesopotamia, on the banks of the Euphrates. In 1894 BC it was captured by an Amorite chief called Sumu-abum. Babylon became the capital of his kingdom, and he became the first king in a long line of rulers. One of the descendants of Sumu-abum was a king called Hammurabi.

Hammurabi became king of Babylon in 1792 BC. He established Babylon as the greatest city in the Near East. Hammurabi also conquered neighbouring cities in north and south Mesopotamia, and Babylon became the capital of a new Mesopotamian empire. One of Hammurabi's most important acts was to draw up a set of laws which everyone in his empire had to follow (see page 29).

The kings who came after Hammurabi gradually lost control of his empire. Cities rebelled, and the empire became weak. Invaders called Kassites, who may have come from central Asia, moved into Mesopotamia and took cities that had belonged to Babylon. In 1595 BC a Kassite king, Agum-Kakrime, seized the throne of Babylon itself.

The Kassite kings ruled Babylon for 400 years. Though they were foreigners, the Kassites maintained Babylonian ways of life. They respected the Mesopotamian gods, which were different from their own, and rebuilt their temples. They kept Babylon as the region's capital. At Dur Kurigalzu, in the north of Mesopotamia, they built a major new city, close to the border with the neighbouring kingdom of Assyria.

The Assyrian Empire reached its greatest extent in the early 700s BC, when it stretched from the Upper Sea (Mediterranean Sea) to the Lower Sea (Persian Gulf).

THE RISE AND FALL OF ASSYRIA

In 1365 BC, Ashuruballit I became king of Assyria – a region that today covers northern Iraq and part of Turkey. His capital city was Ashur, home of the god of the same name. The king's own name meant 'Ashur has preserved life'. Ashuruballit's reign

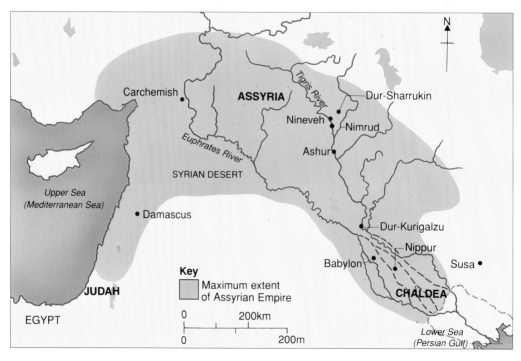

marked the start of Assyria's rise to power. He conquered part of a country called Mitanni which lay to the north of Assyria, and he made contact with Egypt which lay to the west.

Assyrian kings who came after Ashuruballit continued to add land to their growing empire. King Tukulti-Ninurta I captured Babylon, which he looted and burned. Part of the city's population was forced to leave. Under King Ashurnasirpal II, Assyria's empire reached as far as the Mediterranean Sea. He ruled over conquered peoples with great cruelty, forcing them to pay tribute (money) each year. This tribute made Assyria rich. Ashurnasirpal II moved the capital city from Ashur, which was located at the southern edge of the country, to Nimrud, a town in the middle of Assyria on the east bank of the Tigris. He strengthened Nimrud with a wall seven kilometres long, enclosing some 360 hectares. The city had a population of tens of thousands. Within the city was a royal palace and temple complex where, for almost 200 years, the kings of Assyria lived.

Among the later kings was Sennacherib. He made the town of Nineveh the new capital of the Assyrian Empire. At 720 hectares, it covered twice as much land as Nimrud. King Sennacherib built canals to carry water to the city and its farmland, and a grand royal palace in the city centre. It was decorated with painted and sculpted scenes. He put a park around the palace where he grew exotic plants. Sennacherib was a strong ruler. When his eldest son was murdered in Babylon, he destroyed the city. He dug canals to flood it, and scattered the earth on which it stood across the empire.

The last of the great Assyrian kings was Ashurbanipal. His reign is sometimes seen as Assyria's 'golden age' – a time when wonderful works of art were made, and when foreign ambassadors visited to pay their respects at the

Ashurnasirpal II, king of Assyria. Long hair was fashionable for members of the royal court. In his left hand he holds a mace, and in his right a sickle. The mace showed he was king. The sickle was used by the gods for fighting monsters.

These Assyrian soldiers are dressed in armour (see page 45). Archers shoot arrows from behind tall, curved shields. A river flows at their feet.

royal court. Neverthless, it was during Ashurbanipal's reign that the Assyrian Empire began to collapse. Egypt, which had been conquered by the Assyrians, broke free; there was a rebellion in Babylon, and civil wars raged elsewhere. When Ashurbanipal died, in 629 BC, the Assyrian Empire fell apart as invaders attacked it on all sides. And when Nineveh itself was captured, the Assyrian Empire ended for ever.

THE NEW BABYLONIAN EMPIRE

Chaldea was an ancient name for the marshy lands in the far south of Mesopotamia, at the head of the Persian Gulf – present-day southern Iraq and Kuwait. Tribes of settlers who arrived in this region became known as the Chaldeans. Quite where they originally came from is a mystery.

At first, Chaldea was ruled over by Assyrian kings because it was part of their empire. But as the Assyrian Empire weakened, the Chaldean kings seized the moment and began to build an empire of

---

A CLOSER LOOK

Kings' names were carefully chosen, and each had a specific meaning.

- Ashurnasirpal meant 'Ashur is the one who guards the heir to the throne'.
- Ashuruballit meant 'Ashur has preserved life'.
- Ashurbanipal meant 'Ashur is the creator of the heir to the throne'.
- Nabopolassar meant 'Nabu, guard the heir!' – Nabu was the Babylonian god of writing.
- Nebuchadnezzar meant 'Nabu, guard the royal progeny!'
- Sennacherib meant 'Sin has compensated for the death of the brothers' – possibly a reference to elder brothers of the king who had died young. Sin was the Assyrian moon god.
- Tukulti-Ninurta meant 'My trust is Ninurta!' – Ninurta was the Assyrian god of war.

their own. It is called the New Babylonian Empire. When, in 625 BC, King Nabopolassar captured Babylon from the Assyrians, the Chaldeans became the most powerful people in Mesopotamia.

It was Nabopolassar's son who made the greatest impression on the region. He was Nebuchadnezzar II – the king mentioned in the Bible as the destroyer of Jerusalem. He marched against the Egyptians and defeated them at the battle of Carchemish. He rebuilt and enlarged Babylon, which became his capital. The seven-storey ziggurat he built at Babylon is named in the Bible as the Tower of Babel.

After Nebuchadnezzar II died, the New Babylonian Empire went into decline. The kings who came after him could not keep the empire together. Worst of all, a new power was rising in the east – the Persians (see Chapter 10).

This imaginative painting of the Tower of Babel is by the Dutch artist Pieter Bruegel the Elder (c. 1528-69). He has made the ziggurat look more like a Roman amphitheatre than a Mesopotamian mud-brick tower.

GOVERNMENT, SOCIETY AND LAW

As cities grew out of villages, a method of running these new urban centres and organising their populations was needed. The world's first system of government was created.

GOVERNMENT IN MESOPAMIA

The Sumerians devised the earliest form of government. Each of their cities controlled the land around it. Together, the city and its land are called a city-state. Sumer was a country of many city-states, all fiercely independent of one another.

The early days of Mesopotamian government are closely linked to religion. Each city had a temple, dedicated to the city's patron god or goddess. At the head of the city-state was a ruler whom the people believed was the god's representative on earth. He was also the city's chief priest, and he had three titles: *en*, meaning 'the lord', indicating his religious role; *ensis*, meaning 'prince' or 'governor', indicating his role as leader; and *lugal*, meaning 'the great man', indicating his position as leader of the army.

The ruler lived in a palace and had the power to make laws to govern his city. In the early days, he was elected by the people of the city, but as time went by the leader's role became more important. Instead of being an elected official, he began to pass the title on to his son, who passed it to his son, and so on. These

A CLOSER LOOK

In very broad terms, Mesopotamian society was divided into two groups of people – those who owned land, and those who did not. By the time of Hammurabi (see page 21), three basic social classes had emerged: citizens (nobles and freemen who were landowners and heads of households); non-citizens (who did not own land); and slaves (prisoners of war, and individuals who had let themselves be sold into slavery rather than face a life of poverty).

rulers were the first true kings. They believed they had been chosen by the gods, not by the people – so it was their god-given right to rule.

The system of government created by the Sumerians repeated itself throughout the history of Mesopotamia, as different cities rose to domination, led by powerful kings.

Could this be Sargon? Some people think this copper head of an Akkadian ruler depicts the great leader. The beard, hairstyle and diadem indicate the figure is a king. The eyes, ears and nose may have been deliberately damaged by people who came later, to show their supremacy over the old leaders.

SARGON, KING OF AKKAD

Sargon's real name is not known. He took the name 'Sargon' when he became king of Akkad. Sargon (reigned 2334-2279 BC) was the greatest of the Akkadian kings. Very little is known about his early life. According to legend, he was the son of a priestess. Soon after he was born she placed him in a reed basket which she cast adrift on the Euphrates. Baby Sargon was found by a gardener, who raised him as his own son.

As a young man, Sargon worked for the king of Kish, a leading city. He was appointed the king's 'cup-bearer', an important position at the royal court. During a revolt, Sargon overthrew the king and seized power for himself. It is from this time on that he called himself Sargon, meaning 'True King' or 'Legitimate King'. It was his way of emphasising that people should accept no-one else except him as their king. Sargon built a new capital city, named Akkad.

Sargon was a great military leader. His army conquered the land of Sumer to the south, and when its cities came under his control he assumed the title 'King of the Land', in addition to his other titles 'King of Akkad' and 'King of Kish'. To

27

strengthen his position in Sumer, he weakened the conquered cities of Sumer by destroying their defensive walls, and he placed his own officials in charge of them. For the first time in the history of Mesopotamia, the whole area was ruled as one land, because Sargon had united the countries of Akkad and Sumer.

To the north he conquered lands as far as the Mediterranean Sea. Cities were looted and their valuables were taken back to Sargon's capital. He took control of supply routes and his empire grew wealthy. Merchant ships brought pottery, bone ornaments and beads in precious stones from the Indus Valley which lay across the Indian Ocean, from Oman in the Middle East, and from Bahrain and other islands in the Persian Gulf. An account says that, '5400 men ate bread daily before Sargon' – an indication of the size of his court, its officials, and merchant visitors. After reigning for 56 years Sargon died, either of old age, or in a revolt of one of the peoples he had conquered.

LAW IN MESOPOTAMIA

One of the most important duties of a Mesopotamian king was the passing of laws. Laws were necessary to rule a country successfully, and from early on in the history of Mesopotamia collections of laws were issued.

The earliest known collection of laws dates from the time of Ur-Nammu, a powerful Sumerian king who founded the Third Dynasty of Ur (see page 19). His laws were written down in about 2100 BC – although they had probably been in use for very many years before this time. Only 28 of Ur-Nammu's laws are known today. They impose fines on guilty people. For example, one law says: 'If a man has severed with a weapon the bones of another man, he shall pay one mina of silver' (a *mina* was a measure of weight: see page 55).

Under Sumerian law, a person accused of a crime was sent for trial before a panel of judges, who were elders chosen from the community. Witnesses had to

Hammurabi's laws were inscribed in cuneiform on tall stones. On this example, Hammurabi stands before Shamash, the god of justice, who is telling the king to bring law and order to the land.

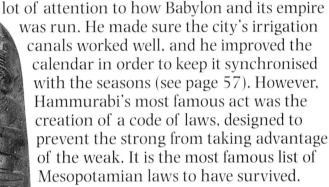

tell the truth – just as in a modern court. The Sumerian system of law seems to have been a fair one, and many systems which came later were based upon it.

THE LAW CODE OF HAMMURABI

Hammurabi, king of Babylon, reigned from 1792 BC to 1750 BC. He was a great organiser, and he paid a lot of attention to how Babylon and its empire was run. He made sure the city's irrigation canals worked well, and he improved the calendar in order to keep it synchronised with the seasons (see page 57). However, Hammurabi's most famous act was the creation of a code of laws, designed to prevent the strong from taking advantage of the weak. It is the most famous list of Mesopotamian laws to have survived.

Hammurabi devised a list of 282 laws, some of which were based on the older Sumerian ones. They were organised into sections dealing with the family, work, property, land, prices and wages, slavery and trade. In the introduction to the list, Hammurabi explained how his system of law was intended to work. His wish was to 'proclaim law throughout the land, eliminate what is bad, and prevent the

A CLOSER LOOK

Hammurabi's laws were carved on stones displayed throughout his empire. People referred to them to find out the punishment for a crime. Here are four of Hammurabi's 282 laws:

● If a man has accused another man and has brought a charge of murder against him, but has not proved it, his accuser shall be put to death.

● If a son has struck his father, they shall cut off his hand.

● If a man has put out the eye of another man, they shall put out his eye.

● If a builder has built a house for a man but has not made his work strong, with the result that the house falls down and kills the owner, the builder shall be put to death.

Laws such as these introduced the idea of retribution, which was where a person could 'get their own back' on someone who had wronged them. Other laws handed out fines as punishments, as had been the custom under Sumerian law.

strong from oppressing the weak'. It established a legal system in Mesopotamia for centuries to come.

ASHURBANIPAL, KING OF ASSYRIA

Ashurbanipal (reigned 668-629 BC) was a military leader and a scholar. He could read and write, and solve complex mathematical problems. But his main claim to fame rests with his eagerness to preserve Mesopotamian culture. During his reign, Ashurbanipal created a large library of cuneiform texts of all sorts, which he housed at Nineveh, his capital (see page 34). He sent collectors to search the temples of Mesopotamia for works of literature and magic, scientific writings and medical reports, all of which were taken back to his library. Some of the texts were already old even in Ashurbanipal's time, dating back 2000 years to the beginning of writing. When archaeologists discovered Ashurbanipal's library in the 1800s, its vast store of 20,000 clay tablets shed new light not only on the history of Assyria, but also on the civilisations of Sumer and Akkad. Had Ashurbanipal not collected these ancient writings, we would know far less about the history of Mesopotamia.

This relief carving shows Ashurbanipal carrying a basket of earth from which the first mud-brick for a new temple at Babylon was to be made.

The Assyrian Empire reached its greatest extent under Ashurbanipal. He conquered Egypt, then raided the country of the Elamites (present-day Iran) where he ransacked Susa, the capital city. The temples of Susa were destroyed, booty was taken, and the land was sowed with salt so that nothing would grow. However, despite these military victories, the end of Ashurbanipal's reign was marked by the start of the collapse of the Assyrian Empire. Within 20 years of his death the empire had broken up and was lost forever.

NEBUCHADNEZZAR II, KING OF CHALDEA

Nebuchadnezzar II (reigned 604-562 BC) was the most important of the Chaldean kings, and one of the most famous figures in ancient history. His exploits are written about in the Bible, but he is best remembered as the builder of the Hanging Gardens of Babylon (see page 36), and for his relations with the Jews.

The Jewish Kingdom of Judah lay between two great powers – Egypt and Babylonia. The Jews were unable to remain either independent or neutral; if they joined one side, they would be attacked by the other. When the Jewish king, Jehoiakim, turned against Babylon and stopped paying taxes, Nebuchadnezzar marched to Jerusalem and captured the city, in 597 BC. Jehoiakim died, but Nebuchadnezzar wanted to exact punishment on the inhabitants of Jerusalem for their rebellious behaviour. The defeated royal family, officials, soldiers and craftworkers were all taken back to Babylon in chains. As many as 10,000 Jews may have been taken into captivity in Babylon.

Ten years later there was a second uprising in Jerusalem. This time, after a siege lasting 18 months, Nebuchadnezzar destroyed the city, burning its temple and palace to the ground. The story of the fall of Jerusalem, and the part played by Nebuchadnezzar, is told in the Old Testament of the Bible by the prophet Jeremiah.

Nebuchadnezzar destroys Jerusalem, as pictured by an artist in the early 1800s.

CITIES OF MESOPOTAMIA

Ur began as a village in about 4500 BC. Over the next 2000 years it mushroomed into a great, oval-shaped, walled city, covering some 60 hectares. By about 2500 BC it had become Sumer's leading city, with a population of about 20,000 people. Within its walls was a maze of narrow streets and winding alleys, packed with houses, shops and markets. The city centre was dominated by a massive temple complex, the centrepiece of which was a mud-brick ziggurat (see box).

Like other Sumerian cities built on the dry plain of southern Mesopotamia, Ur needed an adequate water supply – both for its population and for the patchwork of farmers' fields which surrounded it on

A CLOSER LOOK

Ziggurats were the centre of religious life in every Mesopotamian city. A ziggurat was seen as a link between heaven and earth. The word 'ziggurat' means 'to build high'. It comes from the word *ziqquratum* – a word used by the Babylonians. A ziggurat was a pyramid-shaped tower of several flat platforms, built one on top of the other. The platforms were reached by ramps and staircases. The entire structure was made from millions of sun-dried mud-bricks, held together with wooden beams and reed matting. Some of the outer bricks were glazed in bright colours. At the top of the ziggurat was a small temple, dedicated to the city's god. There was a constant coming and going of priests, temple officials, worshippers and slaves.

The partially restored ziggurat at Ur

all sides. The city was served by a canal, looping around it and linking it to the Euphrates. A network of ditches branched off from the canal, taking water to the fields of wheat, barley, onions and leeks out on the plain. The city's two harbours were shelters for boats which brought foreign merchants from the island of Dilmun (present-day Bahrain), and elsewhere, to trade with the Sumerians.

THE ROYAL CEMETERY OF UR

The British archaeologist Leonard Woolley (1880–1960) excavated at Ur in the 1920s and 1930s. Beneath a thick layer of river silt he found a cemetery where more than 2500 Sumerians were buried. Commoners lay in simple graves, but 16 members of the Sumerian royal family were buried in deep tombs packed with grave goods, which Woolley called the 'Royal Cemetery'.

What surprised and shocked Woolley and his team of excavators was the discovery that each ruler had been buried with their servants, soldiers and musicians. The preparation for a mass burial was carefully worked out. First, a long, sloping shaft was dug down to a pit that would serve as the burial chamber. The chamber was filled with valuable offerings. Then the body of the ruler was placed on

This Sumerian board game came from the 'Royal Cemetery' at Ur. It was made in c. 2600 BC. Two players moved counters around the board in a race game.

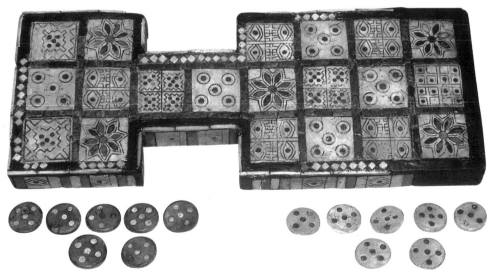

a wooden platform inside the chamber, together with the bodies of his closest attendants, each of whom had drunk poison. The burial chamber was sealed, and a procession of guards with daggers, musicians with lyres, grooms with ox-drawn chariots, soldiers with spears, and women of the court, moved into the shaft. Each carried a small cup of poison. They were prepared to die for their late ruler, to carry on serving him in the life after death. The shaft was filled with soil. One royal grave contained the bodies of 74 attendants, 68 of whom were women. On discovering this mass grave, Woolley and his team of archaeologists dubbed it the 'Great Death Pit'. He could find no signs of resistance among those who had sacrificed their lives – evidence which suggests that the Sumerians would obey their rulers and gods to the grave.

Attendants sacrificed in the Great Death Pit at Ur went to their deaths dressed in expensive clothes. Many of the women wore headdresses of gold and semi-precious stones.

NINEVEH, AN ASSYRIAN CITY

Like Ur, the city of Nineveh began as a village in the prehistoric period from about 6000 BC onwards. More than 5000 years later, the Assyrian king Sennacherib chose Nineveh as his capital, by which time it had grown into a major city covering more than 700 hectares. If the Biblical prophet Jonah is to be believed, at that time Nineveh had a population of 120,000.

King Sennacherib improved the water supply to Nineveh and the surrounding farmland by constructing canals and an aqueduct. At the centre of the town he built a magnificent palace which he called 'The Palace Without Rival'. It was both the home of the Assyrian royal family and the centre of government. Its rooms were lined with painted and sculpted stone reliefs showing scenes of the king

As a young man, Henry Layard travelled throughout the Near East. Here, aged 26, he is dressed as a tribesman from Iran.

defeating his enemies during the siege of Lachish, a town in the Jewish Kingdom of Judah. The siege is described in the Bible, and the images on the walls of Sennacherib's palace are eyewitness accounts of the actions of the Assyrian army, 2700 years ago.

Around the outside of Sennacherib's palace a park was laid out, filled with unusual plants and animals brought from distant lands. But it was Sennacherib's grandson, Ashurbanipal, who gave Nineveh its greatest legacy – a library in which he housed the knowledge of Mesopotamia (see page 30).

French archaeologists, led by doctor and explorer, Paul Emile Botta (1802–70), had been digging at Nineveh for some years by the time a young British traveller arrived there in the 1840s. He was Austen Henry Layard (1817–94), and it was his work which uncovered the royal palaces of Sennacherib and Ashurbanipal. The French team had given up searching for them, but their failure did not deter Layard. His discoveries made him famous.

BABYLON, A CHALDEAN CITY

In the Akkadian language Babylon was called 'Bab-ilim', meaning 'Gate of god'. It was a holy city, the centre of the god Marduk. The city was at its most splendid in the 500s BC during the time of the Chaldeans – a period that lasted less than 100 years following the collapse of the Assyrian Empire.

Nebuchadnezzar II (see page 31) transformed Babylon with an ambitious building programme. Visitors entered the inner city through the Ishtar Gate, its colourful walls decorated with glazed bricks of blue, yellow and white. Once inside the city they passed the fabled Hanging Gardens, a rising terrace planted

A CLOSER LOOK

Tell el-Muqayyar is the modern name for Ur, and Tell Kuyunjik is the name for Nineveh. In these, and other places, the Arabic word *tell* is a clue to the ancient origins of the settlement. It comes from the Babylonian word *tillum*, meaning 'mound'. Because the cities were occupied for thousands of years, they slowly rose above ground level as new buildings were built on the ruins of old ones. This activity created large mounds which rose many metres above ground level. It is into these mounds that archaeologists dig to uncover the remains of the ancient civilisations of Mesopotamia.

CHAPTER FIVE

A CLOSER LOOK

Did the Hanging Gardens of Babylon really exist? The ancient historian Philo said they did, and he named them as one of the Seven Wonders of the World. When the German archaeologist Robert Koldewey (1855–1925) uncovered the ruins of Babylon almost 100 years ago, he found a building which he said once had a garden growing on it. But instead of a grand building, it might only have been a storehouse, kept cool by the vegetation that grew on its roof.

with trees and foliage, fed with water pumped from wells. From there they walked along the street known as 'May the Enemy not have Victory' towards the city centre, where the massive ziggurat to Marduk stood.

As many as 150,000 people may have lived in Babylon, of all nationalities – including thousands of Jews deported from Jerusalem (see page 31). At this time Babylon covered about 405 hectares. People lived in small mud-brick houses, which faced in from the street towards courtyards for privacy. All had flat roofs, and some had rooms for servants and slaves. The city was surrounded by a wall 17 kilometres in circumference.

The Ishtar Gate was the main entrance into the inner city of Babylon. It was faced with glazed bricks showing images of lions and bulls.

A bull from the Ishtar Gate

RELIGION AND MYTHOLOGY

Religion, and the ceremonies associated with it, played an important role in the lives of the Mesopotamians. Much of what we know about their beliefs, and their gods and goddesses, comes from reading stories they wrote. Many Mesopotamian myths (see page 39) have survived on clay tablets.

THE MESOPOTAMIAN UNIVERSE

The Mesopotamians thought that the universe was a sphere, organised into three parts – the sky, the earth and the underworld. These three parts fitted together like the parts of a jigsaw.

The sky was the upper part of the universe. People thought of it as a liquid mass. Fixed within it were the thousands of stars which gave light to the world. The earth was the very centre of the universe. It was seen as a solid place completely surrounded by salty sea. People thought that both the earth and the sea floated on a vast lake of fresh water, which burst through on to the surface of the land to make life-giving rivers and springs. The third part of the universe was the underworld – a dark place and the exact opposite of the sky. The Mesopotamians called

To protect a house and its occupants from demons, people buried small figurines of gods under the floor. This god has written on its arms: 'Enter, spirit of peace!' and 'Depart, spirit of evil!'. Model dogs were also buried to act as guard dogs. They had names such as: 'Expeller of evil!', 'Catcher of the enemy!', 'Don't think, bite!', 'Biter of his foe!', and 'Loud is his bark!'.

it the 'land of no return'. It was where the dead went when they left the 'land of the living'.

Linking the three parts of the universe together were air and water. They were the sources of all life and fertility. They could move freely between the sky, the earth and the underworld.

GODS AND GODDESSES

The Mesopotamians believed that humankind had been created to serve the gods. According to a story told by the Sumerians, people had been moulded from clay by the gods. It was the duty of all people to work for the gods as their slaves. Failure to look after the gods could bring floods, drought, disease or attacks from enemies.

Temples to the gods were built in all towns and cities. Inside these temples were statues and other images of the gods. People thought the gods actually lived inside their statues. This explains why the Mesopotamians treated statues of gods

Sumerian worshippers placed statues such as this one inside temples to pray to the gods on their behalf.

A CLOSER LOOK

There were hundreds of different gods and goddesses in Mesopotamia. Some were extremely popular and were worshipped at many towns and cities: others were less popular and were followed in only one or two towns. An (also called Anu) was god of the sky, and his son, Enki (also called Ea), was god of the earth. His name meant 'Lord Earth'. Enki controlled the lake of fresh water on which the world floated. He was the master of wisdom, the god of arts and crafts, and the protector of humankind. Another son of An was Enlil, whose name meant 'Lord Wind'. He controlled all life by bringing life-giving air for people and animals to breathe. He possessed the Tablet of Destiny which foretold the fate of humankind. He eventually became king of the gods. Marduk, son of Enki, became the main god of the Babylonians. Nanna (also called Sin) was the son of Enlil and, as the moon god, ruled over the calendar.

Adad, the weather god, controlled storms and rain, and Utu (also called Shamash) the sun god, gave light and heat to the world. Inanna (also called Ishtar) was the most important and feared goddess, whose name meant 'Lady of Heaven'. She was the goddess of love and war who had powers of life and death. Ninhursag was the great mother goddess whose name meant 'Lady of the Mountain'. Two other deities were Nabu, the god of scribes and writing, and Ninurta, the god of war and hunting.

and goddesses with great care and respect. The worst that could happen to a statue was that it should be captured and carried off by an enemy. When this happened (as it did from time to time), it was felt the god and his protecting presence had left the town, quite literally leaving it godless. The 'good times' would return only when the god's statue was brought back.

A temple statue was made of wood, decorated with gold. At a secret ceremony, priests said prayers to bring the statue to life. From that moment on the god lived inside its statue. The statue stood on a pedestal inside the sanctuary, which was the temple's holiest room. Other statues in the sanctuary represented the god's family, his servants, and worshippers praying.

THE ART OF TELLING THE FUTURE

The Mesopotamians believed that it was possible to predict the future. The most widely practised method of determining the future was by astrology (reading the stars), but other methods were used, too. Inspecting the entrails of a sacrificed sheep, interpreting dreams, noting the behaviour of birds and other animals, and observing the different directions taken by smoke from burning incense, or oil on water, were all used by priests to foretell events that would happen in the future.

Natural phenomena, such as claps of thunder, rain, hail and earthquakes, were thought of as omens: they were sent by the gods to warn the king about danger to himself or the country. The Assyrians were such believers in these omens that they built weather stations, where scribes recorded their observations on clay tablets. The tablets were sent to the king for interpretation by his priests.

MYTHS OF THE MESOPOTAMIANS

Many stories were told by the people of Mesopotamia, about their gods and about how the world was created. The stories were written in cuneiform on clay tablets (see page 47), and many were stored in libraries at royal palaces, such as at Ashurbanipal's great library in Nineveh. When cuneiform was deciphered in the middle of the 1800s, scholars could read for themselves the myths of the Mesopotamians – and what they read amazed them, casting new light on some of the stories that appear in the Old Testament of the Bible.

THE *EPIC OF GILGAMESH*

The *Epic of Gilgamesh* is the greatest of all Mesopotamian myths, written on 12 large clay tablets in about 3000 lines of cuneiform. It came to light among the ruins of Ashurbanipal's library, built by him in the 600s BC — but the story was already ancient by the time the Assyrian king added it to his collection of Mesopotamian literature.

In the story, Gilgamesh and his friend Enkidu set out to learn the secret of immortality. To begin with they think the way to live forever is by doing great deeds. In one adventure Enkidu kills the demon Humbaba, and in another Gilgamesh slays a bull sent to destroy the city of Uruk. But their bravery does not lead to eternal life, for Enlil, the king of the gods, decides that Enkidu must die as a punishment for killing Humbaba. The death of Enkidu teaches Gilgamesh an important lesson: that no matter how heroic a man is, he remains a mortal whose fate lies in the hands of the gods. Gilgamesh's search for endless life leads him to Utnapishtim, whose name means

In the Epic of Gilgamesh, *Enkidu kills the demon Humbaba. Images of this demon show his face made from the fatty entrails of a sacrificial animal.*

RELIGION AND MYTHOLOGY

The hero Gilgamesh masters a lion. This huge statue is 4.7 metres tall.

have found eternal life'. Ut-napishtim explains to Gilgamesh that long ago Enlil sent a flood to destroy humankind. The god Enki took pity on Ut-napishtim and told him to build a great boat in which to save himself, his family and all the living creatures of the world. On the seventh day of the flood Ut-napishtim first sent out a dove, and then a swallow. Unable to find a safe place to land, both returned to the boat. But when Ut-napishtim released a raven, and it did not return, he knew it must have found dry land. He offered sacrifices as thanks to the gods, and in return Enlil made him immortal, just like the gods themselves.

As for Gilgamesh, he never does discover the secret of immortality for himself, and so he returns to his home city of Uruk in the knowledge that, as a mere mortal, death is inevitable.

A CLOSER LOOK

Is the Bible story of Noah, in Genesis, based on the Mesopotamian story of Ut-napishtim? In 1872, George Smith (1840–76) was working at the British Museum, London, joining together fragments of clay tablets found at Ashurbanipal's library at Nineveh. He came across the tablet with the story of Ut-napishtim and was stunned to read about a flood, a great ship and a dove. The similarity with the story of Noah was unmistakable. Experts believe that both the Ut-napishtim and Noah stories can trace their origins to a single flood story that was told in the ancient Near East at least from the time of the Sumerians. Ut-napishtim and Noah are probably names for the same person.

EVERYDAY LIFE

The evidence for the everyday life of the people of Mesopotamia comes mainly from discoveries made by archaeologists. Objects found buried in the ground are used to build up our understanding about people's daily lives. However, so much evidence has not survived the passage of time that what we do know with any certainty is only a glimpse into the distant world of the Mesopotamians.

Bread made without yeast on sale in the Near East today.

FOOD AND DRINK

Grain was made into flour, from which unleavened bread was baked. Because there was no yeast in the dough, loaves did not rise when baked, so they stayed quite flat. Bread was the staple food from the time of the Sumerians onwards. Wheat and barley grains could also be softened and made into a kind of thick porridge. Other foods were onions, leeks, cucumbers, beans, garlic and lentils. Milk, butter and cheese came from goats and cattle. Dates were eaten fresh, dried, or pressed into a sweet-tasting syrup. Meat came from cattle and sheep. Fish was always popular, caught in rivers, pools, and from the sea.

The main drink was a low-alcohol beer, brewed from wheat or barley. Cuneiform texts refer to

EVERYDAY LIFE

at least 19 different types of Mesopotamian beer. It could be flavoured with dates, honey and spices. Beer was a nutritious drink – a food in its own right. Everyone drank it, including children.

CLOTHING AND MAKE-UP

During the Sumerian period, men went about bare-chested, dressed only in a type of kilt. Later on, this was replaced by a loose-fitting, shirt-like garment. Women wore long shawls and fitted dresses, their hair left loose or coiled around their heads. Both Sumerian men and women wore make-up, especially to emphasise their eyes. Antimony (a mineral) provided a blue-black paint which was applied around the eyes and to the eyebrows and eyelashes. Women coloured their lips and cheeks with red henna, smoothed their skin with pumice stone (a type of volcanic rock), took perfumed baths, and rubbed themselves with oils.

The gold and bead headdress of Queen Pu-Abi, from the Royal Cemetery of Ur (see page 33). The head is modelled from the skull of a Sumerian woman.

MUSIC

Among the thousands of clay tablets found in Mesopotamia, some are musical texts. They have been called the oldest examples of 'sheet music' known to exist. When musicologists studied them in the 1970s, they discovered the music was for stringed instruments called lyres. One tablet, from Ugarit in northern Syria, turned out to be the words and music for the world's oldest song, written around 1400 BC. It was a hymn to a Mesopotamian goddess, composed in a scale of seven notes played in harmony. Experts were surprised to discover that the hymn was in the 'do, re, mi' scale of notes, which is the one used by many musicians today. Until this discovery it was thought that ancient music consisted of single, unharmonised notes. In 1974, musicians gave a performance of the Mesopotamian hymn from Ugarit – its first public performance for more than 3300 years!

A reconstruction of a Sumerian lyre of about 2600 BC.

WARFARE IN MESOPOTAMIA

Wars were fought throughout the long history of Mesopotamia. Cities attacked their neighbours, often in disputes over control of the valuable irrigation canals which brought water to them and their fields. In other wars, armies conquered the lands of their enemies, looted their cities, took the statues of their gods from their temples, and forced their populations into slavery. It was through military campaigns such as these that kings were able to build their empires.

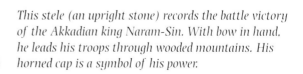

This stele (an upright stone) records the battle victory of the Akkadian king Naram-Sin. With bow in hand, he leads his troops through wooded mountains. His horned cap is a symbol of his power.

EVERYDAY LIFE

Warfare in Mesopotamia reached a high point under the Assyrians, who had an army of up to 50,000 men. Assyrian soldiers wore pointed helmets and tunics, and fought with slings, bows and arrows, and spears. Their shields were made from wicker and leather. Some soldiers wore long robes covered with metal plates, which was an early form of armour. Horses were used for riding and for pulling chariots. At first, Assyrian chariots carried two men – one to drive and the other to fire arrows or throw spears. As time went by, chariots became larger and could carry four soldiers. Horses wore blinkers over their eyes and had bells attached to their harness straps. Breastplates made from bronze or leather hung down from their necks.

An Assyrian soldier's pointed helmet, made of iron

A CLOSER LOOK

The Sumerian army was well organised. Soldiers wore copper helmets, fought with spears and axes, and carried large rectangular shields. In some battles they used slow-moving, two-man chariots, pulled by asses. One side of the 'Royal Standard of Ur', made in about 2600 BC, shows the Sumerian army in detail. Part of the Standard is shown here. At the bottom is a four-wheeled chariot. While the charioteer steers the vehicle over the body of a fallen enemy, his passenger throws spears. In the middle scene prisoners are being pushed along by soldiers carrying spears. In the top panel courtiers walked towards the king. Most Sumerian prisoners of war were executed: any who were spared were kept as slaves.

The war side of the Standard of Ur.

45

ARTS AND CRAFTS

Like most other ancient civilisations, such as those of the Egyptians, Greeks and Romans, the Mesopotamians possessed their own distinctive styles of art, which can be recognised in their artefacts. Archaeologists use these cultural differences to help pinpoint places where objects were made, and to build up a dating framework into which historical events can be fitted.

THE INVENTION OF WRITING

Writing started in Sumer, possibly at the town of Uruk, in about 3300 BC (see page 17). This was a time of great change for the villages of southern Mesopotamia. They were growing into busy towns, and trade was emerging as an important part of their economy. People wanted to know how much grain or how many sheep were entering or leaving their stores and farms, so a method of keeping reliable records was needed. Writing was invented in order to record the business activities of farmers and merchants.

The first type of writing used pictures to represent objects or ideas. These are called ideographs. For example, a picture of a head meant 'head', and two

One of the world's first accountancy documents, from c. 3200 BC. The surface is divided into sections, in which are pictographic signs, some representing numbers.

ARTS AND CRAFTS

wavy lines meant 'water'. Ideographs were slow to write because each picture had to be drawn neatly and carefully. In order to write faster, original pictures with curves were gradually changed into forms that could be written with straight lines only.

WRITING ON CLAY

The Mesopotamians wrote mostly on small pieces of damp clay. Clay was easy to find and cheap to use. A piece of clay could be worked into a flat tablet which fitted into the palm of the writer's hand. A tool called a stylus was used to write on the soft clay. It was made from the stem of a reed, or a piece of wood or bone. Its tip was gently pressed into the soft clay of the tablet to make small wedge-shaped impressions. After it had been written on, a clay tablet was left in the sun to dry, until it was hard.

Wedge-shaped cuneiform writing on a clay tablet. It required skill both to write and read the mass of tiny impressions made by scribes on tablets like this.

When scribes discovered that a stylus with a blunt, wedge-shaped tip made a cleaner, sharper impression in clay, the system of picture writing began to change. In its place came the cuneiform script, made up of wedge-shaped marks. The word cuneiform comes from two Latin words: *cuneus* meaning 'wedge' and *forma* meaning 'shape'.

Clay tablets were used for keeping everyday records and accounts, but they were not the only objects on which the Mesopotamians wrote. Cuneiform was also carved on to hard surfaces such as stone and metal. Cuneiform became the main script of the ancient Near East and it was used

A CLOSER LOOK

When the first cuneiform inscription was published in Europe in the 1600s, it aroused little interest among scholars. They did not believe that the strange wedge-shaped marks were writing. One said they were experiments in making patterns using a triangular shape. Another said they were tracks made by birds! But as more examples of cuneiform were found, scholars realised they were dealing with a type of extinct writing – and so the race to decipher it began. The real breakthrough was made by a British army officer, Henry Rawlinson (1810–95). In the 1840s Rawlinson copied out a large cuneiform inscription carved high on the side of a cliff at Behistun, western Iran. The same cuneiform inscription had been carved in three different languages (Old Persian, Elamite, and Babylonian) and by studying them all, side-by-side, Rawlinson was able to work out what the signs said.

by the peoples of the region – the Sumerians, Akkadians, Babylonians, Assyrians and Persians – for more than 3000 years. The latest inscription written in cuneiform is dated to AD 75, after which time it went out of use.

CYLINDER SEALS

Cylinder seals were invented in Mesopotamia at about the same time as writing. They, too, came about because of the growth of the economy – in this case the need to establish the ownership of property. They were usually made from stone, but shell, ivory and metal were also used. Their surfaces were engraved with intricate patterns, often of gods and animals. When rolled over damp clay they left an impression, or print, of the pattern of the engraving. This impression was a person's 'signature', identifying them as the owner of property such as jars, baskets and boxes. Seals protected a person's property, and owning a seal was a mark of prestige.

A cylinder seal (left) and its impression rolled on clay (right)

ARTS AND CRAFTS

Letter

Clay envelope

LEARNING TO READ AND WRITE

People who could read and write (scribes) were highly thought of in Mesopotamian society – but learning cuneiform script was a long, hard process. As one scribe wrote to his son who wanted to follow in his father's footsteps: 'Of all the human trades that exist on earth... none is more difficult than the art of the scribe.'

Scribes were taught to read and write cuneiform in a school called an *edubba*, which literally means 'tablet-house'. There were more than 500 different cuneiform signs to memorise, and it took years before a scribe was fully trained. While he was learning cuneiform, a pupil at an *edubba* was called a 'son of the tablet-house', and his teacher was the school 'father'. Pupils nearing the end of their training were called 'elder brothers', who acted as both friends and bullies towards the younger pupils in the school. Elder brothers expected the younger pupils to give them presents (bribes): if they did not, then a beating was bound to follow.

The school day lasted from sunrise to sunset. Teaching was strict – pupils who did badly in their studies were caned. Pupils were taught science, literature, mathematics and grammar. Mathematics was an important subject to master (see page 55).

Three different teachers taught it: a 'scribe of accounting' (teaching arithmetical skills such as addition, subtraction and division); a 'scribe of measurement' (teaching skills of geometry and distance); and a 'scribe of the field' (a surveyor who taught how to calculate areas of land).

Cuneiform signs were small and complicated, so pupils had to learn how to write neatly without making mistakes. This they did by copying out inscriptions time and time again. Pupils also had to learn words and phrases by heart, and took examinations to test their memory and knowledge.

POTTERY

The first pots made from baked clay were fashioned in the Near East about 7000 BC. They are some of the oldest ceramic vessels in the world, and their manufacture coincided with the development of village communities, where people lived in permanent settlements (see page 13).

As potters learned how to use clay, the range of pots they made increased. Pieces of broken pottery (potsherds) are the commonest finds made by archaeologists and, as fired clay is virtually indestructible, it is possible to recreate whole pots from a jigsaw of fragments.

Mesopotamian pots included bowls, plates, saucers and jars, in many sizes from small to large. At first pots were handmade, slowly built up from coils or slabs of clay which were pressed into shape. From about 4500 BC, the potter's wheel was introduced, enabling potters to make pots with thinner sides and in more elaborate shapes.

Many pots were left undecorated. They came from the kiln in shades of red and black, the colour of their bodies determined by how much (or how little)

ARTS AND CRAFTS

oxygen had been present during the firing process. Other pots were decorated in a variety of ways. Some were coated with a thin wash of liquid clay (called slip), often in a contrasting colour to the body of the pot. On some pots the slip was used like paint to make patterns on the surface of the vessel. When a pot's surface was rubbed (burnished) with a wooden or bone tool, shiny patterns could be made as the clay became slightly compressed. Other techniques involved impressing unfired pots with stamps, or cutting into the surface.

Styles of pottery are linked with particular groups of people at different times. The style of a pot is used by archaeologists to determine when and where it was made, which is particularly important when studying the prehistoric communities that existed before writing.

WORKING IN STONE

The stonemason's art was highly developed in Mesopotamia. Stones such as alabaster, basalt, diorite, gypsum, jasper and limestone were all used to make statues, cylinder seals and, most notable of all, the scenes of hunts and battles carved on large stone slabs that lined the walls of Assyrian palaces.

Most Assyrian palace reliefs were carved between 870 BC and 620 BC. The palaces, built from perishable mud-brick, contained painted rooms with floors

This stone relief carving shows soldiers escaping from Ashurnasirpal's army by swimming across the River Euphrates. They cross the river supported by inflated animal skins, heading to the fort on the right.

covered by carpets. Set against the walls were two-metre-high panels of carved stone, depicting scenes which were themselves painted.

The most widely-used stone for palace reliefs was a form of gypsum, sometimes known as Mosul marble (the modern town of Mosul lies on the right bank of the Tigris, opposite the ancient city of Nineveh). Greyish-white in colour and finely-grained, blocks were cut from the rock with iron saws. They were then split and shaped, and mounted on the palace walls. The carving was done once the stone was mounted.

The purpose of the palace reliefs was to create an impression of Assyrian power and might. Visitors who saw the reliefs could not fail to be impressed by their scale and grandeur, or to understand their political message – that the Assyrian king was all-powerful, and the Assyrian Empire was all-conquering.

To archaeologists, the images on the stones tell vivid stories about the people of the time: how they dressed, how they were organised, the wars they fought, the technology they possessed, and their religious beliefs. But a word of caution is needed: they also acted as a powerful means of distributing propaganda. A king could enhance his reputation by deliberately exaggerating his success in battle, changing the truth to suit his needs.

The helmet of King Meskalamdug, shaped like a wig, comes from the Royal Cemetery of Ur. It was beaten from a single sheet of gold, the hair pattern being stamped out from the inside in a technique called 'chasing'.

METALWORK

Copper was a valuable resource for the early Mesopotamians who used it to make tools, weapons and decorative objects. The raw material (ore) for making copper was transported down the Euphrates from hills in the north to metalworkers who lived in the south.

When copper is mixed with tin, it forms an alloy called bronze. Bronze is harder than copper and made stronger tools and weapons which stayed sharp longer. The Sumerians made much use of bronze. They discovered that it could be cast in clay or stone moulds, which enabled them to 'mass produce' some items. Casting was used to make axes, daggers and spearheads.

Of all metals, gold survives the best, and many examples of Mesopotamian goldwork have been found. A versatile metal, gold was put to many uses: jewellery, cups and vases were made; daggers, harps, lyres and statues were covered with it or had pieces inlaid for decoration. Metalworkers found out how to make thin sheets of gold (and silver) by beating it out over flat stones. From this sheet metal, they shaped vessels with wide, open mouths, such as dishes and bowls.

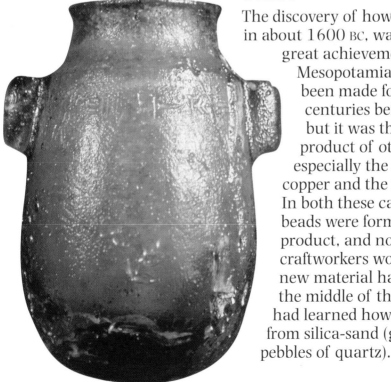

Assyrian green glass vase from Nimrud, c.750 BC. It was made in a mould, then smoothed by grinding and polishing.

Glass

The discovery of how to make glass, in about 1600 BC, was one of the great achievements of the Mesopotamians. Glass had been made for several centuries before this time, but it was the accidental by-product of other processes, especially the smelting of copper and the firing of pottery. In both these cases, small glassy beads were formed as a waste product, and no doubt craftworkers wondered if this new material had any uses. By the middle of the 1000s BC, they had learned how to make glass from silica-sand (ground-up pebbles of quartz).

SCIENCE AND TECHNOLOGY

The search for scientific knowledge was widespread among the civilisations of the Near East. Fundamental principles of mathematics and astronomy were known. In medicine, doctors studied the human body and how to heal it. But probably the most significant aspect of Mesopotamian technology was the invention of the wheel.

THE WHEEL

The wheel was probably invented some time before 3200 BC. The evidence for this comes from the early town of Uruk, where clay tablets have been found on which are scratched pictures of carts with wheels. The first wheels were solid, made from two or three planks of wood shaped into discs held together with wooden or copper brackets. Solid wheels were in use for more than 1000 years in Mesopotamia before lighter wheels with spokes were made, from around 2000 BC onwards.

A Sumerian cart with solid wooden wheels, shown on the Royal Standard of Ur

SCIENCE AND TECHNOLOGY

MATHEMATICS

The Sumerians were the first people to develop a system of arithmetic. The Sumerian system was adapted and improved by the Babylonians, and it spread throughout the ancient Near East. Adding, subtracting and multiplying were important skills when counting goods such as sacks of grain, or numbers of sheep and cattle.

The most widely used number system was based on counting in units of 60. This is called a sexagesimal system. Although 60 might seem a strange counting unit, it is in fact extremely practical because it can be divided exactly by 2, 3, 4, 5, 6, 10, 12, 15, 20 and 30, which makes many calculations quite simple. There was also another counting system, based on counting in tens, hundreds, and thousands, called a decimal system.

To help with calculations, people used multiplication tables. Other tables helped them with division, and with square roots and cube roots of numbers. Tables were written on clay tablets.

WEIGHTS AND MEASURES

Closely connected with counting was the system of weights and measures. This, too, was based on units of 60. In the Babylonian period the basic weight was the *mina* (about 500 grams) which was subdivided into 60 *shekels*. Measures of length were based on the cubit or 'elbow' (about 50 centimetres). The Babylonian 'mile' was the equivalent of about 10 kilometres, which was the distance a person could walk in about two hours.

Assyrian bronze weights in the shape of lions. The largest was equal to 5 mina (about 2.5 kg).

DOCTORS AND MEDICINE

The Mesopotamians believed that illnesses were caused by harmful demons inside a person's body. Some demons were said to cause diseases of the stomach, while others were blamed for illnesses of the limbs, head, or eyes. When a person became ill, they had a choice of two types of medical doctor – the *ashipu* and the *asu*. The *ashipu* was an expert in magic, somewhat like a sorcerer. The *asu* was the practical doctor, who treated patients with herbal remedies made from more than 100 different species of plants.

Gula, the goddess of medicine, surrounded by symbols of other gods

One of the most important roles of the *ashipu* was to diagnose a patient's illness by the use of magic. The *ashipu* decided which demon was causing the illness, and whether it was the result of an error or sin committed by the patient. Once a diagnosis had been made, the *ashipu* set about curing the patient by using magical charms and spells to drive out the harmful demon.

Patients who saw the *asu* received practical treatment. For cuts and wounds the *asu* applied ointments made from plants, spices and animal fats, held on by bandages. The ointments had antiseptic qualities which worked like soaps to ward off infection from bacteria. If the patient had an internal illness, the *asu* gave them a potion to drink. It, too, was made from plant extracts, dissolved in beer, which probably made the medicine go down easier. The *asu* was also skilled in mending broken bones, and in performing minor operations.

From the evidence so far found, most Mesopotamian doctors were men, though a single female doctor is known to have worked in Babylon. There may well have been other women doctors, too. Midwifery was certainly practiced exclusively by women doctors.

SCIENCE AND TECHNOLOGY

THE CALENDAR

Along with many other ancient civilisations, the Mesopotamians used a calendar based on the phases of the moon (new moon, crescent, half moon, waxing, and full moon). This is called a lunar calendar. Their year was divided into 12 months of 29 or 30 days each, and each month began when the new crescent moon was first sighted in the night sky. The problem with a calendar based on the lunar year is that it has 11 days fewer than a year based on the movement of the sun (365 days). To make up the difference, the Mesopotamians added an extra month to their year, about every three years, to keep the lunar calendar synchronised with the solar (sun) calendar. Without this additional month the seasons would begin to change at different times each year. Astronomers compiled lists predicting the future positions of the sun, the moon and the planets. They were worked out for many years ahead, and were used to determine the beginning of months and years.

The oldest map in the world, from c. 600 BC, puts Babylon at the centre of everything, surrounded by neighbouring lands (small circles) and the sea (large circle). The Euphrates is shown as a wide band running from top to bottom.

MAPS AND MAPMAKING

Clues to how the Mesopotamians pictured the shape of the world exist in the form of maps marked out on clay. The so-called Babylonian 'world map' is the oldest map in the world to depict the relative locations of neighbouring countries. Dating from 600 BC, it shows Babylon near the centre of the world. The River Euphrates flows in a broad band across the world, and around are marked the countries of Assyria, Urartu (present-day Armenia), and parts of western Iran. Surrounding the land is the great circle of the Salt Sea, beyond which are marked regions where fabulous beasts were thought to live, and where the sun was not seen.

CHAPTER TEN

PERSIA – THE RISING NEW POWER

The revival of Babylon's fortunes under the Chaldean kings was short lived (see page 24). To the east of their New Babylonian Empire a power was growing that was to dominate the region for centuries to come.

The ruins of Persepolis lie in modern-day Iraq. Persepolis is the Greek name for the city built by the Persian king, Darius. Many fine columned buildings stood at its centre on a large stone platform that rose 15 metres above the surrounding plain.

THE RISE OF THE PERSIANS

The country of Persis, the homeland of the Persians, lay east of Babylon, in present-day Iran. In 559 BC, Cyrus became the Persian king. With his accession to the Persian royal throne the balance of power in the Near East changed. Cyrus waged war on his neighbours, the Medes, who had themselves been at war with the Assyrians. When he captured the city

PERSIA – THE RISING NEW POWER

of Hamadan, the Medes' capital,
he gained control of all their
lands, from the Black Sea in the
west as far as the Indus river
valley in the east.

Cyrus then turned his
attention towards the Lydians
(whose land occupied much of
present-day Turkey). He added
their country to his empire after
defeating them in battle in 547 BC.
His conquest of Lydia pushed
the western boundary of the
Persian Empire as far as the
shores of the Mediterranean and
Aegean seas, bringing him into
hostile contact with the Greek
world for the first time. Cyrus'
next conquest was Mesopotamia
itself. On 23 October 539 BC,
Cyrus and his Persian army
entered the city of Babylon. The
Babylonians were celebrating a
festival and offered little or no
resistance to the invaders. Cyrus
proclaimed himself 'King of the
world – King of Babylon, King of
Sumer and Akkad'.

Cyrus was a wise and righteous
ruler. He allowed the Jews exiled
in Babylon by Nebuchadnezzar to
return to their home city of
Jerusalem (see page 31), a
triumph for which he is praised in
the Bible, in the Old Testament
book of Isaiah. The Greek
historians Herodotus and
Xenophon also wrote about his
life in legendary terms.

*This procession of conquering soldiers from the
Persian army is carved on a stairway leading to
the palace of Darius at Persepolis.*

TIMELINE

Most of the dates in this list can only be given approximately.

BC

c. 14,000	The last Ice Age ends. Rainfall and temperature increases.
c. 10,000	Hunter-gatherers start to harvest wild grains.
c. 9000	Domestication of plants and animals begins.
c. 9000	Jericho, the world's oldest town, is settled.
c. 7000	First pottery made in the Near East.
c. 6500	The first villages appear in southern Mesopotamia.
c. 4500	First use of plough in Mesopotamia.
c. 3700	Uruk, the first town in Mesopotamia emerges.
c. 3300	Picture writing appears.
c. 3200	The wheel is invented.
c. 3100	Cuneiform script develops.
c. 2900 – c. 2300	The Sumerian civilisation flourishes in southern Mesopotamia.
c. 2600	The Royal Cemetery is in use at Ur, where rulers and nobles were buried with valuable grave goods, and their sacrificed attendants.
c. 2600	First use of a four-wheeled war wagon.
c. 2330 – c. 2200	The Akkadian civilisation flourishes in northern Mesopotamia.
2334 – 2279	Reign of Sargon, king of Akkad.
2112 – 2004	The time of the Third Dynasty of Ur.
2004 – 1792	The time of the Amorite kingdoms.
1792 – 1595	The Babylonian Empire flourishes.
1792 – 1750	Reign of Hammurabi, king of Babylon.
c. 1755	Hammurabi's Law Code is carved in stone.
c. 1700	The use of horses revolutionises warfare.
1595 – 1365	The Kassites rule Babylon.
1365 – 629	The Assyrian Empire flourishes.
880	Capital of Assyria moved to Nimrud.
705	Capital of Assyria moved to Nineveh.
668 – 629	Reign of Ashurbanipal, king of Assyria.
625 – 539	The time of the Chaldean or New Babylonian Empire.
612	Fall of Assyrian Empire: Nimrud and Nineveh are sacked.
604 – 562	Reign of Nebuchadnezzar II, king of Chaldea.
539	Babylon is captured by the Persians.
521 – 486	Reign of Darius I (the Great), king of Persia.
334 – 329	Alexander the Great (of Macedonia) conquers Egypt and Persia.

GLOSSARY

alloy two or more metals mixed together to make a different type of metal. Copper mixed with tin makes bronze.

ashipu an expert in magic, somewhat like a sorcerer.

astrology the study of how the stars influence people's lives.

astronomy the study of the stars, planets and other objects in the sky.

asu a doctor who treated patients with herbal remedies.

burnish to rub a pottery vessel before firing to give a smooth, glossy surface.

ceramic made from clay.

city-state a city and its land.

culture a word used by archaeologists to describe groups of people, usually prehistoric, who share common characteristics, such as making the same style of pottery.

cuneiform the script used in Mesopotamia and neighbouring regions for writing on clay tablets.

cylinder seal a tube engraved with a design which was impressed into damp clay when the seal was rolled over it.

decimal a counting system based on units of 10.

domesticated when a crop or animal is changed from its wild form into one that can be grown or reared by farmers.

Ice Age a cold period in the history of the Earth, characterised by ice sheets extending over large areas of land.

ideograph a sign drawn in picture writing, indicating an idea, not the name, of a thing.

law code a text written for a ruler recording the judgments and penalties for various crimes.

Lower Sea this is what the Mesopotamians called the Persian Gulf.

lugal the Sumerian word for 'king'.

lunar calendar the measuring of time based on observing the various phases of the moon.

mina a measure of weight used in the ancient world, equal to about 500 g.

Neanderthals early humans, named after a place in Germany where their skeletons were first identified. They lived from about 100,000 to 40,000 years ago.

Near East term used to describe a region of the south-western part of the continent of Asia, where the heartland of Mesopotamia lay. (Can also be called the Middle East.)

obsidian a naturally-occurring volcanic glass, used for cutting tools.

pictograph a sign in a script whose picture suggests the meaning.

relief carving sculpture in which the design stands out from a flat surface.

sexagesimal a counting system based on units of 60.

solar calendar the measuring of time based on observing the position of the sun in the sky.

stylus a writing implement made from a reed, bone, wood or metal.

tell the Arabic term for a mound consisting of the debris of an ancient settlement. Also called *tel* (Hebrew), *choga* or *tepe* (Persian) and *hüyük* (Turkish).

tribute a type of payment, like a tax, often made by the losers to the winners of a war. It can be in money or goods.

Upper Sea this is what the Mesopotamians called the Mediterranean Sea.

ziggurat a high tower built in stepped stages with a temple at the top.

INDEX

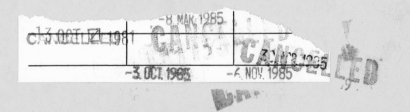

SOCIAL AND ECONOMIC INEQUALITY IN THE SOVIET UNION

SIX STUDIES

SOCIAL AND ECONOMIC INEQUALITY IN THE SOVIET UNION

SIX STUDIES

MURRAY YANOWITCH

MARTIN ROBERTSON

First published in Britain 1977
by Martin Robertson & Company Ltd.
17 Quick Street, London N1 8HL

ISBN: 0-85520-223-8 ✓

Printed in the United States of America

For Lee, Nina, and Philip

CONTENTS

LIST OF TABLES

PREFACE

To begin with the obvious — the Soviet Union is a socially divided society. The collectivities of which it is composed, whether designated as classes, strata, or "socio-occupational groups" (a term favored in recent Soviet writings on social structure), exhibit systematic differences in incomes and living standards, in control over the organization of the work place, in the educational and occupational opportunities open to their children. This can hardly come as a revelation. But what is new is that the social and economic inequalities which permeate Soviet life have become, within limits of course, accessible to study and discussion by Soviet scholars. The principal public justification for the study of inequality is the Party's need for reliable information to implement its function of "scientific management" of the relations between the main social groups in Soviet society. "Social planning" (or "social management"), no less than economic planning, has now been recognized as a distinct and necessary mechanism of control requiring constant guidance by the Party. Whatever the variety of meanings which may be attached to "social planning" and the specific policies pursued in its name, one of its principal functions is that of reconciling the divergent and sometimes conflicting interests of social groups. This is the context in which a considerable Soviet literature on the theme of inequality has emerged in recent years.

Although class and strata divisions are acknowledged to exist in the Soviet Union, the various social groups have no means of directly expressing and defending their own collective interests, of independently organizing to promote these interests. The Party has reserved for itself the right to speak for all. In this situation the writings of sociologists and economists (functioning as contributions to the promotion of efficient "social management") act

as a kind of filter through which some of the inequalities in rewards and opportunities emerge into view, and the grievances, aspirations, and interests of distinct social groups find some opportunities for expression. These are the writings we draw on in the
studies of Soviet economic and social inequalities which follow.

We approach the theme of inequality in the Soviet Union from
two standpoints. One of our objectives is to present in reasonably
systematic form some of the evidence bearing on the unequal position of the principal social groups in the distribution of rewards,
opportunities, and decision-making power, as well as on male-
female differentials in work and family roles. But these "objective" indicators of inequality are not our only concern. Inequality
has also emerged as a public issue in a number of controversies
that have been part of the intellectual ferment of the post-Stalinist
epoch. We examine these controversies for what they reveal about
the tensions, grievances, and conflicts generated by the deep social divisions which are continually reproduced in the Soviet Union.
These discussions have concerned such matters as educational
policy (the advisability of preferential college admission for particular social groups), the need for "democratization" of management, the measures required to overcome women's subordinate
status, and alternative theoretical approaches to the study of Soviet
class structure. The issue of inequality has been a central one in
all of these discussions. Although such discussions can hardly be
characterized as "open debates," they reveal new ideas struggling
for a hearing. The spectrum of views which emerges is itself part
of the evidence of social differentiation. Thus our interest throughout this volume is not only in the "facts" of inequality but also in
some of the ways in which class and strata divisions are reflected
in controversies on social and economic issues.

Moshe Lewin has written that "the vocation of Marxism is the
analysis of class realities, of class forces hiding behind various
facades...." One of the ironies and tragedies of Soviet intellectual life is that Soviet scholars cannot apply this "vocation" to the
analysis of their own society. We have sought to bring together
some of the material that would go into such an effort.

A word on some matters that are not considered in any detail.
We trust that readers will not regard the omission of the familiar
as a fatal flaw in the essays which follow. Thus the privileges and
power associated with membership in the "professional" apparatus
of the Party and state administration receive no special attention
here. We take these for granted. But the privileges of "official-

dom" are only one element of the broader theme of class and strata divisions in the Soviet Union. Each of the following essays is intended as a self-contained study of some aspect of this general theme. The absence of a concluding "synthesis" reflects our conception of these essays as initial steps toward a more comprehensive study of the structure and ideology of inequality in Soviet life.

ACKNOWLEDGMENTS

The author is pleased to acknowledge the financial assistance of the American Council of Learned Societies. He is also grateful to Murray Feshbach for many useful comments and suggestions over the years. Special thanks are due Bertram Silverman, a friend and colleague, for numerous helpful discussions on the broad theme of these essays.

SOCIAL AND ECONOMIC INEQUALITY IN THE SOVIET UNION

SIX STUDIES

Our main concerns throughout this study are some of the principal forms of social and economic inequality in the Soviet version of a socialist society. More specifically, we focus on inequalities between social groups in incomes and living standards, access to schooling, public esteem, opportunities for mobility, and — in a somewhat limited context — participation in decision-making. We also examine some of the ways in which social inequality has emerged as an issue in Soviet public discourse, however restricted the latter may be. Social tensions associated with inequality, which cannot be expressed more directly, have a way of appearing in such discussions even if in muted form.

For source material we rely heavily, although not exclusively, on recent Soviet studies of domestic social structure. The questions posed in this area of Soviet sociological literature, the empirical studies undertaken, as well as the issues which have thus far been avoided reflect a certain "vision" of social structure. How does Soviet social thought portray the structure of its own society? We are, of course, asking the same question that the Polish sociologist Stanislaw Ossowski asked about an earlier period of Soviet history.[1] Given the passage of time since Ossowski's work (written in the early 1950s) and the relatively abundant Soviet literature on social structure in the interim, this question deserves to be asked anew in its own right. Our answer to it, however, will also serve to introduce the kinds of materials we rely on in subsequent chapters for our analysis of some of the principal forms and magnitudes of inequality in current Soviet society.

The Stalinist Heritage

Ossowski characterized the "official Soviet image" of society

3

during the Stalinist period as one "in which there are classes without class antagonisms and without class stratification."[2] The two classes whose existence was recognized were associated with different forms of "socialist property" — the working class with state property and the collective farm peasantry with cooperative property. The third (and final) structural element in this vision of a socialist society was the "socialist intelligentsia," a social group accorded the designation of "stratum" rather than "class." No pretense was made, however, that this was an equalitarian society. This was hardly possible since this mode of perceiving Soviet social structure emerged during a period when "equalitarianism" was a term of opprobrium and income differentials were in the process of being widened. But the existence of substantial income inequalities was not associated with class (or strata) privileges or hierarchy, for it reflected the differing merits of individuals, i.e., their differential contribution to production.

There is a sense, of course, in which one class — the working class — was regarded as having a superior status rooted in its "historic mission." It was associated with a "higher" form of property and played the "leading" role in the transition to communism. But once again, this was "a superiority of merit and not of privileges."[3] It was not connected with the power of one group in the social structure to appropriate the labor of another. The transition to the future communist society was not seen primarily in terms of a reduction in social or economic inequality, or in the increased power of direct producers over the conditions of production, but rather as a process of "merger" of the two forms of socialist property (and thus the disappearance of classes), a rise in the "cultural-technical level" of those engaged in manual labor, and the emergence of material abundance.

We have reproduced here the obviously simplistic and ideological formulations which dominated Soviet representations of domestic social structure from the late 1930s to the early 1960s. Our purpose in restating what may be familiar is to provide a point of departure against which the significance of more recent modes of perceiving the structure of Soviet society may be gauged. How has the old vision changed and what elements of it have been retained? Has a genuinely new vision emerged or is the new merely a gloss on the old — embellished with the jargon and trappings of "concrete sociological research"? How can we account for whatever changes have occurred in modes of "seeing" social classes and strata?

The Limited Acceptance of Stratification

For the earlier period there is no need to distinguish between "popular" and "scientific" representations of social structure. Whether this structure was defined in the holiday pronouncements of a political leader, an article in a Party "theoretical" journal, or a textbook on "historical materialism," the picture was essentially the one we have presented above. With the emergence of sociology as a legitimate intellectual discipline in the 1960s, a distinct "scientific" literature on social structure appears. We shall focus largely on this literature and, more particularly, on those of its representatives who, in our judgment, have done the most serious work on social divisions and the nature of inequality in Soviet society. These include, among others, sociologists like T. Zaslavskaia, O. Shkaratan, Iu. Arutiunian, and their colleagues.

One of the most striking aspects of this literature is the manner in which it has introduced a new terminology and conceptual apparatus into Soviet discussions of social structure without directly repudiating the official Soviet image of earlier years. Thus the concept of Soviet society as a hierarchical structure of social groups capable of being ranked according to their "higher" or "lower" status has been explicitly formulated in this literature. Perhaps the clearest expression of this appears in the work of Zaslavskaia:

The social positions occupied by different strata and classes in the socialist society can be, in principle, represented in the form of a certain hierarchy in which some positions are regarded as higher than others. The foundation for the vertical hierarchy of social positions ... is the complexity ... and responsibility of the work performed, an increase in which is normally accompanied by a rise in required education, increased material rewards, and corresponding changes in the mode of life.[4]

In a similar vein she applies to Soviet society the concept of social groups existing in "social space" whose structure must be described with the aid of vertical as well as horizontal coordinates.[5] Although Zaslavskaia's work has been mainly concerned with the special problem of rural-to-urban migration, it clearly conveys a certain image of social structure as a whole, one whose principal elements are "vertically differentiated" groups arranged on a "ladder of social positions."[6]

Shkaratan, whose work has focused directly on social structure, sees the latter concept as inseparably connected with social inequality. The elements of this structure are "groups of people unequal in social and economic terms...."[7] Indeed, one of the justifications for the study of social structure is that "it is a concept which helps to identify social inequality for the purpose of struggling for its elimination."[8] Moreover, the inequality of social groups is seen by Shkaratan as not only a heritage of capitalism but as being reproduced by socialism.[9]

Even these very general features of the approach embodied in the writings of sociologists like Zaslavskaia and Shkaratan signify a clear break with some elements of the earlier "official vision" of social structure described by Ossowski. This is certainly true of the former conception of a class system which is exclusively horizontally structured, and the view of inequality of rewards as mainly reflecting differing individual merits. Of equal, if not greater, significance is the recognition of the inadequacy of the traditional tripartite division of Soviet society ("two basic classes plus one stratum") as an instrument for analyzing prevailing social differentiation. Although the traditional scheme has not been explicitly rejected, the new sociological literature has sought to identify a multiplicity of "socio-occupational groups" (or "social strata") — eight to ten in some studies — and to portray their differentiation with respect to economic status, cultural levels, value orientations, and general mode of life. The specification of a larger number of distinct social gradations than allowed for in the traditional tripartite scheme has been defended partly on very "practical" grounds — the need for "social planning" to supplement the long-established economic planning. This requires reliable information to deal with such social processes as rural-to-urban migration, city planning, leisure-time activities, youngsters' career plans. The need for the effective "management" of these processes, as well as for policies to promote "social integration," have been invoked to legitimize the disaggregation of the "two basic classes plus one stratum" model of earlier years.

The new approach we are describing may be illustrated by examining the social gradations used in the studies of Shkaratan and Arutiunian. Shkaratan's studies focus on the social structure of industrial enterprises (sample studies of Leningrad machinery plants) and urban populations (three cities in the Tatar Republic). Arutiunian's work centers on the social structure of collective farm and state enterprises in rural localities. The distinct social groups identified in some of these studies are shown in Table 1.1. These groups range from common laborers at one extreme to managerial personnel at the enterprise level at the other. The

Table 1.1

Classification of Socio-occupational Groups in
Soviet Studies of Social Structure

Shkaratan's Studies of Machine-Building Enterprises
1. Managerial personnel (plant directors, department and shop chiefs)
2. Highly skilled scientific and technical personnel (designers)
3. Personnel in skilled mental work (technologists, economists, planning personnel, bookkeepers)
4. Highly skilled workers combining mental and manual functions (adjusters, tuners of automatic lines, repair mechanics)
5. Skilled manual workers in hand work (metal craftsmen, assemblers and fitters, electricians)
6. Skilled manual workers on machinery (machine operators, punch-press operators, press operators, machinists, motor mechanics)
7. Middle-level nonmanual employees (clerical and office personnel, inspectors, sorters)
8. Unskilled manual workers

Arutiunian's Studies of Rural Social Structure
1. Higher-level managerial personnel (collective farm chairmen, directors of state farms, schools, enterprises)
2. Higher-level specialists (agronomists, zootechnicians, engineers, teachers with higher education)
3. Middle-level managerial personnel (heads of departments of state farms, brigade leaders)
4. Middle-level specialists (those with secondary specialized education)
5. Nonmanual employees (clerical staff, cashiers, accountants, supervisors of nurseries)
6. Machine operators (tractor operators, drivers, repair workers)
7. Skilled workers and collective farmers
8. Low-skilled workers and collective farmers
9. Common laborers

Sources: O. I. Shkaratan, Problemy sotsial'noi struktury rabochego klassa SSSR, pp. 377-79; L. S. Bliakhman and O. I. Shkaratan, NTR, rabochii klass, intelligentsiia, pp. 269-70; Iu. V. Arutiunian, "A Social-Ethnic Study," Sovetskaia etnografiia, 1968, no. 4, p. 7; Iu. V. Arutiunian, Sotsial'noe i natsional'noe, pp. 329-30.

data presented in these and similar studies on the economic status, cultural attributes, and life chances of these strata provide us with some of the raw material used in subsequent chapters to analyze the nature of social and economic inequality in Soviet society.

Our concern at this point, however, is with the general vision of Soviet society implied in these new schemes of social classification and the justifications which Soviet sociologists offer for them. The point of departure of the new approach is that "in the social structure of ... our society, along with differences associated with different forms of socialist property, socio-occupational differences rooted in the peculiarities of the socioeconomic division of labor acquire essential importance."[10] The principal basis for social differentiation becomes the "quality of labor." This can be conceived as varying along a manual-mental "continuum," with gradations also depending on the complexity of the labor and the extent to which it requires managerial initiative rather than the performance of preassigned tasks.[11] Adherents of this approach place particular stress on the notion that these are not schemes of "polar divisions" in Soviet society but of "gradual transitions" and "intermediate types."[12] In other words, this mode of representing social structure obviously tends to obscure any sharp discontinuities in both the content of work performed and in the rewards — material and nonmaterial — associated with it.

These divisions into socio-occupational groups (or social strata) are not presented as negating the traditional scheme but as providing a "more complete, detailed, and multifaceted classification"[13] than the tripartite system of working class–collective farm peasantry–intelligentsia allows. In some of their work both Shkaratan and Arutiunian treat all the social groups which they distinguish as constituting elements of the "intraclass structure" of the basic classes. Thus the technical intelligentsia in state industrial enterprises is regarded as a stratum (or a series of strata) within the working class, and its counterpart in collective farms as a stratum of the peasantry.[14] This appears to imply the abandonment of the notion of a single and distinct intelligentsia stratum or to confine this category to those members of the intelligentsia employed in "nonmaterial production" (the arts, teaching, medicine). Although this is the aspect of their writings ("dissolving" a portion of the intelligentsia into the two basic classes) that has been seized upon by their critics among the more traditional Soviet sociologists, there is a more important aspect of their approach which signals a new mode of conceptualizing Soviet social structure. For Arutiunian the socio-occupational group is already "the primary element of social structure."[15] For Shkaratan such groups are the "decisive structure-forming elements" of the urban population he studies in the Tatar Republic and Leningrad.[16] Both of these sociologists suggest the possibility of constructing a "nonclass system" of "intrasocietal groups" as a way of classifying the structural elements of society. Given the diminishing importance of differences in forms of property ownership and the increasing significance of "character of labor" as a socially differentiating factor, the variety of socio-occupational groups may be conceived simultaneously as components of a class system (the "two plus one" scheme) and of society regarded as a multiplicity of social strata cutting across the class system:

> Socio-occupational groups may be examined from different points of view. On the one hand they appear as intraclass groups, i.e., they determine the internal structure of classes. But on the other hand, to the extent that differences between classes are diminishing and contiguous groups are becoming increasingly similar in the character of labor, they may appear as and be regarded as intrasocietal groups — strata. In this approach to structure society represents a multistrata system in which the intelligentsia is one of the social strata. In addition, nonmanual employees, skilled manual workers, low-skilled and unskilled manual workers constitute distinct strata. Naturally, with a more detailed analysis these categories in turn may be broken down into internal strata, particularly in the case of the intelligentsia. [17]

The language and conceptual apparatus of social stratification have thus become part of the Soviet discourse on social structure. Its assimilation into Soviet social thought is evidenced in a variety of forms. Discussions of Western stratification literature, for example, are no longer exclusively critical. Such literature is criticized not for identifying a multiplicity of social strata in capitalist society but for ignoring the principal type of social division — social classes in the Marxian sense — and for relying on "arbitrary characteristics" to distinguish social strata.[18] Expositions of domestic social structure by "official" spokesmen since the mid-1960s have regularly cited the existence of social strata within the basic classes and intelligentsia category.[19] A sociologist like Shkaratan has referred directly to the "stratified, scaled type" of social divisions under socialism, in contrast to the "polarity" of social groups under a regime of private property.[20] Arutiunian has presented a ranking of nine socio-occupational groups according to a synthetic index of social status derived by combining measures of income, education, and "influence within the collective" for each group.[21]

But the conceptualization and empirical study of Soviet stratification have thus far been limited in certain obvious ways. The upper reaches of the social structure have been systematically excluded from even the best of the Soviet studies, and the political and power dimensions of stratification have been largely ignored. This may be readily illustrated by observing the socio-occupational groups identified in Table 1.1. The highest groups encompassed in Arutiunian's studies of rural social structure ("higher-level managerial personnel") include collective farm chairmen, state farm directors, and directors of rural industrial enterprises and schools. Shkaratan's studies of social structure in the machine-building industry isolate a group called "managerial personnel of production collectives," a composite that includes plant directors, department heads, and shop chiefs; but no data on incomes, cultural levels, or social sources of recruitment are presented separately for the individual components of this category. His studies of urban social structure in the Tatar Republic (not shown in Table 1.1) combine "managerial personnel of social and state organizations" and "managerial personnel of production collectives" into one group, again without further specification. Thus empirical studies of what is acknowledged to be a hierarchical social structure are essentially confined to the primary units of economic organization — industrial enterprises and farms. When "quality of labor" or "position in the social division of labor" are presented as the principal criteria of social differentiation, the context is almost invariably the "production collective." Personnel employed in the higher levels of government ministries, planning agencies, the scientific establishment — not to speak of the Party organization — are not included in the "continuum" of socio-occupational strata whose incomes, life styles, and opportunities for intergenerational transmission of status are investigated by Shkaratan, Arutiunian, or any other Soviet sociologist.[22] Those groups whose macroeconomic and macrosocial decisions control the allocation of society's productive resources and its reward structure are excluded from scrutiny.

This does not mean that the power dimension of stratification is completely ignored. Arutiunian, for example, shows that the different socio-occupational groups in rural economic units differ markedly in their perception of their influence "in deciding major questions in the collective."[23] Moreover, we shall see (in Chapter 6) that inequality of power is a legitimate theme in the empirical study of relationships within the family. But once again, as in the case of income and cultural differentiation, a form of inequality appears only at the "collective" (enterprise or family), not the societal level.

The higher strata of Soviet society, which are notable for their absence in the empirical studies of stratification, do make their appearance, however, in the theoretical literature on social structure. Iu. Volkov has identified a special stratum of the intelligentsia professionally employed in performing functions of management, including the "management of social processes." This includes not only plant managers but persons employed in "higher organs of economic management" and in "state organs of administrative-political management not related directly to production." They are distinguished by "the right to make decisions binding on others" and to implement these decisions through the use of coercion, if necessary.[24] Similarly, Shkaratan recognizes the existence of a stratum of "professional executives" that includes "Party and state personnel" not employed in material production but who perform "societal functions corresponding to the requirements of society as a whole taken in its unity."[25] Here we have the essential features of the concept of power which appears in Soviet discussions. Power is something that is invariably used in the public interest. It never appears — at least in a macrosocial context — as a relationship between rulers and subjects.

The "professional executives" obliquely identified by sociologists like Shkaratan and Volkov with the "management of social processes" are precisely the social groups whose relative positions in the distribution of material and cultural values and power over the production process are not specified in Soviet empirical studies of social structure. Thus the basic polarities in this structure between those who control and consume society's economic surplus and those who produce it — between ruling and subordinate "classes" in the Marxian sense — remain concealed from view. Nonetheless the range of inequality revealed when the polar sociooccupational groups within industrial enterprises or farms are compared is obviously substantially greater than that embodied in the "average" indicators for the three heterogeneous groups which constituted Soviet social structure in the former "official" version.

The Interpretation of Inequality

Soviet expressions of attitudes toward social inequality and attempts to justify its continued existence reveal the same readiness to go beyond the simplistic propositions of an earlier period simultaneously with an inability to complete a line of argument or scheme of empirical research. Obvious questions that are implicitly posed by the logic of an argument remain unanswered.

In contrast to the period from the early 1930s to the mid-1950s, recent Soviet discussions of this theme reveal a distinctly egalitarian tone — at least in some respects. Increased "social homogeneity" is invariably presented as a positive value and as descriptive of actual trends in Soviet society. Indeed, a principal criterion of the "maturity" or "progressiveness" of social structure is the "attained level of social homogeneity."[26] Suggestions have been made for incorporating in the state planning mechanism "social indicators" which would specify targets for reductions in inequality in incomes, educational attainments, and cultural levels of social groups.[27] Egalitarian sentiments have been expressed with particular clarity in connection with evidence of social inequalities in access to higher education. Such inequalities not only represent an underutilization of society's intellectual potential, they are also "unjust" and contain the danger of the "self-reproduction" of the intelligentsia.[28] But the theme of removing "injustices" (in the form of social inequality) appears much less frequently than the stress on the further development of the "productive forces" as the basis for achieving "full social equality" in the future. The attainment of a socially homogeneous society is almost always made dependent on continued progress in science and technology which presumably will permit a steady reduction in disparities in conditions of work and rewards.[29] Moreover, the movement toward social equality cannot be an "elemental," i.e., uncontrolled, process. Like all social processes, its pace and forms are necessarily subject to the guidance and regulation of the Party and state.[30] The very mode of characterizing progress toward social equality in a society admittedly divided into classes and strata excludes the possibility that group conflict may be an element in this process. Like the transition to communism, of which it is a part, the reduction of social inequality is an aspect of "social management."

But why should substantial inequalities in rewards continue to exist in Soviet society long after the elimination of private and unequal ownership of the means of production? This should be an important question for Soviet Marxists. If an unequal (ownership) relation to the means of production is no longer the principal source of economic and social differentiation — as it presumably is under capitalism — what is the underlying mechanism that generates and reproduces inequalities in income, cultural levels, and prestige under socialism?

To the extent that Soviet sociologists have directly confronted this question, their discussion has relied on the concept of the "social division of labor."[31] Although from the standpoint of ownership all individuals have an essentially similar relationship to the means of production, they contribute unequally to society's economic and cultural development. This reflects the need to "attach" individuals — often for extended periods — to specific work activities of differing significance to society. The "normal functioning" of the economy, given the still inadequate state of the productive forces, does not permit anything like an equal sharing or rotation of different job functions among the members of the work force. Thus the division of labor into mental and manual, complex and routine, managerial and subordinate job functions becomes a division of society into distinct social groups retaining relatively fixed occupational positions throughout their work careers and contributing unequally to economic and cultural growth. It remains only to ask why the "historically conditioned" inequality of contribution should be accompanied by inequality of rewards. The answer, once again, simply reaffirms the overriding influence of economic backwardness on questions of distribution: Until abundance is achieved (a goal presumably shared by all), society "evaluates and will continue to evaluate its members primarily according to their contribution to the development of social production, i.e., according to the quantity and quality of their labor."[32]

Instead of dismissing this as merely another illustration of the Soviet capacity for mystification and ideological justification for privilege, we prefer to specify just what this approach accomplishes and what it leaves unexplored. Its principal function is to make inequalities in productive contribution, and hence in economic rewards, dependent on position in an "objectively existing" structure of production. The underdeveloped state of this production mechanism limits the number of work positions which can utilize high levels of intellectual and manual skills. Thus by virtue of the jobs which must be filled, individuals have unequal opportunities to develop their own natural talents and to contribute to society's economic and cultural growth.[33] Inequalities of rewards, consequently, are not primarily the results of individual differences in work effort, ideological commitment, or even talent (i.e., they do not reflect merely differences in individual "merit"). They are inherent in a social structure whose main contours are necessarily governed by the structure of production processes. The socialist society not only inherits social and economic inequality from capitalism but reproduces it insofar as the urgency of continued economic growth requires retaining a "social division of labor."[34] This is an aspect of its "immaturity" compared to the communist society of the future.[35]

This is an approach which obviously accepts and justifies existing social and economic inequalities as objectively required by
economic backwardness. Such inequalities, however, are not
treated as the embodiment of justice, and the explicit acknowledg-
ment that they are reproduced by socialism (albeit temporarily)
bespeaks an attempt to grapple with the realities of a stratified
society that has no counterpart in earlier Soviet writings. What
the "social division of labor" approach ignores, however, is the
obvious fact that inequalities of rewards (at least of economic rewards) are determined in the process of political decision-making.
Whatever may be "society's evaluation" of the differential contributions of various socio-occupational groups, the actual structure
of income differentials stems from the decisions of political and
state agencies. How do such agencies translate the relative "contributions" to economic development of, let us say, collective
farmers and industrial executives, or workers in capital goods
and consumer goods industries, into a structure of income differentials? Do not such "contributions" reflect the economic priorities of the income-determining agencies themselves? How do the
heads of such agencies, in their capacity as specialists in "social
management," gauge their own "contribution" (and hence their own
appropriate income levels)? Until Soviet sociologists are able to
confront the issue of power — power over both the production and
distribution process — and the whole mechanism of political
stratification, their reliance on the "social division of labor" to
explain social and economic inequality will conceal at least as
much as it reveals.

A Debate on Social Structure:
The Problem of the Intelligentsia

Recent Soviet efforts to conceptualize social structure in a way
that permits its more serious study have generated a controversy
on the position of the intelligentsia in Soviet society. The course
of this debate illustrates the manner in which progress in Soviet
social thought and empirical research is made by simultaneously
confronting and adapting to long-established ideological propositions.

The legacy of the Stalinist conception of social structure was
particularly unsatisfactory in its treatment of the intelligentsia.
In effect this category covered all individuals not included in the

working class and collective farm peasantry, i.e., all those employed in nonmanual or "mental labor." The serious study of social structure could not proceed without disaggregating a "stratum"
which included within its ranks such diverse groups as clerical
staff, writers and artists, engineers, and state ministers — all
presumably engaged primarily in mental labor. Since the mid-
1960s sociologists have conventionally distinguished between two
categories of mental labor, reserving the title of "intelligentsia"
for the second: (1) routine white-collar jobs, typically in office
and sales occupations, not requiring specialized or advanced education; and (2) skilled mental labor normally requiring a higher
or specialized secondary education.[36] Incumbents of the first category are typically referred to as "nonspecialist" employees (sluzhashchie), while those in the second are "specialists" (or intelligentsia proper).[37] This still leaves considerable heterogeneity in
the intelligentsia category but obviously improves on earlier formulations. A typical exposition of the "basic elements" in Soviet social structure will now cite as distinct social groups the working
class, the collective farm peasantry, employees, and the intelligentsia (with the latter two referred to as strata employed in mental labor).[38]

The controversy that has arisen among Soviet sociologists concerns the issue of the dividing line between the two classes on the
one hand and those employed in mental labor on the other, or more
particularly the "boundaries" of the working class and the relation
of the intelligentsia to these boundaries. Although in its concern
with "correct definitions" the dispute has some of the earmarks
of medieval scholasticism, it is nonetheless significant. In addition to illustrating the way in which new conceptions of social
structure struggle for recognition in Soviet thought, it also raises
issues which have recently occupied the attention of students of
social structure in nonsocialist countries.

Citing the increasing complexity of social structure, the shifting
boundaries of social classes, and the appearance of "mixed types,"
a group of sociologists has argued that some categories of mental
labor should be regarded as strata within the working class. This
position has been most clearly expressed in the writings of S. A.
Kugel' and O. I. Shkaratan:

...while in a professional-technical sense, in the character of its labor, the intelligentsia as a whole remains as a distinct stratum, in a socioeconomic sense
we may observe a very definite tendency for the merger into a single social
group of workers in manual and mental labor employed in state enterprises in
the sphere of material production. Consequently, the technical intelligentsia

may be increasingly regarded as an autonomous stratum of the working class, as part of the aggregate worker. Similar processes are occurring within the collective farm peasantry.[39]

In current Soviet society, considering the socioeconomic and sociopolitical characteristics of the working class, it seems to us appropriate to include in it all workers in both manual and mental labor in branches of material production and circulation employed at enterprises and institutions that are common public property. This approach is based on common characteristics in the process of production. . . .

Thus in certain respects and under specific historical circumstances, the division between workers in mental and manual labor emerges as an aspect of intraclass differences.[40]

Some of the sociologists who support this position have sought to defend it by specifying those changes in the work roles of the intelligentsia which have made for a convergence, and in some cases a "fusion," between this stratum and the working class. Thus the sheer "massification" of the intelligentsia has been invoked (by L. Gordon and E. Klopov) as evidence of the loss of its "elitist" character. Employment in intelligentsia occupations is typically concentrated in large-scale economic units, and specialists are therefore subject to the same kind of work discipline as other employees. Their work roles are now less likely to require their "direct management" of other individuals and often involve the same kind of "fragmentation" as workers' jobs.[41] All of this is presented not to suggest the disappearance of the intelligentsia stratum as a whole but to argue for extending the boundaries of a socially differentiated working class.

Some of the principal figures among Soviet sociologists have consistently opposed such suggestions as constituting an effort to "dissolve" the intelligentsia into the working class. M. N. Rutkevich, in particular, has insisted on the retention of the concept of a separate intelligentsia stratum, all of whose elements — whether lower-level technicians, engineers, or scientists — are distinct from the working class (and peasantry). This position is defended by arguing that the "content of labor" — particularly the extent to which it is predominantly manual or mental in nature — is a "class-forming" factor. The employment of the variegated intelligentsia in skilled mental labor apparently divides it from even the most skilled portions of the working class.[42] For V. S. Semenov, another opponent of those who seek to extend the boundaries of the working class, the latters' arguments suggest the notion of the "proletarianization" (orabochievanie) of all social groups.[43]

Social homogeneity will be increasingly attained, but not through all groups absorbing the attributes of one particular (working) class. For other opponents of the new proposals (G. Glezerman, for example) there are logical difficulties in abandoning the neatness and simplicity of the traditional scheme:

Some writers propose that the intelligentsia should be regarded as a component or stratum within the working class and the cooperative peasantry. But in this interpretation it would appear that the socialist intelligentsia is divided into two parts — a workers' and collective farm intelligentsia, between whom there are class differences. In addition, some of the intelligentsia (people in the free professions and others) cannot be included in either of these classes and therefore do not fit into such a classification.[44]

The main thrust of all these criticisms by spokesmen for the traditional approach is to reaffirm the conceptual integrity of a distinct intelligentsia stratum separated from the working class and peasantry by virtue of its employment in mental labor. In some respects these criticisms present a strange spectacle. In a society which proclaims the working class to be the "leading" class, why should it be so important to exclude from it even the lower levels of an obviously inflated (in a definitional sense) intelligentsia stratum?

Inertia and the normal resistance to abandoning long-established ideological formulations obviously play a role here. But there are other considerations of a political character at work. It is one thing to project the vision of a "socially homogeneous" society and to proudly claim that a "convergence" (sblizhenie) between the working class and the intelligentsia is already in progress. It is quite another to argue that the "boundaries" of the working class have already shifted to absorb elements of the intelligentsia. This thesis, with its unmistakable affinity to the notion of the "proletarianization" of professional strata in the West, implies that "social homogeneity" is being attained through the social descent of the intelligentsia to working-class status. This is not a position that the cautious ideological guardians of Soviet sociology can easily accept. Its implications are troublesome from the standpoint of the interests of the working class as well as the intelligentsia. For many workers the hope of access to intelligentsia status (for their children, if not for themselves) has rested on the economy's rapidly growing demand for engineers and technicians. For the more traditionally minded and politically sensitive sociologists, one of the difficulties in accepting the Kugel'-Shkaratan thesis of shifting class boundaries is its implication that technological advance and economic development involve a demotion to working-class status of precisely those intelligentsia occupations which upwardly mobile workers aspire to enter. In its own way the debate over the boundaries of the working class reflects an underlying tension in Soviet social policy: the need to appeal to the egalitarian sentiments of lower strata (via the constant reaffirmation of the vision of a "socially homogeneous" society) without threatening the material advantages — however limited these sometimes are — and social esteem associated with intelligentsia status. The thesis advanced by sociologists like Shkaratan and Kugel' has been troublesome precisely because it could not be easily reconciled with the second of these objectives.

Whatever may be the difficulties some Soviet sociologists have confronted in abandoning the traditional dichotomy between working class and intelligentsia, it is important to understand the limited methodological objectives of a sociologist like Shkaratan, the chief proponent of extending the boundaries of the working class. He has clearly not suggested that the whole of the intelligentsia be (conceptually) "dissolved" into the two basic classes, nor that important differences in job content, economic status, and life styles between intelligentsia and working-class occupations have disappeared. His objective has been to establish the legitimacy of the manual-mental labor distinction as a "relatively independent" — i.e., "nonclass" — basis for studying social differentiation in Soviet society.[45] Differences in content of labor generate social groups ("socio-occupational groups," "social strata"), but these differences are not class-differentiating attributes. They produce a set of social gradations among those employed on a given type of socialist property. Thus all individuals employed in the Leningrad machinery plants (ranging from common laborers to plant managers) which were the subjects of his research were studied "jointly" as members of a single class divided into social strata according to manual-mental labor gradations. This approach permitted inequalities in economic and social status between the polar groups in Soviet factories to be portrayed as intraclass inequalities. Essentially the same was true of Arutiunian's studies of the social structure of collective and state farms. One cannot help but suspect that the incorporation of the technical intelligentsia into the working class and peasantry by these sociologists was, at least in part, a strategic device designed to make the inequalities which their studies revealed more ideologically acceptable than they otherwise would be. The as-

sumption was that the legitimacy of such studies would be reinforced by an intraclass approach to social inequality.

Confronting the continued opposition of some of the most authoritative figures in Soviet sociology, the proponents of extending class
boundaries to encompass the intelligentsia have retreated from
some of their earlier, more extreme formulations. Thus in some
of his more recent work (1973) Shkaratan labels as "incorrect"
the view that the whole of the "production-technical intelligentsia"
is already part of the working class and affirms the existence of
the intelligentsia as a distinct stratum. Nonetheless he also re-
states — in a somewhat more restricted form — the essence of
the thesis he and Kugel' began to propound in the mid-1960s:

A part of the intelligentsia directly employed in the production process at enterprises may be regarded as a highly educated stratum of the working class.
We refer to technicians, engineers servicing complex aggregates and cyber-
netic devices, laboratory engineers, etc....
An increasing portion of the intelligentsia consists of skilled executors who
are distinguished from workers mainly by the differing relative weight of manual
and mental elements in the labor process.[46]

Thus the issues remain unresolved, and conflicting conceptu-
alizations of the worker-intelligentsia boundary continue to receive a hearing.[47] One of the more significant side effects of the
controversy, however, has been the explicit recognition of the
heterogeneity of the intelligentsia stratum itself. The sociological literature has distinguished at least the following subdivisions
within the intelligentsia category: engineering-technical personnel, administrative-managerial cadres, scientists, personnel in
education and public health, military specialists, and the "creative intelligentsia."[48] As noted earlier, however, only some of
these groups have been included in empirical studies of social
structure. Aside from the obvious absence of data on the economic and social status of military specialists, the most notable
gap in these studies concerns the upper levels of the "administrative-managerial" component of the intelligentsia stratum. Only
in conceptual terms is its presence recognized, and then only
fleetingly.

We may now return to the principal question posed earlier. How
has the original Stalinist conception of social structure been modi-
fied and what elements of it have been retained? The vision of society as a set of functional, nonantagonistic social groups remains
intact as an underlying conception. The distinct social groups,
however, now include not only two classes and a stratum employed

in mental labor but a multiplicity of "socio-occupational strata" within and overlapping the larger social groups. It has become a common practice for studies of social and cultural differentiation in the 1970s to encompass a variety of distinct strata (seven to nine seems to be a typical number), ranging from unskilled laborers to managerial personnel and technical specialists.[49] Inequalities are seen as a function of location in social structure rather than as reflections of individual merit. The differential contributions of the various strata to the system's economic and cultural growth are the basis for (declining but still significant) inequalities in rewards, opportunities, and public esteem. Economic and technological change make for an increasingly "complex" social structure, and thus the precise boundaries of social groups are less clear-cut than formerly. The political dimension of stratification and inequalities in the distribution of power — unlike economic and cultural inequalities — remain largely ignored.

The student of socialist stratification systems must recognize and accept these limits if Soviet materials are to be used to examine such systems. However confining these limits may be, there is much that can be discovered. This we shall now proceed to demonstrate.

Notes

1. Stanislaw Ossowski, Class Structure in the Social Consciousness (London: Routledge and Kegan Paul, 1967), ch. VII.
2. Ibid., p. 142.
3. Ibid., p. 112.
4. Akademiia nauk SSSR, Institut mezhdunarodnogo rabochego dvizheniia, Urbanizatsiia i rabochii klass v usloviiakh nauchno-tekhnicheskoi revoliutsii, Moscow, 1970, p. 103.
5. T. Zaslavskaia ed., Doklady vsesoiuznomu simpoziumu po sotsiologicheskim problemam sela, Novosibirsk, 1968, p. 5.
6. Ibid., p. 39. We rely on one of Zaslavskaia's colleagues, L. D. Antosenkova.
7. O. I. Shkaratan, Problemy sotsial'noi struktury rabochego klassa SSSR, Moscow, 1970, p. 52.
8. Ibid., p. 456.
9. Ibid., p. 153.
10. Iu. V. Arutiunian ed., Sotsial'noe i natsional'noe, Moscow, 1973, p. 7.
11. Ibid., p. 8.
12. O. I. Shkaratan, "The Working Class of Socialist Society in the Epoch of the Scientific-Technical Revolution," Voprosy filosofii, 1968, no. 11, p. 18.
13. Iu. V. Arutiunian, Sotsial'noe i natsional'noe, p. 7.
14. O. I. Shkaratan, Problemy, pp. 118, 120.

15. Iu. V. Arutiunian, Sotsial'naia struktura sel'skogo naseleniia SSSR, Moscow, 1971, p. 99.

16. O. I. Shkaratan, "Problems of Social Structure of the Soviet City," Nauchnye doklady vysshei shkoly, filosofskie nauki, 1970, no. 5, p. 23.

17. Iu. V. Arutiunian, Sotsial'naia struktura, p. 99. The same approach, although formulated in somewhat more abstract terms, appears in O. I. Shkaratan, Problemy, p. 117.

18. E. E. Murniek, "Intraclass Differentiation of the Collective Farm Peasantry," in Akademiia obshchestvennykh nauk pri Ts. K. KPSS, Problemy nauchnogo kommunizma, no. 6, Moscow, 1972, p. 94.

19. M. Yanowitch and W. Fisher, Social Stratification and Mobility in the USSR (White Plains, N. Y.: International Arts and Sciences Press, 1973), p. xix.

20. O. I. Shkaratan, Problemy, p. 38.

21. Iu. V. Arutiunian, Sotsial'naia struktura, pp. 353-55.

22. A partial exception to this statement is M. V. Timiashevskaia's study of scientific personnel in Akademgorodok. See M. Yanowitch and W. Fisher, Social Stratification, pp. 137-52.

23. Iu. V. Arutiunian, Sotsial'naia struktura, pp. 107-11.

24. M. Yanowitch and W. Fisher, Social Stratification, pp. 54-55.

25. O. I. Shkaratan, Problemy, p. 119.

26. V. Ia. El'meev, Problemy sotsial'nogo planirovaniia, Leningrad, 1973, p. 101. See also V. S. Semenov, "New Phenomena in the Social Structure of Soviet Society," in E. F. Sulimov ed., XXIV s"ezda KPSS i problemy nauchnogo kommunizma, Moscow, 1973, p. 55.

27. V. Ia. El'meev, Problemy, pp. 103-5.

28. Ministerstvo vysshego i srednego spetsial'nogo obrazovaniia RSFSR, Gor'kovskii gosudarstvennyi universitet im. N. I. Lobachevskogo, Sotsiologiia i vysshaia shkola, Uchenye zapiski, Issue 100, Gorki, 1970, pp. 11-12.

29. V. S. Semenov, "New Phenomena," p. 63.

30. M. Rutkevich, "The Social Structure of a Developed Socialist Society," Kommunist, 1974, no. 2, p. 83.

31. We rely here on V. Ia. El'meev, V. R. Polozov, and B. R. Riashchenko, Kommunizm i preodelenie razdeleniia mezhdu umstvennym i fizicheskim trudom, Leningrad, 1965, ch. 1; Ural'skii politekhnicheskii institut im. S. M. Kirova, Sotsializm i ravenstvo, Sverdlovsk, 1970, pp. 24-26; O. I. Shkaratan, Problemy, pp. 153-54, 460-64.

32. Ibid., p. 154.

33. Ibid., p. 154.

34. Ibid., p. 153, 460.

35. S. A. Kugel' and O. I. Shkaratan, "Some Methodological Problems of Studying the Social Structure of Society," Nauchnye doklady vysshei shkoly, filosofskie nauki, 1965, no. 1, p. 59.

36. M. N. Rutkevich, "The Concept of the Intelligentsia as a Social Stratum in Socialist Society," Nauchnye doklady vysshei shkoly, filosofskie nauki, 1966, no. 4, p. 22.

37. This matter is somewhat complicated by the occasional practice, in popular literature as well as in economics publications, of using the term "employees" to cover both routine white-collar and intelligentsia occupations.

38. V. S. Semenov, "New Phenomena," p. 49.

39. S. A. Kugel', Novoe v izuchenii sotsial'noi struktury obshchestva, Leningrad, 1968, pp. 24-25.

40. Akademiia nauk SSSR, institut filosofii, Problemy izmeneniia sotsial'noi struktury sovetskogo obshchestva, Moscow, 1968, p. 111.

41. L. Gordon and R. Klopov, "The Social Development of the Working Class of the USSR," Voprosy filosofii, 1972, no. 2, pp. 12-14.

42. M. N. Rutkevich in Nauchnye doklady, 1966, no. 4, pp. 24-25; M. N. Rutkevich, "The Intelligentsia of the Socialist Society," in E. F. Sulimov, XXIV s"ezda, p. 41.

43. V. S. Semenov, "New Phenomena," p. 43.

44. G. E. Glezerman, Istoricheskii materializm i razvitie sotsialisticheskogo obshchestva, 2nd ed., Moscow, 1973, pp. 184-85. By "free professions" Glezerman means writers, composers, lawyers, among others.

45. O. I. Shkaratan, Problemy, p. 117; Voprosy filosofii, 1968, no. 11, p. 22.

46. L. S. Bliakhman and O. I. Shkaratan, NTR, rabochii klass, intelligentsiia, Moscow, 1973, p. 163.

47. For a position essentially similar to that of Shkaratan in the above quotation, see R. I. Kosolapov, Sotsializm, Moscow, 1975, p. 447. In a 1974 article Shkaratan abandons his practice of incorporating elements of the intelligentsia into the working class and treats occupational strata within both of these groups as "the principal strata of the urban population." The key point, however, is that this permits him to study the economic and social position of these strata "jointly," as he had done in his earlier work. See O. I. Shkaratan and V. I. Rukavishnikov, "The Social Structure of the Population of the Soviet City and Trends in its Development (Theoretical Propositions)," Sotsiologicheskie issledovaniia, 1974, no. 2, p. 41.

48. L. S. Bliakhman and O. I. Shkaratan, NTR, rabochii klass, pp. 264-65; M. N. Rutkevich, "Trends in Changes in the Social Structure of Soviet Society," Sotsiologicheskie issledovaniia, 1975, no. 1, p. 68.

49. V. K. Bondarchik ed., Izmeneniia v bytu i kul'ture gorodskogo naseleniia Belorussii, Minsk, 1976, pp. 32-33, 48-51; V. I. Staroverov, Sotsial'no-demograficheskie problemy derevni, Moscow, 1975, p. 115.

What are some of the main patterns and approximate magnitudes of prevailing inequalities in Soviet money earnings and living standards? It should be stressed that what follows is not an attempt at a comprehensive survey of Soviet income structure. Our primary objective is to disclose the relative economic status of some of the principal social groups in Soviet society. Differences in money incomes are obviously not the only source of differential privileges in the Soviet Union. But with the increasing supply and variety of consumer goods and services in recent years, differences in monetary rewards can more readily be translated into differences in real income and distinct styles of life. Hence an examination of income differentials is an integral part of our concern with the broader theme of social inequality in the Soviet Union. As is the case throughout this volume, we are also interested in the attitudes toward inequality which have emerged in the sociological and economic literature. Changes in wage and income policies have created opportunities for the introduction of new ideas and the challenging of old dogmas in Soviet discussions of inequality. We turn to these matters first.

The Nonegalitarian Reduction of Income Inequality

Beginning in 1931 and for approximately 25 years thereafter, wage policy pronouncements and discussions were almost invariably dominated by a single theme: the struggle against "egalitarianism" or "equality-mongering" (uravnilovka). Although wage policy during this period was not confined to widening the gap between high- and low-paid labor, there is unmistakable evidence of increased inequality in the distribution of wage income between

the early 1930s and the late 1950s.[1] Whatever its other functions
— such as the consolidation of social privileges — the continuing
denunciation of egalitarianism was a way of focusing attention on
the need to utilize monetary incentives to promote the development
of scarce skills and disciplined work habits. But like other policies of the period, the antiegalitarian campaign had all the earmarks of a frenzied struggle against "enemies." Egalitarianism
was not only identified as a petty bourgeois and utopian socialist
policy — which was bad enough — but it was also linked with more
ominous forces: "Trotskyites, Zinovievites, Bukharinites, and
other enemies of the people...."[2] Thus the theme of antiegalitari-
anism was an inseparable component of the whole "spirit" of the
Stalinist epoch.

In contrast to the period of the prewar five-year plans and the
early postwar years, there is little doubt that the period since the
late 1950s has seen a reduction in money wage and income differentials. This is suggested both by official statements of policy as
well as by Soviet empirical studies of income inequality. A gradual reduction in inequalities of economic status has now come to be
regarded as a "natural" feature of Soviet economic and cultural
development. Repeated increases in minimum wage levels, reduced ratios of highest-to-lowest basic wage rates, and essential
stability of basic rates for the most highly paid groups of occupations have been characteristic of Soviet wage policy since the late
1950s and into the early 1970s.[3] Some of the statistical evidence
pointing to the implementation of a policy of reducing the gap between high and low income groups since 1956 is shown in Table 2.1.

Although the shrill antiegalitarian tone of the early planning
years has been largely abandoned, the income narrowing policies
of the more recent period are not typically presented as reflecting
the introduction of new principles of wage and salary determination. The overriding (although not exclusive) principle continues
to be "payment in accordance with the quantity and quality of work,"
and the importance of a wage structure which creates a "personal
material interest" in effective work performance remains a constantly reiterated theme.[4] Thus the reduction in wage and salary
differentials since the late 1950s is not presented as a turn to
egalitarian principles of distribution but as a reflection of "objectively conditioned" changes in the skill and educational composition of the labor force and of shifts in economic priorities in favor
of traditionally neglected and low-paid sectors. The literature on
wage structure warns against "arbitrary" reductions in differen-

Table 2.1

Selected Measures of Soviet Wage and Income Differentiation

Years	(1) Decile coefficient of wage differentiation*	(2) Ratio of average wages of 10% highest paid to 10% lowest paid	(3) Decile coefficient of differentiation of family income [†]	(4) Leningrad: Ratio of average wages of 10% highest paid to 10% lowest paid
1956	4.4	8.1		
1959				4.6
1961				4.0
1964	3.7			3.7
1966	3.2		3.8 [‡]	3.6
1968	2.7	5.1		3.3
1970	3.2		3.2	
1972				3.3
1975 (plan)	2.9	4.1		

Sources:

col. 1 — G. S. Sarkisian, Uroven', tempy i proportsii rosta real'nykh dokhodov pri sotsializma, pp. 125, 132.

col. 2 — L. E. Kunel'skii, Sotsial'no-ekonomicheskie problemy zarabotnoi platy, pp. 68-69.

col. 3 — G. S. Sarkisian, Dokhody trudiashchikhsia i sotsial'nye problemy urovnia zhizni naseleniia SSSR, p. 134.

col. 4 — N. M. Tikhonov, Neobkhodimyi produkt v usloviiakh razvitogo sotsializma, p. 169.

*Ratio of the wage exceeded by 10% of workers and nonmanual employees to the wage exceeded by 90%.

[†] Ratio of the income per capita exceeded by 10% of families to that exceeded by 90%.

[‡] 1965.

tials, reductions which become "ends in themselves." Egalitarianism (now exemplified by Chinese efforts to "jump over" necessary stages on the road to communism) normally remains a term of opprobrium.[5] Even the introduction of income supplements for low (per capita) income families must be justified in nonegalitarian terms. It is not seen as a departure from the principle of "distribution according to work" but as necessary to offset the distorting effect on this principle of variations in family size and composition.[6]

The continuing emphasis on the "objective" limits to wage and income equalization and the need to avoid "voluntaristic" behavior in this area serves a dual function. It simultaneously justifies the kind of selective, centrally guided income narrowing policies of recent years, and also sanctions the reproduction of those substantial economic inequalities which still remain as "objectively" required by the socialist principle of distribution. In the nonegalitarian reduction of income inequality, the primary issue is not distributive justice (or as it would have been put in earlier days, "elementary class justice") but the "scientific management" of gradual changes in the distributive process of a "developed" socialist society.

Thus most recent discussions of wage differentials and inequalities in economic status have been contained within the bounds of traditional themes: "payment in accordance with work," the primacy of material incentives, the need to avoid egalitarian tendencies — all part of the heritage of the early planning years. But the intellectual climate of the late 1960s and early 1970s has also permitted some striking departures from customary formulations of the issue of economic inequality. Some of the ideas expressed during this period can only be interpreted as protests against privilege and criticisms of traditional practices governing income differentiation and work incentives.

Iu. V. Arutiunian's studies of social differentiation in the countryside provide an illustration of this critical approach. In a volume published in 1971 Arutiunian posed a question which implied a protest against excessive inequalities in economic status:

> Intelligentsia occupations are attractive not essentially because of their high pay but in themselves, because of the content of the work, the predominance of creative functions. The high quality of the work is, in effect, its own reward.... In this connection a question arises: How justified are additional material rewards for creative labor that is attractive even without them?[7]

We should not be deceived by Arutiunian's singling out of "creative labor." His question appears in the context of a discussion of the desirability of closing the gap ("which does not always seem justified") between high- and low-paid occupational groups in rural society. It is not primarily a criticism of high pay for "creative" labor but of excessive inequalities in rural income structure as a whole.

The same point is implied in the very manner in which some sociologists, in presenting their findings, have illustrated the "particularly large gap" in the living standards of polar social groups. For example, it was hardly necessary to explicitly condemn extreme economic inequalities (nor, obviously, would it have been possible to do so) when a sociologist summarized the advantaged position of managerial personnel and specialists relative to low-skilled manual workers (in a Moldavian study of collective farms in 1970) as follows: the proportions of the former group owning washing machines, vacuum cleaners, and refrigerators were 4.5, 7, and 7 times greater, respectively, than the proportions of the latter group with these items.[8] A criticism of economic privilege was surely implicit in the simple enumeration of such inequalities.

Another illustration of what we have here called the "critical approach" appears in the way that some writers have invoked the sacred principle of "payment in accordance with work." Traditionally this had been used to justify prevailing inequalities or to argue for increased income differentiation. Now it was being invoked for precisely the opposite purpose. For example, the long-standing inferior economic status of collective farmers relative to state farm workers involved "unequal conditions of payment for equal labor"[9] and could not be justified by the socialist principle of distribution. The particular case cited here to illustrate a violation of this principle was less important than the more general point that the unceasing reiteration of this principle had co-existed with arbitrary inequalities of economic status.

Perhaps even more significant was the attempt of some economists to argue that "distribution according to work" could not be an adequate guide to determining the earnings level of all occupational groups. It had to be supplemented by the "law of reimbursement of outlays of labor power." In the language of Marxian economics this meant that the incomes of even the lowest paid groups in the work force must be sufficient to cover "the cost of production and reproduction of labor power." This required a minimum level of compensation for all employed individuals, "independent of the share of their labor contribution to the creation of the social product."[10] Such a level would not only meet the needs of sheer physical subsistence but would provide the minimum amenities required for cultural growth, work morale, and the "normal" reproduction of the work force. The implication was clear. The earnings of the lowest paid occupational groups (presumably determined in accordance with their "labor contribution") had been inadequate to cover the normal costs of production of labor power. Indeed, the very substantial increases required in minimum wage rates (from 40 rubles per month in 1965 to 70 rubles in the early 1970s) offered indirect testimony of the earlier prolonged neglect of "the law of reimbursement...." Such increases could hardly be explained by changes in the "quantity and quality" of work performed by the lowest paid groups in the work force. For the more traditional economists any attempt to limit the "regulating" role of the socialist principle of distribution remains suspect. Hence their readiness to detect "egalitarian tendencies" in the arguments of proponents of the "law of reimbursement...."[11] Whether such suspicions are justified, these arguments certainly do lend support to a policy of reducing inequalities in economic status.

The same can be said about some of the recent sociological literature on work attitudes. This has gone beyond the traditional one-dimensional identification of work incentives with "material interest," an identification that reduced the problem of work incentives to that of establishing a sufficiently differentiated structure of earnings. The new approach appeals for recognition of the fact that with a rise in educational attainments and general living standards there has been a "change in the structure of stimuli to labor."[12] At the risk of trivializing a considerable body of literature in this area, we may summarize one of its principal themes as follows: The greater the "intellectual" and "creative" content of labor (the greater the scope for "self-supervision" and "self-organization"), the less important become the incentive effects of differentials in material rewards. Opportunities for promotion to jobs "richer in content" may be as effective an incentive to efficient work performance as the prospects of increased money wages. Given the attractiveness and high prestige of more "creative" labor, wage increases then become important as a "compensating factor" for individuals forced to remain in "manual, heavy, low-skilled, uninteresting labor," i.e., for the lowest paid sectors of the work force.[13]

The point here is not that material incentives are being questioned or abandoned but that the whole issue of work incentives has now been posed in a manner that is compatible with a reduction in the earnings gap between high- and low-paid groups. Our brief review of some new departures in Soviet discussions of the problem of economic inequality should make it clear that the time is past when such discussions could be confined to invectives against egalitarianism and perfunctory affirmations of "distribution according to work." Although egalitarianism (as uravnilovka) remains beyond the pale [14] (what else can one expect of a tendency once linked to "Trotskyites, Zinovievites, Bukharinites..." and now to the "barracks communism" of the Chinese?), a variety of unusual justifications for the reduction of economic inequalities has emerged. The suspicious (including the conservative Soviet economists cited earlier) may be excused for detecting egalitarian sentiments in at least some of these.

We turn now to the principal concerns of this chapter: inequalities in the economic status of selected occupational strata. We rely on money earnings as well as on some indicators of "real" differences in material well-being (housing facilities, possession of selected household goods). Where possible, our discussion will also seek to relate the observed inequalities in economic status to cultural and style-of-life differences among social strata.

Wage Differentiation in Industry: General Features

Most of our discussion of inequalities in incomes and living standards will draw on the local studies of industrial enterprises and urban and rural communities which Soviet sociologists and economists have conducted since 1965. These studies, with their comparatively detailed breakdown of occupational groups, are a much richer source of information on Soviet stratification patterns than the official all-Union labor statistics. Nonetheless a brief survey of the relative earnings status of the broad occupational categories in the industrial work force singled out in official labor statistics [15] will provide a useful introduction to the local material which follows. It will serve to identify some of the important general features of Soviet income differentiation which our analysis of the local studies will elaborate and consider in greater detail.

The principal occupational categories distinguished in the official industrial labor statistics include workers, engineering-technical personnel, and employees (sluzhashchie). Each of these categories, of course, encompasses a highly heterogeneous composite of occupational titles. Engineering-technical personnel in industry, for example, include not only engineers and lower-level technicians but also plant managers and other high-ranking managerial personnel. The employees category in industry includes mainly low-ranking white-collar personnel in clerical and office jobs, but also embraces some groups requiring specialized training such as economists and accountants. Broadly speaking, the contrast between workers on the one hand and employees and engineering-technical personnel on the other may be regarded as a manual-nonmanual division within the industrial labor force, with engineering-technical personnel typically representing the

29

higher-level nonmanual occupations ("specialists"). Soviet discussions frequently treat the relative wage positions of workers and engineering-technical personnel as symbolic of the gap between manual and higher-level "mental labor" in Soviet industry.

Perhaps the most clearly established trend in Soviet occupational wage structure is the steadily diminishing relative wage advantage of engineering-technical personnel over manual workers (see Table 2.2). While the average earnings of the former were more than double the wages of workers in the immediate prewar period, a continuing erosion of the money wage differential between these two groups reduced the earnings advantage of engineering-technical personnel to approximately 30% in the early 1970s. The earnings level of the clerical and office occupations in industry designated as "employees" has been below that of manual workers throughout most of the postwar period, standing at approximately 80-85% of workers' wages in recent years.

Table 2.2

Average Monthly Wages of Workers, Engineering-Technical Personnel, and Employees in Soviet Industry

Years	Average monthly wages, in rubles			Wages of engineering-technical personnel in % of workers'	Wages of employees in % of workers'
	workers	engineering-technical personnel	employees		
1955	76.2	126.4	67.8	166	89
1960	89.8	133.0	73.2	148	82
1965	101.7	148.4	85.8	146	84
1970	130.6	178.0	111.6	136	85
1973	145.6	184.9	118.5	127	81

Sources: Tsentral'noe statisticheskoe upravlenie, Trud v SSSR, pp. 138-39; Narodnoe khoziaistvo SSSR v 1973 g., p. 586.

The relatively low and declining earnings differential between workers and engineering-technical personnel deserves further attention. Soviet writers often present it as illustrating the increasing equality in economic status of manual and mental labor. It is true, of course, that the average earnings figures for engineering-technical personnel conceal substantial variations in earnings within the broad range of occupations included in this heterogeneous category and thus understate the privileged economic status of individuals in the higher-ranking managerial and specialists' positions. But this has always been the case, while

closing of diff a
response to econ
climate as much as Stalins
working of the

Differentiation of Incomes

Thanks
smart-ass,
but we ain't
interested.

the narrow gap between the average earnings of engineering-
technical personnel and workers is a relatively recent phenomenon. A number of factors have been at work here. In recent years
the narrowing wage gap reflects, at least in part, a deliberate policy of freezing the maximum basic wage rates (although not the
premiums) of the top-ranking managerial positions in the engineering-technical category.[16] For the lower-ranking positions
large increases in the supply of engineering and technical school
graduates have permitted a policy of moderate wage increases.
Whatever it may conceal, the narrowing wage differential cited
here reflects a kind of "proletarianization" of the lower rungs of
the engineering-technical category in the sense of a loss of traditional earnings superiority over manual workers.

The changing composition of the young people who enter the labor force as manual workers has also operated to raise the earnings of the latter closer to those of engineering-technical personnel. These new workers are no longer predominantly rural migrants or even the children of rural migrants eager to obtain
whatever nonagricultural jobs might be available. An increasing
proportion are secondary-school graduates who aspire to admission to higher educational institutions and are reluctant to accept
the many semiskilled and unskilled workers' jobs which remain
to be filled in the Soviet economy. The need for industrial enterprises to attract and retain such workers has also contributed to
a reduction in the relative wage advantage of engineering-technical
personnel.

The traditional Soviet policy of unbalanced economic development, with its markedly unequal priorities for different economic
sectors, has also had a distinctive impact on the occupational
earnings differentials we are considering here. One of the familiar manifestations of the highly uneven pattern of Soviet economic
development has been substantial inequalities in earnings between
all occupational groups employed in heavy industry on the one hand
and light and food industry on the other. Although these inequalities have recently been reduced,[17] they remain considerable. When
these interindustry wage differentials are considered in juxtaposi-
tion with the recently diminished earnings gap between workers
and engineering-technical personnel, they reveal a complex pattern of differentiation that has not received the attention it deserves (see Table 2.3). The highly uneven sectoral priorities
characteristic of Soviet development strategy have created specially favored groups of manual workers in "leading" industries

31

Table 2.3

Average Monthly Wages of Workers and Engineering-Technical Personnel
in Selected Branches of Soviet Industry, 1969

Industrial sector	Average monthly wages, in rubles		Wages of engineering-technical personnel in % of workers'
	workers	engineering-technical personnel	
All-industry	125	172	138
Coal	210	281	134
Ferrous metallurgy	145	206	142
Lumber	143	166	116
Oil extraction	128	217	169
Machine building	125	165	131
Chemical and petrochemical	125	187	150
Building materials	123	155	126
Pulp and paper	122	177	145
Woodworking	118	146	124
Electric power	117	195	166
Food	109	168	154
Light industry:	100	138	138
textiles	105	148	141
leather and shoe	110	146	133
garment	91	125	137

Sources: Derived from V. E. Komarov, Ekonomicheskie problemy podgotovki i ispol'zovaniia kadrov spetsialistov, p. 190.

(a "labor aristocracy"?) whose economic status not only is considerably higher than that of most other groups of workers but whose earnings levels are above those of nonmanual specialists in low-priority sectors. Thus the average earnings of workers in the most highly paid sectors of Soviet industry (coal, steel, oil) exceed those of engineering-technical personnel in the less-favored sectors. For a particularly privileged group of workers such as coal miners, average earnings are higher than those received by engineering-technical employees in most industries. Thus differences between "low" and "high" earnings do not simply mirror the difference between employment in manual workers' versus nonmanual specialists' occupations. Although our discussion has been confined to industrial employment, it should be obvious that both the working class and the intelligentsia (in its official definition as "specialists" in mental labor) are highly fragmented social entities.

We now turn to material which permits us to disaggregate the broad occupational groupings examined thus far, to consider other indicators of economic status than money wages, and to incorporate occupational strata outside the industrial sector into our analysis of the economic dimension of Soviet stratification.

Urban Strata: Earnings and Living Standards

The studies of urban strata by a group of Soviet sociologists headed by O. I. Shkaratan (discussed briefly in Chapter 1) are of invaluable assistance in disaggregating the rather general categories considered above into more discrete occupational groups. Conducted in 1965-70, these sample studies of the social structure of industrial (machine-building) enterprises in Leningrad and of urban employment as a whole in several cities of the Tatar Republic distinguish eight or nine "socio-occupational groups." In Leningrad these include four manual strata (ranging from unskilled to "highly skilled" workers) and four nonmanual (ranging from clerical and office employees to managerial personnel). In the cities of the Tatar Republic individuals in "creative" occupations are added as a distinct group (although their earnings are not revealed), and other nonindustrial strata (teachers and doctors, for example) are distributed among some of the socio-occupational classifications employed in the Leningrad studies. Whatever their limitations — and we shall consider some of them below — these sample studies obviously yield a fuller picture of urban social differentiation than the material examined thus far.

Although our principal interest is in inequalities in the earnings and living standards of these strata, a preliminary glance at some of their other characteristics — or "personal attributes," as we shall refer to them — seems justified. We refer, in particular, to such attributes as sex, Party membership, and education. Occupational differentials in the distribution of these attributes are of interest in their own right and are related to the inequalities in economic status on which we shall focus below. Tables 2.4 and 2.5 reveal some of these personal attributes as well as the earnings status of occupational groups in Leningrad machinery plants and in two cities of the Tatar Republic [18] in the period 1965-70.

The extent of female representation differs markedly among the various occupational strata. It is highest in unskilled manual jobs and the simpler office and clerical occupations, where the female

Table 2.4

Socio-occupational Groups in Leningrad Machine-Building Plants, 1965 and 1970:
Party Membership, Education, and Monthly Wages, in Rubles

No.	Socio-occupational groups*	1965			1970		
		Party member-ship (in %)†	years of education	monthly wages (in rubles)	Party member-ship (in %)†	years of education	monthly wages (in rubles)
1	Managerial personnel	60.8	13.6	172.9		13.4	191.0
2	Highly skilled scientific and technical personnel	40.2	14.0	127.0		14.1	133.0
3	Personnel in skilled mental work	42.8	12.5	109.8		12.8	131.0
4	Highly skilled workers	37.6	8.8	129.0	44.3	9.8	142.0
5	Skilled workers in hand work	37.9	8.3	120.0	34.6	8.7	140.0
6	Skilled workers on machines	39.5	8.2	107.5	35.4	8.4	142.0
7	Middle-level non-manual personnel	27.1	9.1	83.6			90.0
8	Unskilled manual workers	13.8	6.5	97.5	12.2	5.6	106.0

Sources: 1965: O. I. Shkaratan in Voprosy filosofii, 1967, no. 1, p. 36.
1970: I. P. Trufanov, Problemy byta gorodskogo naseleniia SSSR, pp. 61-62; L. S. Bliakhman and O. I. Shkaratan, NTR, rabochii klass, intelligentsiia, pp. 203, 271.

*For greater detail on the particular occupations included in the various groups see Table 1.1 in Chapter 1.
†Includes Komsomol as well as Party members.

34

Table 2.5

Socio-occupational Groups in Two Cities of the Tatar Republic, 1967: Sex, Education, and Monthly Wages, in Rubles

No.	Socio-occupational Groups*	Kazan			Al'met'evsk		
		% women	years of education	monthly wages (in rubles)	% women	years of education	monthly wages (in rubles)
1	Managerial personnel	28.0	12.9	164.3	20.5	12.9	178.3
2	Highly skilled personnel in "creative" occupations	39.5	14.0		25.0	15.0	
3	Highly skilled scientific and technical personnel	30.6	14.3	156.9	45.5	14.6†	146.3
4	Personnel in skilled mental work	69.4	14.0†	111.0	66.6	13.3†	111.7
5	Highly skilled workers	13.3	10.2†	97.9	29.7	11.4†	115.6
6	Skilled workers in hand work	31.3	7.8	99.9	40.3	7.6	95.8
7	Skilled workers on machines	42.3	7.0	99.1	14.5	7.5	114.6
8	Middle-level nonmanual personnel	88.9	9.3	75.7	84.2	9.4	77.4
9	Unskilled manual workers and low-skilled nonmanual personnel	77.9	7.0	73.8	83.4	6.1	62.9

Sources: Iu. V. Arutiunian, Sotsial'noe i natsional'noe, pp. 88, 168, 323-24; L. S. Bliakhman and O. I. Shkaratan, p. 271; O. I. Shkaratan in Sovetskaia etnografiia, 1970, no. 3, p. 10.

*In addition to the particular occupations cited in Table 1.1, these groups include at least the following: teachers and doctors in group No. 4; college teachers in group No. 3; sales personnel in group No. 8. Although this is not stated explicitly, it is implied in L. S. Bliakhman and O. I. Shkaratan, p. 270.

†Simple average of figures for Russians and Tatars.

share is in the neighborhood of four-fifths or more (see Table 2.5). In the Tatar Republic women also predominate among personnel in "skilled mental work," which in this area includes teachers and doctors — traditional female work roles — along with engineering and accounting positions. But the highest positions in the occupational spectrum — "managerial personnel" — as well as skilled workers' jobs, are largely staffed by men.

The frequency of Party membership also reveals considerable variation, especially between the polar occupational groups. While it is comparatively rare at the bottom of the occupational hierarchy, i.e., among unskilled workers and employees in routine nonmanual positions, some 60% of the individuals in managerial jobs are Party members (judging by Shkaratan's studies of Leningrad machinery enterprises). This share would undoubtedly rise if we could distinguish the highest-level positions in the managerial category (plant directors, for example). However, the frequency of Party membership among nonmanual "specialists" below managerial rank differs little from that among skilled workers.

The principal features of strata differences in educational attainment may be summarized as follows: Skilled manual workers and "middle-level" office employees typically have 7-10 years of schooling, while for higher-ranking nonmanual and managerial personnel the comparable figures are 12-15 years. Unskilled manual jobs are typically filled by individuals with 5-7 years of schooling. In Leningrad the educational level of office and clerical employees (apparently chiefly women) exceeds that of all categories of blue-collar workers, while in the Tatar Republic the only group of manual workers with higher levels of education than office and other "middle-level" nonmanual employees is that classified as "highly skilled." Among the higher-ranking nonmanual occupations (groups 1-3 in Leningrad and 1-4 in the Tatar Republic in Tables 2.4 and 2.5) the top of the educational hierarchy is usually occupied by "highly skilled scientific and technical personnel," a group whose educational level consistently exceeds that of the managerial category.

What do these studies of urban strata reveal about Soviet patterns of inequality in economic status? Any occupational classification is necessarily somewhat arbitrary and cannot help but affect the picture of wage inequalities which emerges. This is especially the case under Soviet circumstances, in which extreme inequalities in earnings cannot readily be revealed. Thus the earnings gap between polar occupational groups is obviously understated in these studies. The monthly wages of the highest-paid occupational stratum (managerial personnel) appear to be only two to three times those of the lowest paid. This is certainly closer to reality than the gap revealed when "average" workers are compared with the heterogeneous engineering-technical personnel category, but it is an understatement nonetheless (as we shall demonstrate below).

However, these studies provide rather convincing evidence of another feature of the Soviet earnings structure which can be accepted with some confidence. The division between manual and nonmanual occupational roles as such is not accompanied by sharply distinct earnings levels of these broad groups. A consistent feature of the earnings hierarchy is the relatively low position of individuals in routine nonmanual jobs. In Leningrad this group ("middle-level nonmanual personnel") occupied the bottom of the earnings ladder in both 1965 and 1970. This meant that their monthly earnings were exceeded by unskilled as well as by skilled manual workers. [19] In the Tatar Republic, where the lowest-skilled nonmanual occupations were classified jointly with unskilled laborers, the earnings of middle-level nonmanual employees (which in this area included sales employees as well as clerical and office occupations) were second from the bottom. Thus the lowest rungs of the earnings ladder are shared by manual and nonmanual groups, which are also those with the highest proportion of female workers. Given the relatively high educational level of middle-rank nonmanual employees we noted earlier, it is apparent that the earnings hierarchy diverges from the hierarchy of educational attainment.

The same point may be further illustrated by noting the relative wage and educational levels of skilled manual workers on the one hand and of nonmanual "specialists" on the other. There is no significant break in earnings levels as we move from skilled manual workers to "specialists" in nonmanual occupations. Indeed, there is evidence of considerable overlapping in the earnings positions of these groups. In Leningrad and Al'met'evsk, for example, the average earnings of at least some categories of "skilled" and "highly skilled" manual workers exceeded the earnings of nonmanual groups below the rank of managerial personnel, while in Kazan the earnings differential in favor of specialists in "skilled mental work" was relatively small (about 11%). Although the moderate earnings differential between skilled manual workers and nonmanual specialists undoubtedly reflects the particular occupational groups distinguished in these studies,[20] our impression is that it is a common feature of the Soviet earnings structure. In any case it is in marked contrast to the rather sharp break in the educational levels of these strata (see Tables 2.4 and 2.5). The extended education required for access to the lower-ranking layers of the "intelligentsia" does not appear to be accompanied by any significant wage advantage in its favor.

This does not mean, of course, that large inequalities in earnings are absent. One of the principal limitations of the Soviet studies of urban strata on which we have drawn is that they fail to distinguish the specific positions to be found at the poles of the occupational hierarchy and thus tend to understate the range of inequality in earnings. As noted earlier, the average earnings of highest-paid strata appear to be only some two to three times those of the lowest.[21] But this comparatively low ratio reflects, at least in part, the heterogeneous collection of jobs included in Shkaratan's top-ranking occupational stratum: "managerial personnel" (in the Leningrad studies the latter is a composite of shop chiefs, department heads, and plant directors). A closer estimate of the magnitude of the earnings gap between polar groups in these studies is suggested by the fact that individuals in the upper 10% of the earnings distribution of "managerial personnel" were paid some three to four times the average wages received by the lowest-skilled manual and nonmanual groups.[22]

The range of inequality is further extended when we consider the privileged position (in terms of monetary rewards) of two "elite" groups at the upper extreme of the occupational hierarchy: directors of industrial enterprises and scientists at research institutes. Enterprise directors are frequently paid at "personal rates" (personal'nye oklady). These rates are literally "personal" in the sense that they are not established for a particular job title but for individuals with "outstanding knowledge and experience" in their field. Soviet sources make it clear that "personal rates" (set in excess of officially authorized "occupational rates") are a "mass phenomenon" for directors of large industrial enterprises.[23] The earnings of scientists at research institutes may be taken as representing the economic status of an "elite" group outside industrial employment. If we examine jointly the "personal rates" of factory directors, the earnings of particular categories of Leningrad scientists, Shkaratan's occupational groups in Leningrad machinery plants, and the minimum rates of plant cleanup personnel (uborshchitsy), we may derive a closer approxi-

Table 2.6

Monthly Wages* of Selected Occupational Groups, Leningrad,
1967-68, 1970

Occupational groups	Monthly wages (in rubles)
Scientific personnel of research institute, 1967/68 †	
head of department	422
head of laboratory	366
senior scientific associate	261
junior scientific associate	92
Groups employed in industrial enterprises, 1970 ‡	
directors of "large industrial enterprises"	450-500
managerial personnel	191
engineering-technical personnel and other "specialists"	
in nonmanual work	132
skilled manual workers	141
unskilled manual workers	106
clerical, office employees	90
cleanup personnel	60

Sources: Some of the figures are taken directly or derived from Table 2.4. Others are from Leningradskii ordena Lenina i ordena trudovogo krasnogo znameni gosudarstvennyi universitet imeni A. A. Zhdanova, Khozraschet v sovremennykh usloviiakh upravleniia promyshlennost'iu, p. 110; L. E. Kunel'skii, Zarplata, dokhody, stimulirovanie, p. 29; S. V. Sharutin, "Some Problems of Improving the Organization of Wages of Engineering-Technical Personnel," in Uchenye zapiski kafedr obshchestvennykh nauk vuzov Leningrada, politicheskaia ekonomiia, Issue XIV, Raspredelitel'nye otnosheniia sotsializma i ikh razvitie na sovremennom etape, p. 132.

*All figures except for directors of enterprises and cleanup personnel are monthly earnings. For these two groups the figures are for "personal rates" and minimum basic rates respectively.

† The figures for scientists apply to the D. I. Mendeleev All-Union Scientific Research Institute of Metrology. We have taken an average of 1967 and 1968 since the figures fluctuate rather markedly from year to year.

‡ The figures for all groups except directors are cited in our sources as applicable to machine-building enterprises. The figure for directors appears in a 1973 publication, and we assume it was in effect in 1970. The figure for cleanup personnel was authorized in 1968, and we assume it was still in effect in 1970.

mation of the extremes in economic status which prevailed in major Soviet urban centers during the late 1960s and early 1970s (see Table 2.6). Such a comparison, although certainly not embracing the highest incomes received in the Soviet Union, obviously reveals a much wider range of inequality than anything we have

cited thus far. Thus the monthly "personal rates" of factory directors and the earnings of department heads in scientific research institutes were some four to five times the earnings of
low-skilled industrial employees and "junior" scientific personnel, and some seven to eight times the legal minimum basic wage
rate (the rate at which plant cleanup personnel were paid). It is
also clear that there was a wide earnings gap between the "masses"
of nonmanual specialists and those in higher-level managerial and
administrative positions. Quite apart from the occupational groups
at the bottom of the earnings ladder, the distinction between is-
polniteli and rukovoditeli — between "executors" (whether in
manual or mental labor) of the decisions of others and "leaders"
or "managers" with the power to make decisions and to command
others — is a source of significant inequalities in earnings. Whatever the impact of other sources of privilege, prevailing inequalities in money earnings seem more than adequate to continually
fuel egalitarian sentiments among the mass of the Soviet population.

Thus far we have relied largely on earnings differentials as indicators of inequalities in the economic status of occupational strata.
To what extent are the various strata characterized by inequalities
in living standards and style-of-life differences as these are reflected in such indicators as housing characteristics and possession of selected consumer durable goods? Once again we draw on
the kinds of sample studies of urban communities utilized above.
This necessarily limits the distinct social groups which can be
compared, but there is no other way to proceed.

The supply of housing facilities to the various occupational
strata included in Shkaratan's Leningrad studies of 1965 and 1970
was distributed in a relatively egalitarian manner when such facilities are measured in terms of housing space (in square meters
per capita). Thus in Leningrad the availability of housing space
in 1965 to the different strata varied within the narrow range of
6.0 to 7.0 square meters per capita, with the lower figure applying to families of manual workers and the higher to families of
managerial personnel. Although strata inequalities in the distribution of housing space in this city appear to have increased between 1965 and 1970 (ranging in the latter year from 6.4 to 8.8
square meters per capita for workers and managerial strata, respectively), the extent of inequality still appears relatively moderate. However, unlike the pattern of differentiation in money
earnings, inequalities in housing space were consistently in favor
of nonmanual strata. Thus not only those in managerial positions

but also the principal categories of engineering-technical personnel and higher-level office employees (individuals in "skilled
mental work") had larger housing quarters (per family member)
than manual workers, whether skilled or unskilled.[24]

But this measure of the distribution of housing facilities surely
understates strata differences in housing characteristics. Soviet
writers regard the provision of families with separate apartments
(rather than communal apartments shared by more than one family, dormitory facilities, or individual homes) as the principal
symbol of progress in solving the Soviet housing problem. Suppose we rely on this criterion as an indicator of strata differences
in housing characteristics. The advantaged position of individuals
in intelligentsia occupations then emerges even more clearly. Not
only the Leningrad studies but several others (see Table 2.7) make
it apparent that access to separate apartments is considerably
more frequent among nonmanual specialists than among working-
class families. In some studies the inequalities in this respect
are striking, certainly greater than can be accounted for by occupational differences in money earnings or per capita income.
Thus a 1970 survey of "typical cities" found that more than four-
fifths of engineering-technical personnel lived in separate apartments, while the comparable figure for manual workers was approximately one-third. In Shkaratan's Leningrad study of the
same year some one-fifth to one-fourth of manual workers' families lived in separate apartments of two or more rooms, while
more than one-half of managerial families had access to such
apartments. It is hardly surprising that a Soviet writer, describing the distribution of separate apartments between workers and
"personnel in skilled mental work" in the Tatar Republic in the
late 1960s, should have referred to it as "highly uneven":[25] in
Kazan the proportions of these groups residing in separate apartments of two or more rooms were 16% and 41%, respectively.

Differences of this magnitude undoubtedly reflect the privileged
treatment accorded to individuals in higher-level nonmanual occupations by authorities entrusted with allocating housing facilities.
But it would be a mistake to attribute this pattern of housing differentials exclusively to the priorities of such authorities. Cultural differences between working-class and higher-strata families also play a role here. We are aware of the danger of invok-
ing "culture" to explain whatever is not obviously explainable by
other means. But to ignore this factor is to oversimplify matters.
Access to separate apartment dwellings is not likely to appear

Social and Economic Inequality

Table 2.7

Proportions of Various Occupational Groups Living
in Separate Apartments (in %)*

Year and coverage of study	% of each group living in separate apartment
Urals industrial enterprises, 1967 †	
workers	46
engineering-technical personnel	77
Kazan, 1967	
skilled workers ‡	16
personnel in skilled mental work	41
Leningrad machine-building plants, 1970	
unskilled workers	20
skilled workers ‡	24
engineering-technical personnel and other	
specialists §	33
managerial personnel	54
Survey of "typical cities," 1970	
workers	34
engineering-technical personnel	84
other intelligentsia and employees	53

Sources: M. N. Rutkevich ed., Sotsial'nye razlichiia i ikh preodolenie,
p. 111; I. P. Trufanov, pp. 71-72; Iu. V. Arutiunian, Sotsial'noe i natsional'noe,
pp. 177-78; L. A. Gordon et al., "Developed Socialism: The Well-Being of
Workers," Rabochii klass i sovremennyi mir, 1974, no. 3, p. 19.

*In the Urals study the apartments are described as "well-equipped separate
apartments"; in Leningrad and Kazan, as separate apartments of two or more
rooms; in the survey of "typical cities," as "separate apartments."

† Simple average of figures for skilled workers in hand work and skilled
Aluminum Plant and the Urals Heavy Machinery Plant.

‡ Simple average of figures for skilled workers in hand work and skilled
workers on machines.

§ Simple average of figures for occupational groups Nos. 2 and 3 in Table 2.4.

equally urgent to social groups that differ markedly in educational
levels and frequency of peasant social origins. One illustration of
the influence of cultural factors on housing patterns emerges in
the studies of urban strata in the Tatar Republic in the late 1960s.
Manual workers, many of them of rural origins, were much more
likely to reside in their own private homes — sometimes built by
themselves on small land allotments provided by municipal authorities and usually equipped with inferior amenities — than nonmanual strata whose preferences ran in the direction of separate apartments. Essentially the same situation was found in the "typical
cities" survey cited earlier.[26] Our point, of course, is not that

workers "prefer" inferior housing but that the occupationally based criteria of housing authorities interact with differences in duration of urban residence and cultural factors to create marked social inequalities in urban housing patterns.

The various urban strata are also characterized by distinct patterns of ownership of consumer durable goods. These do not simply mirror inequalities in financial resources (or in "political access") of different social groups; there is a "cultural" phenomenon at work here as well.

In most of the studies available to us, information on the distribution of consumer durables among social groups appears in the form of holdings of selected goods by broad occupational categories: workers and engineering-technical personnel, or workers and several subgroups within the broad "mental labor" category, but usually excluding the upper and lower extremes of the occupational hierarchy. Evidence from a variety of such studies suggests that certain types of consumer durables were more or less uniformly distributed among these broad occupational groups in the late 1960s and early 1970s, at least within given urban communities. This common core of goods included items like sewing machines, radios, and television sets. Substantial inequalities appeared, however, in the possession of other items, particularly equipment designed to aid in housework: washing machines, vacuum cleaners, refrigerators. For example, in the Urals studies of industrial enterprises in the late 1960s (the findings in other areas could be used to illustrate the same point), the proportions of manual workers owning these items were reported as follows: refrigerators — 20%, washing machines — 57%, vacuum cleaners — 11%; among technical specialists the proportions were 56%, 82%, and 37%, respectively.[27]

Such inequalities, as noted earlier, were not a simple reflection of differences between social groups in money earnings or income per capita. The fact is that manual and nonmanual strata — particularly when the latter category is confined to employees with higher education — are often distinct cultural groups whose differing value systems are reflected in differential patterns of consumption of goods other than "necessities," even when their income levels are essentially similar.

The Kazan studies provide clear evidence of this kind of social differentiation. Thus workers' families with per capita incomes of up to 100 rubles per month attached greater importance to the possession of TV sets than did higher-level nonmanual personnel

43

at comparable income levels. On the other hand, goods designed to assist in the performance of household chores (vacuum cleaners, washing machines, refrigerators) were more frequently owned by nonmanual than manual workers at all income levels. To some extent this pattern of ownership is clearly associated with the larger housing space and more frequent residence in separate (noncommunal) apartments available to nonmanual families. But it also suggests that intelligentsia families attach greater importance to releasing time from household chores, whether to meet the demands on their time imposed by professional job status or their greater participation in cultural activities, or both. It also points to the prevalence of more traditional attitudes toward female household roles in the families of manual than nonmanual workers at comparable income levels. An obvious, if somewhat trivial, illustration of the impact of "culture" as distinct from income, as a differentiating variable affecting consumption and style-of-life patterns, also appears in the more frequent possession of musical instruments and photographic equipment among nonmanual strata and the greater proclivity of workers for motorcycles.[28] While a more comprehensive study of contrasts in the modes of life and "cultural consumption" of different social strata must await a thorough analysis of Soviet time-budget studies, our brief survey of patterns of ownership of consumer durables suggests that such contrasts are not a simple reflex of inequalities in monetary rewards. The division between manual and (upper) nonmanual work roles is an important source of social differentiation even when it is not accompanied by significant income differentiation.

However, the ownership of consumer durables and "cultural" goods by all occupational groups may be significantly affected by the unequal priorities accorded to different communities. A study of Akademgorodok, a center of Soviet scientific research near Novosibirsk, reveals something about the living standards of a group that is among the most privileged in the Soviet occupational hierarchy: heads of scientific institutes and higher educational institutions, senior research personnel. But given the special efforts that are made to provide such a favored community with the latest amenities, even the low-skilled manual and nonmanual strata employed here enjoy higher living standards than such groups do elsewhere. Hence a comparison of the living standards of polar occupational strata in Akademgorodok is likely to understate the range of inequalities between urban strata in the society at large.

Moreover, it would be naïve to believe that a simple listing of the
goods owned, without regard to quality or special sources of access, reveals the extent of the privileged position of "elite" groups.
With these qualifications in mind, the Akademgorodok data provide
interesting evidence of differentiation in living standards. Table
2.8 shows the holdings of selected goods by individuals at the extremes of the occupational hierarchy in this community at the end
of the 1960s.

Table 2.8

Ownership of Consumer Durables and "Cultural" Goods:
Akademgorodok, Late 1960s*

Consumer durables and "cultural" goods	% of group owning indicated items	
	directors of research institutes, schools, hospitals; senior research personnel†	low-skilled workers and service personnel
Radio	100	87
Washing machine	90	75
Sewing machine	75	80
Television set	68	80
Bicycle, motorcycle, or motorscooter	50	40
Refrigerator	85	52
Library (more than 100 books)	90	25
Vacuum cleaner	68	10
Piano, accordian	45	8
Automobile or motorboat	22	8

Source: Akademiia nauk SSSR, Institut mezhdunarodnogo rabochego dvizheniia,
Urbanizatsiia i rabochii klass v usloviiakh nauchno-tekhnicheskoi revoliutsii,
pp. 286, 288.

*The precise date of the study, which appeared in a source published in 1970,
is not specified.

†Among the other groups included here were directors of enterprises, "chief
specialists," chief physicians, and leading Party workers.

As in other areas there were relatively small differences in the
extent to which the various occupational groups owned a basic core
of household items. But in Akademgorodok this basic core included
a wider range of goods than elsewhere. Even low-skilled manual
and service workers were relatively well supplied with an item
like washing machines (75% of these workers owned this item, a
distinctly higher share than the figure for "average" workers in
other studies). [29] The other side of this relatively uniform distribution of a basic core of consumer durables (which also included the familiar radio, sewing machine, and TV set, with a

45

smaller proportion of scientists than workers owning the last two items) was a markedly unequal distribution of other labor-saving household goods, "cultural" goods (books, musical instruments), and items that under Soviet circumstances were clearly luxury goods: automobiles and motorboats. Without denying the obvious role of inequalities in monetary rewards and privileged access to superior housing facilities in explaining these patterns of owner-ship, the Akademgorodok study reinforces the impression con-veyed earlier: socio-occupational strata — particularly the polar groups — are also culturally differentiated groups characterized by distinct modes of life and patterns of consumption.

What are some of the conclusions to be drawn from our review of Soviet inequalities in earnings and living standards, and what are some of their implications for broader aspects of Soviet stratification?

Although our discussion has centered on inequalities associated with occupational position, it is clear that monetary rewards (as well as access to goods) may be substantially affected by the par-ticular sector in which occupational strata are employed. The un-equal priorities accorded to different economic sectors by polit-ical authorities means that "high" and "low" earnings are not a simple expression of "high" and "low" skill, education, or objec-tively measured "quantity of output." This may be an obvious point, but it is a way of emphasizing the existence of overlapping strands in Soviet patterns of economic inequality. Thus the earn-ings of manual workers in the steel and coal industries are in ex-cess of those received by technical strata in lower-priority in-dustries, and the access to consumer durables by manual workers employed in a "science center" like Akademgorodok may place them in an advantaged position relative to mental as well as manual workers employed in less-favored sectors. This source of inequality in economic status has probably diminished in re-cent years (at least insofar as interindustry differentials are con-cerned) with the emphasis on a more "balanced" pattern of eco-nomic development appropriate to a "mature socialist society," but it remains an important element in the pattern of economic inequalities. It also serves as a constant reminder of the "polit-ically" directed nature of Soviet income stratification and the possibility of abrupt changes in the relative economic position of occupational strata.

One of the principal features of the reward structure within par-ticular sectors or communities is the absence of a clear — or at least, significant — "break" between the earnings position of manual and nonmanual strata. If we confine ourselves exclusively to the socio-occupational groups considered in the Leningrad and Tatar Republic studies, as well as the managerial and scientists' categories distinguished in Table 2.6, the following three-tiered earnings hierarchy emerges. The bottom rung of the hierarchy is occupied by low-skilled manual workers and those in routine clerical and office jobs not requiring extended training. The second tier encompasses a wide range of occupations, including skilled workers, technical strata (engineering-technical personnel below the top management group), and higher-ranking office staff (economists, accountants). The apex of the hierarchy includes managerial personnel (plant directors and department heads) and senior scientific workers. The first two of these groupings embrace both manual and nonmanual occupations, and there are substantial differences in educational attainments within all of the groupings. Earnings inequalities between the extremes of this hierarchy, as well as between the principal strata in the second tier (skilled workers and technical staffs), have almost certainly diminished since the mid-1950s.

Whatever the underlying factors making for this policy of narrowing earnings inequalities, its public justification is often couched in the traditional rhetoric used in Soviet discussions of the transition to the future communist society — the movement toward a "socially homogeneous society" and the elimination of "essential distinctions" between manual and mental labor. Whether Soviet society in recent years has actually moved toward increased social homogeneity, however, is highly problematic. This is quite apart from the undiminished material privileges of "elite" social groups. The increasing accessibility and variety of consumer goods, housing facilities, and "cultural" goods have created new opportunities for social differentiation, opportunities for translating even reduced inequalities in monetary rewards and substantial differences in educational levels and "value orientations" (to use a favorite Soviet term) into distinct modes of life. It is here that the contrasting characteristics of manual strata and nonmanual "specialists" may assume the form of a major social division in urban communities.

A Note on Rural Income Differentiation

The relatively depressed economic status of the Soviet rural population as a whole, and of the collective farm peasantry in particular, have long been recognized in both Western and Soviet literature on urban-rural differentials in living standards. But to some extent the focus on the relative backwardness of the Soviet rural community has obscured the existence of substantial social and economic differentiation in the countryside. To state the obvious — whatever may have been the case in the early years of collectivization — the Soviet rural community is not now a homogeneous mass living in equally shared deprivation. Despite the socialization or "cooperativization" of land and the comparatively limited scope for the division of labor inherent in agricultural operations, the Soviet countryside is characterized by large inequalities in economic status rooted in differing work roles in the production process. This theme in all its complexity deserves a much more thorough examination than we shall give it here. We confine ourselves to some of the broad patterns of inequality in incomes and living standards. What are the relative positions of the principal rural strata in the distribution of economic rewards?

The main Soviet studies of rural social structure which began to emerge in the late 1960s distinguished essentially four socio-occupational strata. The principal social cleavage was recognized as that between mental and manual labor, with each of these two broad categories being further subdivided into a skilled and unskilled component. The resulting fourfold social division was applied in some studies to both collective and state farms, as well as to nonagricultural enterprises and institutions in rural areas.[30] The number of distinct strata was expanded in the studies of V. Arutiunian. Since Arutiunian's work is perhaps the richest available source of information on the relative incomes and living standards of rural strata, a brief examination of the socio-occupational groups he distinguishes and the personal attributes (sex, Party membership, education) of their "membership" will be helpful. The picture which emerges in one region — the Tatar Republic — will suffice (see Table 2.9), since the distribution of these attributes among the various strata appears essentially similar in the other regions studied.

The simple fourfold social division of other studies has been replaced here by an expanded set of nine distinct socio-occupational groups, ranging from common laborers to higher-level managerial personnel. Perhaps most significant is the recognition of the latter as a distinct stratum (confined to collective farm chairmen, directors of state farms and of nonagricultural rural

Table 2.9

Sex Composition, Party Membership, and Education of Rural
Socio-occupational Groups: Tatar Republic, 1967

Socio-occupational groups*	% women	% Party members[†]	Years of education	
			Tatars	Russians
Higher-level managerial personnel	24.0	84	10.0	
Middle-level managerial personnel	19.6	62	8.4	8.2
Higher-level specialists	67.5	61	13.4	12.8
Middle-level specialists	75.9	35	10.4	10.7
Nonmanual employees	65.9	36	8.5	8.4
Machinery operators	1.5	15	6.2	5.6
Skilled manual personnel	25.6	10	5.3	5.3
Low-skilled manual personnel	66.0	7	5.1	4.0
Common laborers	70.8	5	5.1	3.4

Source: Material on sex composition and years of education is from Iu. V. Arutiunian, Sotsial'noe i natsional'noe, pp. 56-239; figures on Party membership are from Sovetskaia etnografiia, 1968, no. 4, p. 9.

*For greater detail on the particular occupations included in these groups, see Table 1.1 in Chapter 1.

†These figures apply only to men.

enterprises) whose unique position in rural social structure requires special study. As the apex of the occupational hierarchy, it is treated as separate from middle-level managerial personnel (brigade leaders, department heads) and technical specialists (agronomists, veterinarians, engineering personnel), with the latter being further divided into "higher" and "lower" categories. A distinct nonmanual employees stratum (clerical personnel, staff of day-nurseries) and four groups of manual workers complete the set of nine rural socio-occupational groups. The resulting multiplicity of distinct strata conveys an image of rural social structure in which there are no sharp divisions between adjoining social groups, but it also underscores the potentially wide range of inequality between the extremes of this structure. The very groups singled out by Arutiunian (and even those sociologists who worked with the four-group scheme) thus reintroduced the vision of a highly differentiated rural community — a theme which had lain dormant since the precollectivization period, but which dominated sociological studies of the countryside in the 1920s.

As noted earlier for urban strata, there are marked variations in the frequency of Party membership and the sex composition of the different rural social groups. The uneven distribution of Party membership is especially striking. Farm laborers and other low-skilled rural workers are rarely Party members. As we move up the occupational ladder, Party membership increases, reaching more than four-fifths among higher-level managerial staffs. Although women accounted for the bulk of the rural labor force in the Tatar Republic study, they were substantially underrepresented in managerial positions.[31] This does not mean, however, that women were rarely found among the more skilled groups but that where their role was important in such groups, it was likely to be among "specialists" rather than among managerial personnel. As in urban areas, women also accounted for a disproportionately high share of the lowest-skilled manual and nonmanual jobs.

Unfortunately, when we turn to our principal interest here — rural inequalities in economic status — the most privileged group disappears from view as a distinct stratum. Even in Arutiunian's useful studies, the earnings of higher-level managers are merged with those of lower-paid specialists. In other studies the managerial stratum becomes an indistinguishable component of the broad category "personnel in skilled mental labor." The result is that the range of inequality between the extremes of the occupational hierarchy is usually obscured. With this qualification in mind, the earnings figures shown in Table 2.10 provide an illuminating picture of broad patterns of inequality between socio-occupational groups employed in agricultural enterprises in the late 1960s.[32] It should be borne in mind that the discussion which follows is confined to earnings from the "socialized sector" and thus ignores the returns (in money income and consumption) derived from private household plots.

Even when farm managers cannot be distinguished as a separate group, a considerable spread is apparent between the earnings of the top and bottom of the occupational ladder. In most of the areas studied the earnings of the highest-paid occupational groups (managers and specialists combined, or personnel in "skilled mental labor") were more than three times the earnings of farm laborers; in the studies of the Belorussian and Tatar Republic collective farms the earnings ratios of these groups approached 4:1. Unlike the situation in urban industrial enterprises examined earlier, there is no evidence of any significant overlap between the earnings of farm specialists and the more skilled groups of the under-

Table 2.10

Average Monthly Earnings, in Rubles, of Socio-occupational Groups
in Agricultural Enterprises: Selected Regions, Late 1960s*

Socio-occupational group	Monthly earnings (in rubles)	
	collective farms	state farms
Tatar Republic, 1967		
higher-level managers and specialists	110.4	129.1
middle-level managers and specialists	89.3	100.1
nonmanual employees	67.8	64.4
machinery operators	62.3	74.5
skilled and low-skilled manual personnel	55.9	63.1
common laborers	30.6	39.8
Kalinin Region, 1967		
higher-level managers and specialists	116.9	126.2
middle-level managers and specialists	81.9	88.9
nonmanual employees	56.3	73.3
machinery operators	69.7	77.0
skilled and low-skilled manual personnel	52.1	65.6
common laborers	34.4	40.6
Krasnodar Territory, 1967		
higher-level managers and specialists	133.2	126.1
middle-level managers and specialists	99.6	95.8
nonmanual employees	76.3	69.1
machinery operators	84.7	78.3
skilled and low-skilled manual personnel	77.7	70.4
common laborers	55.0	51.8
Belorussian SSR, 1969		
skilled mental labor	162.6	
low-skilled and unskilled mental labor	72.5	
skilled manual labor	85.0	
low-skilled and unskilled manual labor	44.3	

Sources: Iu. V. Arutiunian, Sotsial'naia struktura, p. 119; E. N. Sapil'nikov,
"The Social Structure of the Rural Population and the Path of its Development,"
Voprosy filosofii, 1971, no. 11, p. 34.

*These figures apply to earnings from the "socialized sector" only, i.e., they
exclude incomes from private household plots.

lying nonspecialist work force. Thus the earnings of middle-level
managers and specialists are consistently above those of the highest-paid nonspecialist category: farm machinery operators. The
pay of the latter, in turn, is usually roughly double that of farm
laborers. The laborers' category is always at the bottom of the
earnings hierarchy in agricultural enterprises, never exceeding,
as it sometimes does in industrial enterprises, the earnings posi-

tion of nonmanual employees in lower-level clerical and office jobs.

For reasons spelled out above, the pattern of earnings differentials just reviewed understates the relatively privileged economic status of the highest managerial group in the rural community. Some idea of the spread in earnings between the mass of farm laborers and this managerial group is provided by information on the average yearly pay of collective farm chairmen and common laborers in the Ukraine in 1970. The earnings of these groups and several others in the collective farm work force were reported as follows (in rubles per year):[33]

collective farm chairmen	2,700
chief specialists	1,935
work brigade leaders, heads of livestock departments	1,268
agronomists	1,260
tractor operators, motor vehicle drivers	1,081
office and store-keeping personnel	780
common laborers	531

Thus the "socialized sector" (or in its official designation, the "cooperative sector") of Soviet agriculture admittedly generates an earnings spread on the order of 5:1 between its top managerial stratum and the mass of the farm work force in laborers' jobs, as well as a highly differentiated earnings structure between "middle management" and technical specialists on the one hand and farm laborers. Of course, a fuller picture of strata inequalities in economic status would have to encompass much more than we have considered here — differences in family size, earner-dependent ratios, and the role of the private household plot (lichnoe podsobnoe khoziaistvo). We do not undertake such an examination here, except for a brief word on the private plot.

Incomes from private plots constituted approximately one-third of the total incomes of collective farm families and one-fifth in the case of state farm families in 1970.[34] Among the mass of the work force in unskilled or low-skilled farm jobs, the cultivation of these household plots is clearly required to meet sheer subsistence needs. But whether household production significantly reduces the income inequalities generated in "socialized" farm production is a matter of dispute among Soviet writers on rural social structure. Arutiunian, for example, denies that the cultivation of household plots reduces income differences between "groups in skilled and unskilled labor, manual and mental labor, in the collective farm sector."[35] Part of the explanation may be that, although the lowest paid groups spend a considerably larger proportion of their time in the cultivation of household plots, the higher-ranking occupational groups are apparently in a better position to obtain access to resources from the "socialized sector" — transport, fodder, etc. — for use in private production.[36] However, Arutiunian is disputed by another writer on rural affairs who finds that household production "promotes the equalization of incomes of collective farmers in different social groups."[37]

Whatever the reduction in real income differentials, if any, associated with the cultivation of household plots, a simple exercise will show that substantial inequalities must remain between the polar occupational groups. If we assume (simply for the sake of this exercise) that farm managers' real income is modestly confined to what they can "purchase" with their annual money earnings reported on page 52 above, while the cultivation of household plots by farm laborers adds to their income an amount equivalent to what they receive from the "socialized sector," the income spread between these two groups remains close to 3:1. Whatever the actual magnitude of final income differentials between these groups, the very manner in which the large inequalities in monetary rewards inherent in "socialized" farm activities are reduced (again, if they are reduced at all) serves to accent the differentiation in modes of life of rural strata.

Although we have focused chiefly on money earnings, available evidence on strata differences in material conditions of life only reinforces the picture of deep divisions in the economic status of rural social groups. Thus farm administrators and specialists (in a Moldavian study of 1970) were reported to have roomier and better-equipped housing quarters for their smaller families.[38] In some of the areas studied by Arutiunian in 1967 there were striking inequalities in the possession of household amenities. For example, in state farms of the Krasnodar Territory refrigerators were owned by 44% of managers and specialists and 4% of laborers; in Kalinin Region the figures for ownership of washing machines were 69% and 11%, respectively. The frequency of ownership of these items on collective farms was generally lower, but the degree of inequality was of the same order or even greater. The ownership of TV sets among rural strata was also highly uneven (generally 3:1 or more in favor of managers and specialists).[39] Obviously the distribution of these few items in a scattering of sample studies is a crude indicator of differences in overall levels of living, but it is sufficient to illustrate the highly unequal distribution of symbols of recent progress in the material well-being of the Soviet countryside. It seems clear that inequalities in both money earnings and living standards parallel inequalities in power over the organization of the work process. This is one meaning of "distribution in accordance with labor."

One of the questions which arises from our brief review of rural economic differentiation is a historical one. Were the inequalities between "kulak" and "bedniak" in precollectivized agriculture — inequalities in real income, in power over the production process and the everyday affairs of the rural community — any greater than those which now prevail between the top managerial-specialist stratum and the mass of peasant "direct producers"? Soviet students of rural social structure are in the best position to answer this question, for it is their work which has provided the raw material for such a comparative study.

Notes

1. M. Yanowitch, "The Soviet Income Revolution," Slavic Review, December, 1963, pp. 683-97.

2. A. Liapin, Trud pri sotsializme, Moscow, 1951, p. 60.

3. L. E. Kunel'skii, Sotsial'no-ekonomicheskie problemy zarabotnoi platy, Moscow, 1972, p. 72; Sotsialisticheskii trud, 1975, no. 1, p. 12; N. E. Rabkina and N. M. Rimashevskaia, Osnovy differentsiatsii zarabotnoi platy i dokhodov naseleniia, Moscow, 1972, p. 55; S. Shkurko, "New Conditions of Payment of Labor," Voprosy ekonomiki, 1975, no. 10, p. 4. The policy of continuing to reduce wage differentials may have been halted by approximately 1970, but such differentials were clearly lower in the early 1970s than in the late 1950s.

4. N. E. Rabkina and N. M. Rimashevskaia, pp. 14, 18-19.

5. Akademiia nauk SSSR, Institut filosofii, Sotsialisticheskoe obshchestvo, Moscow, 1975, pp. 217-19.

6. N. E. Rabkina and N. M. Rimashevskaia, p. 51.

7. Iu. V. Arutiunian, Sotsial'naia struktura, p. 240.

8. M. D. Kartofianu, "The Influence of Social Differences on the Everyday Life of the Rural Population," in Akademiia nauk Moldavskoi SSR, Problemy izmeneniia sotsial'noi struktury sovetskogo obshchestva, Kishinev, 1971, p. 69.

9. Iu. V. Arutiunian, Sotsial'naia struktura, p. 113.

10. B. M. Levin, Sotsial'no-ekonomicheskie potrebnosti: zakonomernosti formirovaniia i razvitiia, Moscow, 1974, p. 165. For an earlier version of this position, see V. N. Iagodkin ed., Ekonomicheskie problemy podgotovki kvalifitsirovannykh rabochikh kadrov v sovremennykh usloviiakh, Moscow, 1967, pp. 8-28.

11. I. I. Kuzminov, V. S. Dunaev, and V. V. Tsakynov eds., Ekonomicheskii zakon raspredeleniia po trudu, Moscow, 1975, p. 18. Their principal

grounds for opposition to this "law," however, are that it implicitly treats labor power as a commodity in a socialist society, whose "value," like that of other commodities, is determined by its labor cost of production. For a response to this argument, see V. N. Iagodkin, pp. 20, 22.

12. See the identical formulations in Z. Fainburg, "The Current Stage of the Scientific-Technical Revolution and Social Planning," in Nauchno-tekhnicheskaia revoliutsiia i sotsial'nyi progress, Moscow, 1972, p. 196; and L. S. Bliakhman, "Production Interests of Youth," in Obshchestvo i molodezh', Moscow, 1973, p. 136.

13. Z. Fainburg, pp. 197-98.

14. However, the "egalitarian (egalitarnoi and in quotation marks in the Russian text) mission" of socialism has been acknowledged in at least one recent work, if only to illustrate the "contradiction" between the goal of establishing "full social equality" and the means required to do so — "the economic inequality of specific individuals in the sphere of distribution." See Akademiia nauk SSSR, Sotsialisticheskoe obshchestvo, p. 73.

15. By official labor statistics we mean the kind of material issued by the Central Statistical Administration. The most recent large collection of such statistics appears in this agency's 1968 publication, Trud v SSSR.

16. L. E. Kunel'skii, Zarplata, dokhody, stimulirovanie, Moscow, 1968, pp. 27-29.

17. N. E. Rabkina and N. M. Rimashevskaia, p. 56. More recent evidence of the continuing decline in interindustry wage differentials appears in Sotsialisticheskii trud, 1975, no. 1, p. 9.

18. Shkaratan's sample of incumbents of some occupational positions included in his study of Menzelinsk in the Tatar Republic seems extremely small. In any case the data for this city do not reveal any striking departures from the patterns revealed in Table 2.5 for Kazan and Al'met'evsk. See Iu. V. Arutiunian, Sotsial'noe i natsional'noe, pp. 323-24.

19. Shkaratan's studies, on which we rely here, do not include any groups classified as semiskilled manual workers.

20. In particular, the 1970 data for Leningrad can hardly be accepted as representing the typical relationship between the earnings of manual workers and nonmanual specialists. Both "skilled" and "highly skilled" workers' earnings are shown to be in excess of the earnings of all nonmanual specialists other than managerial personnel. Although this cannot be accepted as typical, it does not negate the principal point we are making here — the contrast between the moderate earnings gap and the rather sharp break in educational attainment levels of skilled workers and nonmanual specialists.

21. The use of per capita incomes yields an even more egalitarian picture of occupational differences in economic status than reliance on average earnings. Thus in all cities covered in Shkaratan's studies, the percentage differences between the per capita incomes of individuals in the highest- and lowest-ranking occupational strata were considerably less than differences in their average earnings. While the narrow spread in per capita incomes in these studies understates still further the range of inequalities in economic status in Soviet society at large, it points to an important feature of family income structure. The lowest wage positions (routine nonmanual and low-skilled manual jobs) are largely filled by women whose earnings are typically less than the earnings of their husbands. The highest-paid positions are likely to be occupied by men whose wives earn less than they do. In the absence of marked differences in family

size and composition, this factor operates to reduce per capita income differences between individuals at the extremes of the occupational hierarchy. It does not follow, of course, that the overall distribution of family income per capita in the Soviet Union is in fact more equal than the distribution of earnings (see Table 2.1). For a comparison of the wage and per capita income figures in Shkaratan's studies, see Iu. V. Arutiunian, Sotsial'noe i national'noe, pp. 168-70, and I. P. Trufanov, Problemy byta gorodskogo naseleniia SSSR, Leningrad, 1973, pp. 61-66.

22) The 1970 study of Leningrad machine-building plants showed 10.6% of managerial personnel earning "more than" 250 rubles per month. See I. P. Trufanov, 1973, p. 62. The estimate we make here assumes that the average earnings of the top 10% of managerial personnel were in the neighborhood of 300-325 rubles per month. We take the earnings of unskilled workers and "middle-level nonmanual employees" as representative of the bottom of the occupational hierarchy.

23. S. V. Sharutin, "Some Problems of Improving the Organization of Wages of Engineering-Technical Personnel," in Uchenye zapiski kafedr obshchestvennykh nauk vuzov Leningrada, politicheskaia ekonomiia, Issue XIV, Raspredelitel'nye otnosheniia sotsializma i ikh razvitie na sovremennom etape, Leningrad, 1973, p. 132.

24. The figures in this paragraph are based on material in O. I. Shkaratan, Problemy, p. 416; I. P. Trufanov, pp. 70-71.

25. Iu. V. Arutiunian, Sotsial'noe i natsional'noe, p. 177.

26. Iu. V. Arutiunian, Sotsial'noe i natsional'noe, p. 178; L. Gordon et al., "Developed Socialism: The Well-Being of Workers," Rabochii klass i sovremennyi mir, 1974, no. 3, p. 19.

27. These are simple averages of the figures reported for two industrial enterprises in M. N. Rutkevich ed., Sotsial'nye razlichiia i ikh preodolenie, Sverdlovsk, 1969, p. 109. For broadly similar findings in other areas, see the sources cited in Table 2.7.

28. Iu. V. Arutiunian, Sotsial'noe i natsional'noe, pp. 164-65.

29. Compare with the findings of a study of industrial enterprises conducted at about the same time. M. N. Rutkevich ed., Sotsial'nye razlichiia, p. 109. Also see the findings of a somewhat later study of the ownership of consumer durables by urban workers. L. Gordon et al., p. 24.

30. Iu. V. Arutiunian, "Social Structure of the Rural Population," Voprosy filosofii, 1966, no. 5; E. N. Sapil'nikov, "The Social Structure of the Rural Population and the Path of its Development," Voprosy filosofii, 1971, no. 11; M. D. Kartofianu, Novyi byt Moldavskogo sela, Kishinev, 1973.

31. The figures in Table 2.9 almost certainly overstate the share of women in top managerial positions in agricultural enterprises. The Tatar Republic study included rural educational institutions, and this probably raised the representation of women in managerial positions. See Chapter 6.

32. We ignore the earnings data available in Arutiunian's studies for rural groups outside agriculture. Such groups encompass a highly diverse range of occupations (in rural industrial enterprises and schools) classified into five or six broad occupational strata. The information in Arutiunian's work on this sector appears much less useful than that on the agricultural sector.

33. This is a partial listing of a more complete set of jobs and earnings levels which appears in B. I. Paskhaver, Rentnye problemy v SSSR, Kiev, 1972, pp. 175-76.

34. S. L. Seniavskii, Izmeneniia v sotsial'noi strukture sovetskogo obshche-stva, Moscow, 1973, p. 269.

35. Iu. V. Arutiunian, Opyt sotsiologicheskogo izucheniia sela, Moscow, 1968, p. 54. He is somewhat less definite on this matter in his Sotsial'naia struktura, pp. 132-33, but the implication seems to be the same.

36. Iu. V. Arutiunian, Sotsial'naia struktura, p. 133.

37. E. N. Sapil'nikov, p. 37.

38. See M. D. Kartofianu, Novyi byt, pp. 48-52; Iu. V. Arutiunian, Sotsial'naia struktura, p. 210. In Kartofianu's Moldavian study of 1970 the proportion of farm managers and specialists living in homes of three or more rooms was distinctly greater than among "unskilled personnel in manual labor," but "...80% of the families of personnel in mental labor have one or two children, while among personnel in manual labor such families constitute 51%...."

39. Iu. V. Arutiunian, Sotsial'naia struktura, p. 210.

3 SOCIAL INEQUALITY IN ACCESS TO SCHOOLING

Thus far we have been concerned chiefly with inequalities in monetary rewards and living standards associated with different positions in the occupational structure. Any serious study of Soviet social inequality must also consider the "openness" of the system, i.e., the extent to which the unequally rewarded positions in the social division of labor are accessible to the children of different social groups. Hence in this and the following chapter we turn our attention to the process of recruitment to occupational positions and the degree of generational transmission of economic and social privileges.

The distinction between inequalities of reward and inequalities of access to differentially rewarded positions may appear to be an obvious one. But the relationship between these two types of inequality bears on the important issue of whether Soviet society — or any society — may be appropriately characterized as a "class system." Whatever the full range of meanings which has been attached to this concept, it obviously implies not simply the existence of inequalities in income and power at a given time but also of institutional mechanisms which reproduce such inequalities in a manner that facilitates a high degree of continuity of privileged (and underprivileged) positions across generations. In the absence of such continuities, as Frank Parkin suggests, "it would still be possible for inequality to persist, but not class stratification in the conventional meaning of that term."[1]

What is the degree and mechanism of transmission of socio-occupational status in a society in which the private ownership and control of property and capital are essentially absent? We shall attempt a more comprehensive answer to this question — for the Soviet Union — than has thus far been provided. Two kinds of material are available for our purpose: (a) the amount and type of schooling typically received by children reared in families of differing social positions; (b) the social origins of individuals holding different positions in the occupational hierarchy, as well as the occupational status of individuals reared in families of differing social positions. This chapter focuses chiefly on the first of these.

One of the functions of the Soviet educational system is to promote economic growth by allocating young people among the various positions in an increasingly differentiated occupational structure. Since the resources available for education are limited and effective performance in various job functions requires different minimum amounts and types of formal schooling, we would expect to find considerable inequality in the length of schooling received by different groups of Soviet youth. To the extent that this "allocative" function of schooling is operative, it also appears natural to confine extended and "specialized" schooling to the "most capable" youth,[2] i.e., those whose academic performance at lower levels of schooling and whose scores on competitive entrance examinations to higher levels of schooling are superior to those of their classmates. The occupational careers open to those with extended schooling are, of course, the more desirable ones — although not always because of any significant income advantages they involve — and the competition for scarce vacancies at higher levels of schooling is frequently intense.

An educational system structured along these lines in a stratified society — Soviet or non-Soviet — has a strong tendency to transmit economic and social inequalities across generations even when all levels of schooling are tuition free. The mechanism of social "self-recruitment" is a familiar one. The critical link is the family unit and its position in the hierarchy of classes and strata. Young people are socialized in families which differ in incomes, consumption patterns, cultural levels, and physical surroundings, as well as in the values and expectations they transmit to children. These differences in family socialization patterns cannot help but strongly affect the school performance of children, their occupational aspirations, the age at which they leave school, and their ultimate occupational destinations.[3] There is no need to ignore the influence of other socializing institutions (preschool child-care institutions, for example) to see that what we have called the "allocative" function of Soviet schooling, combined with significant disparities in family economic and cultural levels, makes for a high degree of inheritance of socio-occupational status.

But the "allocative" role of Soviet schooling is not its only function. There is another that is no less real for the ideological rhetoric in which it is frequently clothed. We may call it the "egalitarian" function of Soviet schooling ("mobility promoting" or "inheritance limiting" may be more appropriate but also more awkward designations for this function). As we have noted earlier, one of the principal criteria of the "transition to communism" is the increasing "social homogeneity" of Soviet society. In this context the extent of equality in the educational attainments of different social strata and in the access of their children to advanced levels of schooling are regarded as specific indicators of progress toward the goal of a socially homogeneous society.[4] Moreover, Soviet educational philosophy explicitly rejects the notion that intellectual capacities and "natural" talents and abilities are disproportionately concentrated among particular classes and strata of Soviet society.[5] Thus any significant disparities between the social composition of students in the higher grades of the educational system and the social structure of the society at large are viewed as "disproportions" requiring Party and state intervention for their correction.[6] This is particularly the case where the disproportions concern the relative shares of children from working-class — the "leading class" — and intelligentsia families. The frequent reiteration of these egalitarian values in both the "popular" and "professional" literature on education has been used to defend policies whose intended impact is to counter, at least partially, the generational transmission of social and economic inequality through the school system. Although we discuss these policies and the controversies surrounding them in some detail below, we may anticipate our later discussion by noting that they include: the "social regulation" of student selection to higher educational institutions and to special schools for "talented youth," adherence to the principle of a "single" school system which generally avoids premature specialization and the early "sorting out" of pupils, and a steady rise in the minimum length of schooling regarded as "obligatory" for all youth. These and similar policies are associated with the conception of the Soviet school system as an "instrument for promoting the social homogeneity of our society."[7]

There is obviously an ongoing tension between the "allocative" and "egalitarian" functions of the Soviet educational system. Although the relative influence of these two orientations has varied in different periods, both are part of the continuing heritage of the Soviet school system, and their joint impact makes it impossible to characterize this system in simplistic terms (as either exclusively "elitist" or "egalitarian"). It is the interplay and tension between these orientations which guide this chapter's analysis of the data, controversies, and policies bearing on access to schooling.

Secondary Education

The completion of the eighth grade of the general-education school marks the attainment of an "incomplete secondary education" in the Soviet Union. By the beginning of the 1970s some 85-90% of school-age children were receiving the "universal" obligatory minimum of eight years of schooling.[8] It is at this point — the completion of the eighth grade — that the initial stage of the "social selection" process leading to the attainment of adult occupational status becomes apparent. There are essentially four paths open to Soviet youngsters at this juncture:

1. Entry to the ninth grade of the ten-year general-education school. This is the route traditionally taken by those who will seek admission to a higher educational institution (vuz). Although most tenth-grade graduates have not gained admission to a vuz in recent years, at least not immediately after graduation, the great majority of vuz entrants are drawn from this group. Thus entry to the ninth grade provides the greatest opportunity for the ultimate attainment of a higher education and of eventual status as a higher-level "specialist."

2. Admission to a specialized secondary school (tekhnikum). These schools provide three or four years of training, leading mainly to semiprofessional occupational status (technician, nurse, accountant, agronomist), although in recent years an increasing proportion of their graduates have flowed into skilled workers' occupations. Like graduates of the general-secondary schools, these youngsters receive a "complete secondary education" and are thus eligible to apply for admission to a vuz, but this is a less likely path to higher education. The tekhnikum is the main channel of access to the lower levels of "specialist" status — or what might loosely be called the "middle strata" in the West.

3. Attendance at a lower-level[9] vocational school (proftekhuchilishche) preparing students for employment in semiskilled and skilled workers' occupations. Until 1969 graduates of these schools were not considered to have received a "complete secondary education" and thus could not gain entry to a higher education. This dis-

ability began to be removed in that year as some of these schools sought to combine vocational training with general-secondary education by lengthening the course of study from 12-18 months to three years. This path remains the least likely route (of the three discussed thus far) to a higher education.

4. Full-time employment. This may be combined with part-time (evening or correspondence) schooling, if desired, in any of the secondary educational institutions described above.

The following figures for 1970 (which may also be taken as approximately true for the early 1970s) show the proportion of eighth-grade graduates following the various paths available to them (in %):[10]

entry to ninth grade of general-secondary school	60.1
entry to specialized-secondary school	11.1
full-time work or vocational school:	28.9
work	12.5
vocational school	16.4

Thus in the early 1970s some 85% of Soviet youngsters continued full-time schooling beyond the eighth grade, with perhaps three-fourths doing so in institutions that provided a "complete secondary education." Although youngsters are essentially "free" to choose any of the above paths (only the tekhnikum requires an entrance examination), the actual route chosen is necessarily affected by a variety of local circumstances. Thus not all types of schooling are equally accessible in rural areas and small towns. On the other hand, the scarcity of attractive job opportunities for 15-16-year-olds in outlying areas leads some youngsters to enroll in the ninth grade of a general-secondary school independently of any desire for extended education. But beyond these local influences we may observe a "sorting out" of youngsters which reflects a variety of circumstances related to the occupational status and educational level of the child's parents: the family's immediate need for additional income, the youngster's academic performance in grades 1-8, the career aspirations transmitted by family socialization patterns.

It is a token of the Soviet concern with the issue of generational transmission of occupational status that a number of sociological studies have focused on this "sorting out" process — both at the eighth-grade and at higher levels of schooling. Although scattered data are available for a relatively wide range of areas, we shall draw chiefly on the more systematic studies conducted in Leningrad, Novosibirsk, and several industrial centers in the Urals:

Table 3.1

Educational Paths Taken or Planned by Eighth-grade Graduates,
by Occupational Status of Parents (in %)

Parental occupational status*	Educational paths followed or planned by eighth-grade graduates, in %			
	ninth grade of general-secondary school	secondary specialized school	vocational school or work	total
Actual educational path				
Sverdlovsk, 1965				
workers	49.6	50.4		100
specialists	69.5	30.5		100
Nizhnyi Tagil, 1968				
workers	51.8	13.8	34.4	100
nonspecialist employees	43.0	15.2	41.8	100
specialists	75.6	18.7	5.7	100
Leningrad, 1968				
low-skilled and unskilled workers, and nonspecialist employees	25	25	50	100
skilled workers	52	27	21	100
specialists in jobs requiring secondary specialized education	70	15	15	100
specialists in jobs requiring higher education	86	11	3	100
Planned educational path				
Cheliabinsk, 1974				
workers	55.5	21.7	22.8	100
nonspecialist employees	59.3	22.4	18.3	100
specialists	64.3	30.0	5.7	100

Sources: E. K. Vasil'eva, Sotsial'no-professional'nyi uroven' gorodskoi molo-
dezhi, p. 41; M. Rutkevich and F. Fillipov, Sotsial'nye peremeshcheniia, p. 214;
M. Rutkevich ed., Zhiznennye plany molodezhi, p. 81; V. G. Afanas'ev et al.,
Problemy nauchnogo kommunizma, no. 9, p. 51.

*In the Leningrad study, where mother and father had differing occupational
positions the higher status is shown. The method used to determine parental
occupational status in the other cities is not clear but probably involved taking
the father's status where both parents were present in the household and the
mother's where the father was absent.

Sverdlovsk, Nizhnyi Tagil, and Cheliabinsk.

What is the impact of parental social position on the paths followed by youngsters as they complete the eighth grade? Table 3.1,
which shows the educational routes followed (in the late 1960s) or
planned (in the early 1970s) by youngsters, exhibits some of the

main features of this initial "social selection" process. Perhaps its most obvious aspect is that the higher-ranking occupational groups ("specialists," those holding jobs which normally require a higher or specialized secondary education) typically send a distinctly larger proportion of their children to the ninth grade of the general-secondary school than do workers and nonspecialist employees. This, it will be recalled, is the path offering greatest promise of eventual access to higher education. Thus some 70% or more of specialists' children went on to the ninth grade, while the corresponding figure for the children of workers and lower-level nonmanual employees was closer to 40-50%. When the data permit us to distinguish subgroups within the "specialists" and "workers" categories, the impact of parental occupational status seems even greater. Thus in Leningrad in 1968 more than four-fifths of the children of specialists with higher education went on to the ninth grade, while only one-fourth of the children of low-skilled workers followed this route. When the data are limited to youngsters' "plans," as distinct from the educational paths actually followed, differences between social groups appear somewhat muted. But even here there can be no mistaking the more "ambitious" aspirations of intelligentsia than of working-class children.

The other side of this process, of course, is the substantial proportion of workers' and lower-level employees' children for whom completion of the eighth grade signals entry into the work force or a brief stay at a vocational school (proftekhuchilishche) prior to full-time employment in workers' occupations. If the situation portrayed in Table 3.1 is at all typical of that prevailing in urban areas in the late 1960s and early 1970s, it suggests that some 25-50% of workers' and nonspecialist employees' children either began to work or entered a workers' vocational school upon completion of an eighth-grade education. Among children reared in intelligentsia families (following Soviet usage for the moment, we treat "intelligentsia" and "specialists" as equivalent categories), on the other hand, the proportion taking this path at the age of 15-16 was altogether insignificant (3% in Leningrad among children of higher-level specialists).

The impact of material and cultural inequalities among adults on youngsters' opportunities for extended education becomes particularly clear when we consider the relationship between parental occupational status, the academic performance of schoolchildren, and the proportions of eighth-grade graduates going on to the ninth grade. It is normal for children who perform particularly well in their early schooling to be encouraged to continue their general education beyond the eighth grade in the hope of eventual access to higher education. On the other hand, those whose school performance is distinctly inferior are more likely to begin work at this point or enroll in a vocational school. There is abundant evidence in the Soviet literature that in the early grades (through grade 8) pupil performance among children reared in intelligentsia families is superior to that of working-class children.[11] But it is also true that at given levels of pupil performance there are marked disparities in the proportions of youngsters continuing their general education, and these disparities are related to parental occupational status.

Soviet schoolchildren are evaluated along a grading scale ranging from 1 to 5. The Leningrad study referred to earlier divided eighth-year students into two groups: those with grade scores of 3.5 and higher, and those below this level. The proportions of each group continuing their general-secondary education were then derived separately for pupils of differing social background. The results provided unmistakable evidence of substantial social inequalities in access to advanced general education (and hence in future opportunities for higher education) among youngsters with similar levels of academic performance (see Table 3.2).

Table 3.2

Parental Occupational Status and Pupil Performance of
Eighth-grade Graduates Entering the Ninth Grade
of General Education Schools, Leningrad, 1968

Parental occupational status	Proportions of youngsters entering ninth grade with various rating scores (in %)*	
	score of less than 3.5	score of 3.5 or more
Low-skilled and unskilled workers, and nonspecialist employees	19	41
Skilled workers	38	69
Specialists in jobs requiring secondary specialized education	50	80
Specialists in jobs requiring higher education	77	89

Source: E. K. Vasil'eva, Sotsial'no-professional'nyi uroven', p. 41.
*Point scores range from 1 to 5.

Among upper-strata children (those whose parents were employed in jobs requiring a higher education) differences in grade

scores had relatively little impact on the proportions continuing
their general-secondary education. More than three-fourths of
both "high" and "low" scoring students in this group took this path.
Among lower-strata children, on the other hand, a "low" grade
score was much more likely to discourage further general education (only 19% of low-skilled workers' children with "low" grades
continued their general education, compared to 77% of upper-strata
children). Not only were higher-strata children more likely to
enter the ninth grade than lower-strata children with comparable
scores, but the highest-ranking groups in the occupational hierarchy sent a larger proportion of their "low" scoring children to
the ninth grade than working-class parents sent of their "high"
scoring children (Table 3.2).

We must warn, however, against exaggerating the extent of unequal opportunities for extended education at this point in the
schooling process. The Soviet Union, at least in recent years, is
clearly not a society which "tracks" most working-class children
— upon completion of the eighth grade — into types of schooling
which rigidly separate their career paths from those of intelligentsia children. The fact is that most urban children, including
working-class children, have continued their schooling in recent
years in institutions which provide a "complete" secondary education (the general-secondary school or the tekhnikum),[12] thereby
leaving open the possibility of achieving intelligentsia status at a
later stage in the occupational attainment process. Those whose
occupational fates are more or less "sealed" upon completion of
the eighth grade (by virtue of their entry into the work force or
transfer to a workers' vocational school) are drawn largely from
the lowest-skilled strata of workers' families. Those disparities
in career prospects which do appear upon completion of the eighth
grade mark the initial, not the final or decisive, stage in a more
extended process that simultaneously reproduces social inequalities and offers the prospect of social mobility to considerable
numbers of working-class youth. This point must be stressed if
we are to understand the tensions which emerge at a later stage
in the schooling process.

What groups of youngsters complete a general-secondary education — i.e., graduate from the tenth grade — and how does the
social composition of these groups differ from those who pursue
other types of schooling? Although only two years of full-time
schooling — corresponding to grades 9 and 10 — are normally required for completion of the daytime secondary school, there was

apparently a considerable "dropout" rate in these grades in the late 1960s and early 1970s. During the 1966/67 and 1967/68 academic years, for example, some 18-20% of ninth-grade students failed to continue their schooling in the tenth grade.[13] There is every reason to assume that this dropping out occurred more frequently among working-class children than among those reared in intelligentsia families. When we recall that the latter group was also more likely to enter the upper grades of the general-secondary school than the former (see Table 3.1), we are not surprised to find that the social origins of tenth-grade graduates — who form the major pool of applicants for a higher education — are more "selective" than those of eighth-grade graduates. Whatever data are available to us suggest that the direction of change as we move from the eighth to the tenth grade is invariably the same: a declining component of working-class children and an increasing share of children reared in families of nonmanual occupational strata.[14]

It seems clear that the latter group constituted a majority of the students in graduating classes of general-secondary schools throughout the latter half of the 1960s and perhaps later. Even in some of the country's largest urban centers, where we might expect this level of schooling to be most accessible to workers' families, working-class children accounted for less than one-half of graduating classes (see Table 3.3). The share of workers in the total employed population of these cities, on the other hand, was in the range of 60-75%. But there is no reason to regard these graduates as representing a highly selective social "elite." Although workers' children were a minority of graduates, they were a sizable minority (some 38-48% in cities like Leningrad, Novosibirsk, and Sverdlovsk). Further, the white-collar majority in these classes included not only "specialists'" children but also youngsters reared in families of lower-level clerical, office, and sales employees ("nonspecialist employees"). We are stressing again that one of the major problems in Soviet education in recent years is precisely the fact that a considerable proportion of lower-strata youngsters retain the hope of attaining the highest levels in the occupational hierarchy until a relatively late state in the socialization process.

How does the social composition of students at other pre-vuz levels of schooling (beyond the eighth grade) differ from that observed among graduates of general-secondary schools? In contrast to the latter group, the tekhnikum (specialized secondary

Table 3.3

Distribution of Students Graduating from Tenth Grade of General-
Secondary Schools, by Parental Occupational Status (in %)

Parental occupational status	Distribution of graduating students by parental occupational status (in %)		
	Sverdlovsk 1965	Novosibirsk 1966	Leningrad 1968
Workers	38.9	48.2	48.5
Nonspecialist employees	19.2	25.4	51.5
Specialists	33.3	26.4	
Others*	8.6		
Total	100.0	100.0	100.0

Sources: M. Rutkevich in Voprosy filosofii, 1967, no. 6, p. 20; L. F. Liss, "On the Stability of Characteristics and Specific Features of the Social Origin of University Applicants," in Institut istorii, filologii i filosofii SO AN SSSR, Sotsial'noe prognozirovanie v oblasti obrazovaniia, p. 39; Partiinaia organizatsiia i rabochie Leningrada, p. 413.

*Includes children of pensioners, cases in which children were orphans, and cases in which parents belonged to "mixed" occupational categories. This classification appears only in the sources of the Sverdlovsk data.

school) is predominantly a working-class institution. In those areas for which data are available at the close of the 1960s, the working-class component among the student body of these institutions was typically on the order of 60-70%.[15] This is an important point, for the tekhnikum is the principal source of recruitment to the lower-ranking intelligentsia occupations, or what Soviet writers call "middle-level specialists"[16] (there appear to be no "lower-level specialists"). Graduation from a tekhnikum has an important advantage over graduation from a general-secondary school for working-class youth with upwardly mobile aspirations. It promises "early professionalization" (some three or four years after completing the eighth grade) in such occupations as technician, nurse, laboratory assistant, or even schoolteacher. At the very least it offers the prospect of attainment of skilled-worker status. For graduates of general-secondary schools, on the other hand, failure on competitive entrance examinations to a higher educational institution normally requires entry into the work force without a specialty, while success means an additional four or five years of schooling prior to attainment of intelligentsia occupational status. It is hardly surprising, therefore, that workers' children have predominated in the tekhnikum, while nonmanual strata have supplied the majority of general-education graduates.

The lower-level vocational schools (proftekhuchilishche), which train youngsters for workers' trades and thus promise a more modest occupational status than either the specialized or general-secondary schools, have an overwhelmingly working-class student body. In at least some cities workers' children approach 90% of the student population in these schools.[17] In none of the cities for which comparable data are available for specialized or general-secondary schools does the share of working-class children come close to such a figure. It is also clear that insofar as children of relatively "high" social origins "descend" to workers' occupations, they do so not through the conscious selection of schooling in workers' trades but chiefly through failure to complete a general or specialized secondary education, or failure to gain admission to a vuz.

We may summarize the relationship between pupils' social background and type of schooling up to this point in the following broad terms: the more "promising" the future occupational status associated with completion of any given type of schooling, the lower is the share of manual workers' children and the higher the proportion of nonmanual strata in the student body. Although our discussion has been confined largely to the schooling of urban children, there is no reason to assume that the inclusion of rural youngsters would alter the essential picture presented here. The fact that rural children are less likely to continue their secondary education beyond the eighth grade than urban children is surely related to the larger relative share of manual occupational strata in the rural than in the urban work force (as well as a relative scarcity of secondary schools with upper-level classes in rural areas and the poorer quality of rural than of urban teachers).[18]

Social Determinants of Differential Schooling

It is all too easy to explain these disparities in amount and type of schooling received by children of diverse social origins by referring in general terms to differences in the "cultural environments" and material rewards of the principal occupational strata. But such broad "explanations," however intuitively reasonable they may seem, tell us nothing about the specific mechanisms which lead to social inequalities in access to advanced schooling and hence to the higher levels of the occupational hierarchy. Our objective here is to identify more precisely at least some of the factors which account for the unequal life chances of children reared in different classes and strata.

It is not at all obvious why there should be marked differences in the social composition of different types of schooling in Soviet society. There is clearly no formal segregation of schoolchildren by class background. There is no obvious counterpart to the network of private schools which permits well-to-do families in other societies to "prepare" their children for privileged economic and social status. Although substantial income inequalities may be observed between the extremes of the occupational ladder, our discussion in Chapter 2 also noted the considerable overlapping of worker and intelligentsia incomes in the middle ranges of the occupational structure. There is also the often-repeated commitment of Soviet educational authorities — which we can assume to be genuine — to equality of educational opportunity and the rejection of the notion that "natural talents" are unequally distributed across social groups. Why, then, even before the final stage of competitive selection for higher education, do we find the kind of social differentiation in schooling which produced (at least until the early 1970s) nonmanual majorities in general-secondary schools and worker majorities in the vocational schools?

One factor operating in this direction is, quite simply, that the plans of upper-strata parents for the schooling and work careers of their children are distinctly more ambitious than those of working-class and peasant parents. Obviously the link between parents' plans and children's school performance is not a simple and direct one, but there can be little doubt that differences in these plans are translated into different degrees of support and encouragement for youngsters' "academic" attainments and expectations. A number of Soviet studies have documented the relationship between the occupational status of families and their career plans for children. One such study — conducted in the Sverdlovsk region in 1966 — is particularly revealing since it provides a more detailed breakdown of social groups than is common in such studies (see Table 3.4). Intelligentsia ("specialists") parents in this region, almost without exception, expected their children to receive a higher or secondary specialized education and hence to inherit their own occupational status. More than 90% of the highest-strata families ("specialists with a higher education") envisaged a higher education for their children. Although most lower-strata families (peasants, unskilled workers) also aspired to nonmanual occupations for their children, only some

35-45% considered a higher education as appropriate for them. Thus parental pressure on children to complete a general-secondary education (the principal means of access to a vuz) must have been distinctly weaker among worker and peasant families than among those in the higher-ranking nonmanual occupations.

Table 3.4

Parents' Educational Plans for Children, by Occupational Status of Parents, Sverdlovsk Region, 1966*

Occupational status of parents	Educational plans of parents for children (in %)					
	higher	secondary specialized	general secondary	incomplete secondary	other†	total
Collective farmers	36.2	20.4	24.4	16.6	2.4	100
Workers	64.9	19.9	8.5	4.2	2.5	100
Nonspecialist employees	70.6	28.6	0.8			100
Specialists with second-ary specialized edu-cation	85.6	13.6	0.4	0.4		100
Specialists with higher education	93.5	6.5				100

Source: M. Rutkevich ed., Protsessy izmeneniia sotsial'noi struktury v sovetskom obshchestve, pp. 145, 149.

*The year to which these figures apply is not given directly in the source used, but judging by other materials on Sverdlovsk in this source it is 1966.

†Undecided or could not answer.

These differences in families' educational plans obviously reflect different perceptions of the opportunity structure rooted in the occupational experience of adult family members, as well as the greater assistance in schoolwork which the more educated nonmanual families are able to offer their children. Quite apart from their direct impact on youngsters' schooling, these unequally ambitious educational plans are only one aspect of a much broader range of class and strata differences in family socialization patterns and hence in the values, expectations, and opportunities transmitted to children. A recent Leningrad study has indicated some of the more obvious forms which such differential socialization assumes:

With an increase in the educational (and hence in the occupational — M. Y.) level of parents, there is a rise in the frequency of attendance at theaters and museums, and the children are more likely to be involved in hobby groups. Together with this there is a decline in the proportion of children who are excessively involved in viewing movies.[19]

The impact of these disparities in parental plans for children's schooling and the range of cultural experiences to which they are exposed is also reinforced by differences in the physical surroundings of youngsters reared in different social groups. Although we referred earlier (see Chapter 2) to the relatively egalitarian distribution of housing space in given locales, the advantages of larger-sized and separate (as distinct from communal) apartments are more frequently available to the higher levels of the occupational hierarchy. A 1967-68 study of the housing characteristics of Leningrad families with children in the third to tenth grades reveals some of these advantages.[20] Families in which at least one parent held a job requiring a higher education were two to three times as likely to live in relatively large apartments (of three rooms or more) as low-skilled workers. Their access to separate apartments was also somewhat more frequent than that of less-educated and less-skilled groups — although their advantage here was comparatively modest (39-48% of families with a highly educated parent lived in such apartments, compared to 31-36% among the less educated). Manual workers and lower-level nonmanual employees were less likely than "specialists" to have a separate work area set aside for their children of school age. If it is appropriate to consider the presence of a nonworking adult in the household as an advantage — and the author of the Leningrad study apparently thought it was — higher-strata families also tended to have a more favorable household situation in this respect. On balance it seems clear that the physical conditions of household life among upper-strata families are more conducive to children's "success" at school than is the case among lower-ranking occupational groups. This is most apparent, however, when we compare the two extremes of the occupational hierarchy (groups with higher education versus low-skilled workers). It is less clear — indeed significant differences tend to disappear — when we compare skilled workers and nonspecialist employees, on the one hand, with the tail end of intelligentsia occupations (those with specialized secondary education) on the other. The more advantaged physical surroundings of the highest strata are no small matter, however, as children approach the higher grades of secondary school, with their increasingly heavy academic "load."

We are not surprised, of course, to discover that youngsters reared in intelligentsia households typically have environmental advantages of both a cultural and material nature compared to working-class and peasant youths. But given a school system that is formally a relatively "open" one at all levels prior to higher education and clearly not explicitly class-selective in nature, the specification of these advantages helps account for the social differentiation in schooling described earlier: namely, the predominance of nonmanual strata in the upper grades of general-secondary schools and the greater tendency of working-class youth to seek early labor market entry and specialized vocational education.

Issues and Controversies in Secondary Education

Our interest here is not only in documenting social inequality in Soviet schooling but also in the reaction to this issue in Soviet public discourse, particularly the tensions, controversies, and policy measures it has generated in recent years. How have Soviet concerns with unequal schooling been reflected in educational discussions and policy-making in the past decade?

The policy of implementing "universal" secondary education since the mid-1960s, although not yet wholly successful, has obviously operated to reduce inequalities in the amount of (pre-vuz) schooling received by youngsters of differing social origins. According to Soviet claims, the proportion of the corresponding age group completing a secondary education rose from 45% in 1965 to approximately 70% in the early 1970s.[21] Since nonmanual strata were disproportionately represented in the graduating classes of general-secondary schools in the late 1960s (as we demonstrated above), the continuing effort to "universalize" secondary education has been presented in the Soviet educational literature as a step toward "full social equality" in education. The egalitarian rhetoric associated with this campaign, the seriousness with which it is regarded, as well as some of its attendant difficulties are well conveyed in a local Party leader's report on secondary education in his republic (Estonia):

Upon visiting schools we sometimes hear complaints from individual teachers to the effect that some pupils are allegedly incapable of assimilating the program of secondary education. However, life itself and the practice of many schools, as well as the ... results of sociological studies, convince us of the lack of validity of these views. The reasons for the poor progress of some pupils lie in the fact that our schools have not yet been able to properly equalize the differences associated with family upbringing of children and the conditions of everyday life. As a result, teachers often behave mistakenly by being too hasty in judging the intellectual abilities of children. ... Our position must be that the whole system of education and upbringing must be used to realize the social policy of the Party, directed toward reducing inequalities connected with differences in family upbringing, toward equalizing opportunities for education. . . .

Education is among the greatest values provided by socialist society, and the Soviet school must strive for its more equal distribution among all youth.[22]

The general objective of "universalizing" secondary schooling has been widely heralded and, at least in public discussions of educational issues, universally accepted. But the question of the appropriate forms of secondary education has been a source of continuing controversies, and the problem of social inequality has been at the heart of these controversies. The latter can best be understood as reflecting the tension between what we earlier referred to as the "allocative" and the "egalitarian" functions of Soviet schooling. The controversies have arisen when educational reform proposals designed to improve the "allocative" or "efficiency" aspects of the Soviet school system have appeared to conflict with its equality-promoting function. More specifically, policies which promised to improve the "fit" between types of schooling provided and the structure of available jobs, or to promote the more effective nurturing of revealed "talent," also threatened to be socially discriminatory. The controversies that emerged illustrate the role which the officially sanctioned value of social equality plays in public discussion of educational issues and, to some extent, in educational policy-making. Two illustrations will suffice.

In 1966 a sociologist (N. Aitov) working in the area of the sociology of education proposed the "rationalization" of secondary education by the introduction of a dual-track system of schooling beyond the eighth grade. Under Aitov's proposal approximately one-third of the children would continue their secondary education in institutions that would be explicitly college-preparatory schools. Admission to these schools would be by competitive examinations, and their curriculum would be geared to the areas of specialization of particular higher educational institutions. They would be "schools of physics and mathematics, engineering subjects, chemistry, the humanities, biology, etc." The remaining two-thirds of eighth-grade graduates would attend vocational schools designed to train "highly skilled workers for all branches of the national economy."[23] Although graduates of these schools could apply for admission to a vuz (after having "worked for a prescribed period"), they would be trained primarily for workers' trades rather than in the more "academic" disciplines available in the college-preparatory schools. Thus at the age of 15 schoolchildren would be channeled into two broad groups of occupations by means of a system of differentiated secondary education which in most cases would determine the lifetime careers available to them.

Aitov's justification for his proposal was grounded primarily in the occupational requirements of the Soviet economy for the foreseeable future. If post-eighth-grade schooling was to become "universal," it had to be recognized that most secondary-school graduates would not gain admission to higher education. Instead of functioning primarily as stepping stones to vuz admission, the higher levels of secondary school (grades 9 and 10) would have to serve mainly as workers' training institutions since the economy had many more workers' jobs to fill than intelligentsia positions. One-third of the corresponding age group would provide a sufficient base for recruitment to the latter.

Aitov was well aware of the kinds of criticism that his proposal might encounter. Would not a socialist society be reinforcing social inequality by introducing a mechanism of early selection of schoolchildren traditionally associated with the "class-bound" educational systems of capitalist societies? Aitov sought to disarm potential critics by arguing that the "last remnants" of social inequality in the Soviet Union were, in fact, disappearing as a consequence of reduced income differentials and the rising educational attainment levels of workers and peasants. Although his proposal assumed inherently unequal intellectual capacities among children ("everybody recognizes this, but rarely do we speak about it openly"), the dual-track system would not be socially discriminatory since both capable and incapable individuals "may be found equally among the children of professors and the children of collective farmers. . . ."[24]

Aitov's attempt to forestall criticism of his proposal on the grounds of its alleged conflict with the egalitarian functions of Soviet education was to no avail. Among the harshest critics were the secretary of the Komsomol (the Communist Youth League) and the journal of the Russian Federation's Ministry of Education. The proposal would mean unequal secondary schooling for workers and vuz-bound youth, and hence was in conflict with the "principle of the unity of the Soviet school system." The Komsomol would "decisively oppose" any attempt to cast doubt on the policy of a "complete" secondary education for all workers.[25]

A somewhat more reasoned criticism, based on explicitly egalitarian grounds, was offered by the sociologist N. Novoselov. Any attempt to separate vuz-bound students from future workers as early as the eighth grade could easily increase the still-remaining class differences in aspirations for and access to advanced education. Given the relatively small number of vuz-preparatory schools under Aitov's scheme and the vast distances over which they would have to be distributed, higher-income families would be at an advantage in sending their children to these schools. Furthermore, Novoselov argued, "there is no absolutely reliable method of determining abilities" which would justify dividing youngsters at this stage into future workers and the college bound. Secondary schools should be chiefly "general-education" schools providing an essentially "uniform" education for all children.[26] They should provide their students with a "vocational orientation" but should avoid early "professionalization." Another of Aitov's critics argued that the organization of the school system should not be geared exclusively to "production requirements" but to "social requirements" as well. This meant that workers needed an education not only "to effectively master technology but to actively participate in social life, to be politically mature, to consciously assimilate the values of spiritual life."[27] Thus a Soviet version of the need for "training for citizenship" was invoked against Aitov's proposal to split the school system after the eighth grade into distinct "vocational" and "academic" tracks (with most youngsters being channeled into the former).

How much attention state and educational authorities paid to this discussion is not clear. But the decisions adopted by these authorities in the late sixties and early seventies do suggest some movement in the direction of Aitov's proposal, although its more extreme aspects (the conversion of most general-education schools into vocational schools) were obviously rejected. A 1969 decree sought to increase the attractiveness of workers' vocational schools by providing for their gradual transformation into "vocational-technical schools with a secondary education," thereby making their graduates eligible for admission to higher education.[28] However, unlike Aitov's proposal, the general-education schools would remain the principal channel for achieving "universal" secondary education. These schools were scheduled to account for approximately 70% of all secondary-school graduates in 1975.[29] It is quite possible, therefore, that state authorities were sensitive to the principal criticism which Aitov's opponents had made: his proposal's potential for reinforcing class and strata inequalities in schooling. But the main problem to which Aitov's proposal was addressed — the fact that with a predominantly "general" secondary education most youngsters would enter the work force without a specialty — remained unresolved.

The issue of whether differentiated secondary schooling (beyond the seventh or eighth grades) is socially discriminatory under Soviet conditions has also been raised in another connection. Some of the country's leading universities have established what in some Western societies would be called "elite" high schools. In Soviet parlance these are "specialized" schools offering "talented" and carefully selected — through competitive examinations — youngsters intensive programs of study in mathematics, physics, and biology.[30] By the early 1970s such schools, some of which are boarding schools, were operating under the aegis of at least the following universities: Novosibirsk, Moscow, Leningrad, Kiev, and Tbilisi. Similarly, secondary schools in which the bulk of instruction is offered in a foreign language exist in several of the country's larger cities. A distinctive feature of these institutions — both the science and foreign language schools — is that their graduates' chances of admission to a vuz (particularly the sponsoring university) are substantially greater than for graduates of "nonspecialized" schools. This reflects not only the highly selective nature of their student body but also the participation of university faculty (at least in Novosibirsk) on their teaching staffs and in their curriculum development. These are obviously highly privileged institutions, and sufficiently comprehensive data on the social composition of their student population would tell us much about the seriousness of the Soviet commitment to equality of opportunity at all levels of schooling.

The scanty information available on this score presents a mixed picture, but one which also underscores Soviet sensitivities to the issue of social inequality in education. Perhaps the most celebrated of the "specialized" science schools, the Physics-Mathematics School attached to Novosibirsk State University, has apparently made genuine efforts to increase the share of peasant and working-class youngsters among its student body since its founding in 1963. In that year only 11% of entering students were drawn from rural areas and "workers' settlements"; by 1965 this figure had risen to 20%, and a 1971 publication claimed that "now" it stood at 40%.[31] The most recent claim (1973) of supporters of this kind of education is that some 60% of students entering the Novosibirsk Physics-Mathematics School were of nonintelligentsia social background.[32] It is not clear, however, how typical this institution is in this regard, and there is some evidence that children of intelligentsia parents predominate in many, if not most, "specialized" schools.[33] But it is significant that the presence of a large contingent of lower-

strata children in at least some of these institutions is offered as
a defense of "specialized" schooling and as an argument for extending this kind of secondary education. Such a defense has been,
at least in part, a response to the critics of schools for the "gifted."

Among the skeptics, if not explicit critics, in the early 1970s
was V. N. Stoletov, the president of the Academy of Pedagogical
Sciences. He argued that "schools for gifted children" in capitalist societies functioned mainly as a means of social selection, and
the only justification for those that had been established in the Soviet Union thus far was strictly their function as a "pedagogical
experiment." But the time had come to subject these schools to
an "objective pedagogical evaluation," especially since "a number
of scholars have already seriously criticized" them. His own position was that "only if instruction was identical for all (Stoletov's
emphasis) young people up to their majority could the problem of
abilities and natural gifts be objectively resolved." Questions
bearing on the whole issue of natural talents could only be adequately answered "given the creation of appropriate socioeconomic
circumstances," presumably involving a higher degree of equality
than had thus far been attained. Until then he favored a single
general-education school for all young people through the age of 17
and greater attention to the development of "talented teachers."
Stoletov's argument here was in direct conflict with those defenders
of "specialized" schools for whom the "preservation, nurturing, and
development of talents" required the abandonment of "conveyorlike,"
standardized education.[34]

Despite the apparent opposition, or at the very least hesitation,
of powerful voices like Stoletov's, there is no sign that the "specialized" schools are being cut back. If anything the opposite is
the case. Proponents of these schools apparently no longer regard
them as purely experimental in nature and have recently suggested
that those already functioning can serve as "a base for the development of a mass network of physics-mathematics schools."[35]
Whether this happens, the argument for the legitimacy of these
"specialized" schools has rested, in no small measure, on their
alleged ability to offset earlier inequalities in children's schooling
and family and social environments by appropriate methods of selection and instruction.[36]

The flurry of controversy over both the Aitov proposals and the
issue of special schooling for gifted children suggests that recent
years have seen increasing pressures for the differentiation of
secondary schooling within the framework of an officially sanc-

tioned "uniform" system of education. Both the proponents and critics of increasing differentiation have sought to buttress their arguments by drawing on the rhetoric of "equality of opportunity" — and in the case of proponents, by seeking to demonstrate that the increased differentiation of secondary schooling is compatible with the reduction of social inequality. The broader issue posed by these discussions might be formulated as follows: In a society with substantial inequalities in the incomes, cultural levels, and educational attainments of adults, will not the increasing fragmentation of secondary schooling into forms that range from special schools for the "talented" at one extreme to vocational schools for workers' trades at the other necessarily reinforce the inheritance of parental occupational status? Or, to put it somewhat more succinctly, is there not an ongoing tension between the "allocative" and the "egalitarian" functions of schooling under Soviet circumstances?

Thus far the response of Soviet authorities to this issue has been, as noted earlier, to rely largely on the general-education schools as the principal vehicle for attaining "universal" secondary education. In recent years, however, some encouragement has been given to early "professionalization" via the expansion of workers' vocational schooling and the acceptance of the principle of selective vuz-preparatory schools. Whether the "differential" or the "uniform" emphasis prevails, the approach to the goal of "universality" of secondary education in some form means that success or failure in access to higher education is becoming an increasingly important turning point in the process of adult status attainment. To this we now turn.

Access to Higher Education

When Soviet ruling authorities determine that a particular issue is an appropriate one for social research and for discussion in both the professional and "popular" press, the results can be highly illuminating. Such has been the case in recent years with the issue of inequalities in access to higher education. Not only has the legitimation of this research produced an abundance of data on Soviet social differentiation, but the accompanying discussions have also offered revealing glimpses of conflicting attitudes toward social inequality. It is probably no exaggeration to say that in recent years the principal context of most serious Soviet discussions of social inequality has been the problem of access to higher education.

There is a fairly obvious reason for the emergence of this issue. The past two decades have seen a profound change in the quantitative relationship between the number of secondary school graduates and the size of entering classes to higher educational institutions. In the early 1950s most youngsters completing a secondary education — ten years of schooling — could expect admission to a vuz. This was not so much a reflection of the widespread availability of higher education as it was of the relatively small proportion of youngsters graduating from secondary schools. Little more than 10% of the corresponding age group was able to even reach the upper grades (9 and 10) of these schools in the early 1950s.[37] Two decades later Soviet authorities were able to claim that most youngsters were obtaining a complete secondary education. But the capacity of vuzy to accept new entrants has increased at a much slower rate than the increase in high school graduates. The result has been a sharp decline in the proportion of the latter going on to a higher education. The greatly heightened competition for admission to relatively scarce vuz vacancies is clearly revealed by the following figures showing the proportion of full-time vuz admissions to secondary-school graduations (in %):[38]

1950-53	65
1960-63	33
1970-73	19

Thus as the Soviet Union has moved closer to "mass" secondary education, the proportion of high school graduates able to continue full-time schooling at a vuz has fallen from approximately two-thirds to one-fifth.[39] In this situation increased attention has naturally focused on a whole complex of factors bearing on the selection process for higher education, and in particular the impact of this process on the social structure of the vuz student body. In earlier years, however small the number of working-class and peasant youngsters completing secondary school, a significant proportion could expect to gain entry to higher education. However, in more recent years the failure of vuz admissions to keep up with secondary school graduations, combined with a student selection process based largely on competitive entrance examinations, has threatened to cut into lower-strata graduates' opportunities for vuz admission more sharply than those of the typically better prepared youngsters from intelligentsia families. At a time when increasing numbers of lower-strata youth were graduating from high school, the traditional path open to such graduates (entry to intelligentsia occupational status via a vuz education) appeared to become less accessible. Partly in recognition of this problem, Soviet authorities in 1959 altered vuz admissions procedures so as to provide preferential treatment for graduates with work experience — a policy that tended to favor lower-strata youngsters in the competition for vuz entry. This policy had its own drawbacks, however — a decline in the "quality" of entering students — and was abandoned some five years later. Thus in the mid-1960s the problem of the disadvantaged position of lower-strata youth in the increasingly intense competition for vuz admission reasserted itself.

All this constitutes the setting which helps to explain why recent Soviet discussions of the problem of social inequality have often focused on the issue of student selection for higher education. What do these studies and controversies reveal, both about the reality of class inequalities and about Soviet attitudes toward them? How have Soviet authorities responded to the issues raised? We shall consider these questions in turn.

The mechanisms making for unequal access of different strata to vuz admission begin to operate before the onset of the formal selection procedure. A process of "self-selection" is at work which removes a considerable number of high school graduates from the competition for vuz entry. Whether they are discouraged by their poor academic performance in high school, by their family's urgent need for additional breadwinners, or by the trauma associated with the high probability of failure in the intense competition, such youngsters simply do not apply for admission. As we might expect, this "discouraged" group is most often found among lower-strata families. Soviet studies of the plans of graduating high school students consistently show a smaller proportion of working-class than of intelligentsia youngsters intending to apply for vuz admission. The results of some of these are shown in Table 3.5. They suggest that youngsters from intelligentsia families are almost invariably highly "ambitious," with some 70-90% planning to apply for vuz admission. While many high school graduates of working-class background also typically have such aspirations (at least one-third but usually more), the proportion of vuz aspirants among them is less stable and distinctly below the comparable indicator for intelligentsia children. In the case of the studies shown in Table 3.5, working-class graduates were also consistently less confident of vuz admission than young-

Table 3.5

Proportion of Secondary School Graduating Students Planning to Continue
Full-time Schooling at Higher Educational Institution (in %)

Location and parental background	Graduating students planning to enter higher educational institution (in %)
Sverdlovsk	
1965: workers	74
nonspecialist employees	83
specialists	91
1967:* workers	40
nonspecialist employees	54
specialists	81
1970: workers	62
nonspecialist employees	68
specialists	83
Cheliabinsk	
1974: workers	34.4
nonspecialist employees	38.0
specialists	71.0
Leningrad region †	
1965: rural residents	56.9
urban residents	86.2

Sources: M. Rutkevich, "Social Sources of Replenishment of the Soviet Intelligentsia," Voprosy filosofii, 1967, no. 6, p. 20; M. Rutkevich and F. Filippov, Sotsial'nye peremeshcheniia, p. 230; F. Filippov, "Changes in the Social Profile and Composition of the Soviet Intelligentsia," in Problemy razvitiia sotsial'noi struktury obshchestva v Sovetskom soiuze i Pol'she, p. 203; V. V. Vodzinskaia, "On the Question of the Social Conditioning of Occupational Choice," in Chelovek i obshchestvo, Issue II, p. 76; V. G. Afanas'ev et al., Problemy nauchnogo kommunizma, no. 9, p. 51.

*These figures are calculated as simple averages of the proportions of students planning to attend a higher educational institution in two districts of the city (the Kirov and Ordzhonikidze districts).

†These figures apply to youngsters planning full-time study in any form, whether at a higher educational institution or tekhnikum. It is clear from the context, however, that most plan on the former.

sters from lower-ranking white-collar families. Similarly, rural high school graduates were less likely to plan on continued full-time schooling than their urban peers. Although the data in Table 3.5, on which we rely here, refer to youngsters' "plans," there is every reason to expect that strata differences in actual vuz applications paralleled — at least approximately — the differences in youngsters' plans.

The process of "self-selection" works in other ways as well.

Among those who do apply for vuz admission there is apparently some tendency for lower-strata youth to avoid the competition for entry to some of the more prestigious and presumably "rigorous" institutions. There is no other obvious explanation for the unusually low proportions of working-class and peasant youth among applicants to institutions like Leningrad and Novosibirsk state universities. Less than one-third of such applicants were drawn from manual strata in the late 1960s.[40] As we shall see below, the normal proportion of working-class and peasant youths among vuz applicants clearly exceeds this figure. But the latter is further evidence of the variety of forms which the selection process, broadly understood, assumes.

The results of the more formal selection procedures (entrance examinations, interviews, examination of high school records) also have an unequal impact on youngsters from different occupational strata. When comparisons are made between the social composition of applicants to particular vuzy and the composition of incoming (admitted) students to these institutions, the latter group typically appears to be less "representative" than the former, i.e., the share of lower-strata youth among entering students is normally less than their share among total applicants. This conclusion rests on the admittedly fragmentary but nonetheless convincing evidence shown in Table 3.6. Wherever workers' children appear in this table as a distinct group of applicants and of admitted students, their share of the former exceeds their share of the latter. The same is true of peasants' children, with one interesting exception. For the sample of Leningrad vuzy shown in this table, peasant children are a larger proportion of incoming students than of applicants. It is very likely that the process of "self-selection" was at work here in another form: the relatively few peasant children who thought it worth applying to Leningrad higher educational institutions must have been an unusually able lot.

The results of the formal selection process are in most cases precisely what we would expect, given the central importance of competitive entrance examinations of an "academic" character in the criteria for admission. The higher the educational level of applicants' parents, the greater is the probability of children's success on entrance examinations (see Table 3.7 for an illustration). Hence the increasing share of intelligentsia children as we move from "applications" to "admissions," and the typically decreasing share of worker and peasant children. In some cases

Table 3.6

Parental Occupational Status of Applicants for Admission and of
Students Admitted to Selected Higher Educational Institutions (in %)*

Institution and parental occupational status	Distribution of applicants (in %)	Distribution of admitted students (in %)
Kazan University, 1962		
workers	34.0	32.1
collective farmers	20.3	15.1
employees (specialists and nonspecialists)	45.7	52.8
Rostov University, 1966		
workers and employees (nonspecialists)	57.7	47.0
collective farmers	15.2	2.6
specialists	27.1	50.4
Saratov Medical Institute, 1966-76		
workers	23.8	20.5
collective farmers	10.5	9.6
employees (specialists and nonspecialists)	65.7	69.9
Leningrad, 1968 (sample of 5 vuzy)		
workers	32.0	29.8
collective farmers	9.3	11.7
nonspecialist employees	11.7	10.7
specialists	39.4	42.0
other	5.1	4.7
undetermined	2.5	1.1

Sources: Kazan: N. Aitov, "Social Aspects of Receiving an Education in the USSR," in Akademiia nauk SSSR, Sotsial'nye issledovaniia, no. 2, p. 192. Rostov: B. Rubin and Iu. Kolesnikov, Student glazami sotsiologa, p. 70. Saratov: Calculated from material in A. V. Zelepukin, "Formation and Social Functions of the Soviet Intelligentsia," in I. N. Chikhichina ed., Sotsial'no-klassovaia struktura i politicheskaia organizatsiia sotsialisticheskogo obshchestva, p. 104. Leningrad: G. A. Zhuravleva, "Some Problems of Youth's Orientation to Higher Educational Institutions," in Molodezh' i obrazovanie, p. 191.

*The figures for Kazan University refer explicitly to day-time applicants and students. For the other institutions the context implies day-time study, although it is uncertain whether this is actually the case.

the relatively modest change in the share of the latter two groups (see Table 3.6 where these groups represented some one-third to one-half of both "applications" and "admissions" at Leningrad, Kazan, and Saratov vuzy) probably reflects the operation of policies of "social regulation" of admissions designed to insure some minimum representation for lower-strata students. These policies will be discussed later.

The more successful examination performance of higher-strata youths does not simply mirror their generally superior earlier

Table 3.7

Proportion of Applicants Passing Entrance Examinations to
Novosibirsk State University, by Educational Level of Parents (in %)

Educational level of parents*	Proportion of applicants passing entrance examinations (in %)		
	1967	1968	1970
Higher	57	66	71
Specialized secondary	41	54	50
General secondary	37	43	42
Incomplete secondary	28	48	36
Primary or less	23	38	33

Source: L. Liss, "The Social Conditioning of Occupational Choice," in Tartuskii gosudarstvennyi universitet, Materialy konferentsii 'kommunisticheskoe
vospitanie studenchestva', p. 149.
*Figures apply to cases in which both parents have the same educational level.

academic preparation, buttressed by a more "cultured" family environment. It also reflects the greater frequency with which intelligentsia families rely on private "coaches" — presumably
paid — to help prepare their children for entrance examinations.
A 1967 study of entering students of Gorki State University described this unequal utilization of private tutoring services as
follows:

> Among first-year students from employees' families, every fourth one pre-
> pared (for the examination — M. Y.) with a tutor; among those from workers'
> families — one out of every twenty, while none of those from peasants' families
> relied on the assistance of a tutor. The higher the level of parents' education ...
> the higher the percentage preparing with a tutor: with an education of up to four
> grades — 2.5%; with a complete secondary education — 12.9%; with a secondary
> specialized education — 17.2%; and with a higher education — 36%.[41]

Thus graduation from secondary school is one of those critical
turning points at which the advantages of "higher" social origins
work in a variety of ways to transmit status inequalities across
generations. Differences in initial aspirations for advanced
schooling, in assistance received in preparation for entrance examinations, and in performance on these examinations all operate
to favor higher-strata youngsters in the competition for access to
higher education. While policies of "social regulation" of vuz admissions (discussed below) may reduce these advantages somewhat, they clearly do not reverse them. Among the variety of recent Soviet studies which have revealed the impact of the class
position of high school graduates on their opportunities for advanced schooling, we may rely here on two which appear to have

been the most carefully designed — those for the Novosibirsk Region and the city of Leningrad. The probability of vuz admission in the late 1960s for different strata of high school graduates in these two areas is shown in Table 3.8. These findings deserve close attention and our discussion immediately below is based on them.

Table 3.8

Probability of Admission to a Higher Educational Institution
of Secondary School Graduates in the Year of Their Graduation,
Novosibirsk Region and Leningrad (in %)*

Location and occupational status of parents of graduates	% of secondary school graduates admitted to higher education
Novosibirsk (city), 1969	
intelligentsia	68
workers	45
Novosibirsk Region, smaller cities, 1969	
intelligentsia	24
workers	20
Novosibirsk Region, rural areas, 1969	
intelligentsia	45
workers	21
Leningrad, "higher" performing students,[†] 1968	
specialists in jobs requiring higher education	73
specialists in jobs requiring secondary specialized education	61
skilled workers	44
low-skilled and unskilled workers, and nonspecialist employees	21
Leningrad, "lower" performing students,[‡] 1968	
specialists in jobs requiring higher education	40
specialists in jobs requiring secondary specialized education	34
skilled workers	16
low-skilled and unskilled workers, and nonspecialist employees	7

Sources: G. Antonova, "Social Mobility of Secondary School Graduates (From Materials of Novosibirsk Region)," in Tartuskii gosudarstvennyi universitet, Materialy konferentsii 'kommunisticheskoe vospitanie studenchestva', p. 112; E. K. Vasil'eva, Sotsial'no-professional'nyi uroven', p. 42.

*The figures for Novosibirsk apply to male students admitted for full-time study; those for Leningrad, to all students admitted to any form of higher education.

† Those whose academic grade average in secondary school was 3.5 or higher (out of a maximum of 5).

‡Those whose academic grade average in secondary school was less than 3.5.

Whether the distinct groups investigated were urban graduates or rural graduates, "higher" performers or "lower" performers in secondary school, within each of these groups the probability of admission to a higher educational institution was greater for youngsters of intelligentsia parents than for lower-strata graduates. Youngsters from a major university center like Novosibirsk had distinctly greater opportunities for access to higher education than small-town and rural graduates in the same region. The advantages of residence in a large city were so marked that the vuz opportunities of even working-class youngsters in Novosibirsk equaled or exceeded those of specialists' children in adjoining small towns and rural communities. While the "better" performing high school students were more likely to continue their education than "poorer" (academically speaking) students, intelligentsia youngsters in Leningrad with inferior high school performance had greater opportunities for vuz admission than children of unskilled workers with higher academic ratings.

It would obviously be foolish to indulge in excessive generalization on the basis of these studies alone. But at the very least they suggest a wide range of variation in the opportunities for higher education of different strata. In large cities (such as Leningrad and Novosibirsk) with extensive networks of vuzy, some two-thirds or more of the youngsters whose parents have a higher education can expect admission to a vuz in the year of their high school graduation. In rural areas and towns in the vicinity of such cities, the comparable indicator for children of manual strata is probably closer to one-fifth, as it is for the children of the lowest strata (the unskilled) of workers' in large cities.

Thus at successive key junctures on the path to more advanced schooling (the eighth and tenth grades) the selection process — both formal and informal — eliminates larger proportions of workers' and peasants' children than of specialists' children. It is clear therefore that lower-strata children are underrepresented in higher educational institutions. But how marked is this underrepresentation? This is a critical question since it bears directly on the issue of the extent to which working-class and peasant children fill the more privileged positions in the occupational hierarchy. A recent study of class inequalities in Western countries has treated "the proportion of working-class youths in the full-time student population... [as] perhaps the best single index of the openness of the educational system as a whole."[42] Suppose we apply this criterion of "openness" to the Soviet educational system — indeed to Soviet society generally — modifying it only to include peasant along with working-class youths. Our estimates below of the share of these groups in the total student population must be regarded, of course, only as reasonable approximations. But they will also reveal an interesting distinction between more "elite" and more "representative" institutions.

For the society at large the principal components of "class structure" and their relative importance in 1970 were as follows (in % of total employment):[43]

workers	60.0
collective farmers	15.2
nonspecialist employees	10.6
specialists	14.2

Thus manual strata made up some 75% of the employed population, with the larger part of the remaining group (14%) constituting the Soviet version of the "intelligentsia" (specialists) and the smaller part the group of lower-level nonmanual employees.

From the mass of data available on the social composition of vuz enrollment, we confine ourselves largely to cases in which "specialists" can be distinguished from "nonspecialist employees" (there seems little point in treating plant directors and sales clerks as belonging to the same social group). In the light of the above figures on the class structure of the society at large, it seems clear that lower-strata youths are especially underrepresented at some of the country's leading universities based in large cities. At all universities in the late 1960s for which the share of specialists' children could be separately derived, this group was the largest single component of the student population. Table 3.9 shows the social composition of this population. The relative share of working-class and peasant youths in the student body of these universities was generally in the neighborhood of 30%, or less than one-half the share of workers and peasants in the population at large. The proportion of specialists' children, on the other hand, approached 50% or more in some cases, and was typically some two and one-half to three and one-half times the relative share of the intelligentsia in the total population.[44] However, it is also quite certain that university-type institutions, with their concentration on the sciences, mathematics, and the humanities, are more "elitist" in their social composition than the many engineering and agricultural "technical institutes." The relative share of workers' children among the students of these engineering vuzy and of peasant youths at agricultural institutes appears

Table 3.9

Occupational Status of Parents of Soviet University Students, Late 1960s*

University	Occupational status of students' parents (in %)					
	specialists	non-specialist employees	workers	collective farmers	career military personnel	others
Rostov State University, 1966	50.4	47.0		2.6		
Gorki State University, 1967	46.4	25.6	25.3	1.3		1.4
Novosibirsk State University, 1968	51.0	12.5	26.0	2.8		7.9
Perm State University, 1969	31.5	29.5	29.4	4.2		5.4
Urals State University (Sverdlovsk), 1969	39.0	9.1	27.1	0.9	4.1	19.8

Sources: Rostov: B. Rubin and Iu. Kolesnikov, p. 70. Gorki: K. N. Minkina, M. G. Sizova, and A. A. Terent'ev, "The Social Characteristics of First-year University Students," in Gor'kovskii Gosudarstvennyi Universitet im. N. I. Lobachevskogo, Sotsiologiia i vysshaia shkola, Uchenye zapiski, Issue 100, pp. 21-22. Novosibirsk: L. F. Liss, "On the Stability of Characteristics and Specific Features of the Social Origins of University Applicants," from Institut istorii, filologii i filosofii SO AN SSSR, Sotsial'noe prognozirovanie v oblasti obrazovaniia, p. 34. The figure for collective farmers is computed as a residual by deducting from the total employed in manual labor the figures shown here for various categories of workers. Perm: Calculated from S. V. Vladimirov,"The Attitudes toward an Occupation, Depending on the Motives for Its Selection," in Perm State University, Trud i lichnost' pri sotsializme, Issue II, Uchenye zapiski, no. 295, p. 109. Urals: M. Rutkevich and L. Sennikova, "The Social Conditioning of Motives for Entering a Higher Educational Institution and the Choice of a Future Occupation," in Motivatsiia zhiznedeiatel'nosti studenta, p. 112.

*Parents' status was determined according to father's occupation at Novosibirsk and Urals state universities. In other cases the method of determining occupational status was not indicated. For Rostov, Gorki, and Urals state universities the figures refer to first-year students; for Perm State University — to a sample of 35% of students in all departments; for Novosibirsk State University — to applicants for admission. For Perm State University the figures explicitly refer to day-time students; in other cases this is suggested by the context although it is uncertain.

to be consistently higher than it is at universities in the same region. Table 3.10 provides some of the evidence which supports this conclusion. Drawing on all the evidence available to us — but with no pretense at precision — we would suggest a figure on the order of 35-40% as a reasonable estimate of the relative share

Social and Economic Inequality

Table 3.10

Proportion of Students of Working-class Origin at Selected Soviet
Higher Educational Institutions, Late 1960s*

Educational institution	% of students of working-class origin
Sverdlovsk Region, 1969	
Urals State University	27.1
Urals Polytechnical Institute	31.4
Sverdlovsk Mining Institute	40.1
Institute of Railroad Engineering	41.5
Lumber Industry Engineering Institute	35.5
Sverdlovsk Agricultural Institute	42.9
Novosibirsk Region, 1966-70†	
Novosibirsk State University	19-28
Novosibirsk Electrical Engineering Institute	37-47
Novosibirsk Institute of Railroad Engineering	55-63
Kharkov (city), 1968	
Kharkov State University	40.4
Kharkov Polytechnical Institute	49.0

Sources: Sverdlovsk: M. Rutkevich and L. Sennikova, p. 112. Novosibirsk:
L. Liss, "The Social Conditioning of Occupational Choice," in Tartuskii gosudarstvennyi Universitet, Materialy konferentsii 'kommunisticheskoe vospitanie
studenchestva', p. 143. Kharkov: N. I. Sazonov ed., Kritika antimarksistkikh
vzgliadov po voprosam sotsial'no-politicheskogo razvitiia sovetskogo obshchestva, p. 82.
*The figures for Kharkov explicitly refer to day-time students; in other cases
this is suggested by the context but is uncertain. For Sverdlovsk and Kharkov
the figures refer to first-year students; for Novosibirsk, probably to all students.
† These figures apply to "workers and their children." This tends to overesti-
mate the share of students of working-class social origins since it includes the
children of nonmanual employees and peasants who were employed as workers
before admittance to a higher educational institution.

of working-class and peasant youths in the total full-time college
student population in the late 1960s. Most vuz students at this
time were being recruited from nonmanual strata (both intelligentsia and lower-level nonspecialist employees), with intelligentsia
youths alone probably accounting for close to one-half the total
— or about three times this group's share of the population at
large. The most underrepresented section of the population by
far was the collective farm peasantry.[45]

Although youths of both working-class and peasant origins are
obviously underrepresented in the college student population, we
must guard against exaggerating the extent to which this popula-

tion is drawn from a narrowly based and highly privileged stratum. It is important at this point to recall the rather broad meaning assigned to the intelligentsia category (whose children supply a disproportionately large share of vuz students) in Soviet parlance. This group includes not only scientists, engineers, academic personnel, and higher-level managers, but also a large group of individuals who would be classified as "middle strata" in Western societies (technicians, teachers, agronomists, etc.). Moreover, the institutions training the next generation of these "middle-level specialists" are attended largely by youngsters of working-class social background. It must also be recognized that the large minority of students of manual-strata origin in Soviet vuzy compares rather favorably with similar indicators for the more economically developed noncommunist countries of Western Europe in the 1950s and 1960s.[46] Nonetheless a society which proclaims the "leading role" of the working class in the construction of a new social order must reconcile its official ideology with the reality of this group's significant underrepresentation in institutions training the higher ranks of the future intelligentsia. The tensions associated with this process are reflected in recent Soviet attitudes and policies concerning the need for "social regulation" of vuz admissions. The urgency of such regulation must seem all the more pressing during periods when some elements among the intelligentsia exhibit signs of disaffection.

The Issue of "Social Regulation" of the Student Population

Soviet reactions to the problem of social inequalities in access to higher education have reflected a clash between "egalitarian" and "meritocratic" orientations. Although this distinction is not always simple and clear-cut, it does provide a useful way of identifying the range of Soviet reactions to existing social inequalities.

The studies of the sociologist V. N. Shubkin and his colleagues in the Novosibirsk region in the early 1960s sparked a controversy which continued throughout that decade and into the 1970s. These studies were among the first to find that despite vuz admissions policies — in effect since 1959 — which favored entry for youths with prior work experience, the opportunities for a postsecondary education for children of urban intelligentsia were significantly greater than those of working-class and especially peasant youths. Shubkin posed the problem as follows:

On the one hand, we must provide all youth with equal opportunities for receiving an education. On the other, as a result of inequalities in the material conditions of families, in the education of parents, in the structure of families, in places of residence, in location of educational institutions, in levels of teaching, etc., young people with equal abilities but with differing levels of preparation actually have unequal opportunities for receiving an education.[47]

Writing in 1965, he warned that the heightened competition for vuz admission expected in the next few years could lead to a decline in the proportion of working-class and peasant youths admitted unless special measures designed to offset this tendency were promptly adopted. Although he disclaimed any suggestion that particular social groups be given preferential treatment "regardless of their knowledge," his call for the "social planning" of education was clearly an appeal for a more representative student population.[48]

The "meritocratic" response to Shubkin's position was taken up in 1966-67 by a group of Sverdlovsk sociologists led by M. N. Rutkevich. The latter explicitly rejected the need for any form of preferential admissions based on the social origins of applicants. The "social regulation" of the student population — justified in earlier years — was inappropriate in a developed socialist society which "had attained full equality of rights for its citizens whatever their social position and social origin." In such a society the criteria for admission to higher education should be identical for all:

In our view, the only kind of regulation which should prevail in the selection of youth for higher educational institutions is through the method of competitive examinations conducted with complete impartiality ... without any preferences based on work experience or other similar factors. Requirements must be uniform for all applicants without exception. Those who perform best on entrance examinations should be admitted to a vuz, with particular attention being paid to test results in subjects related to the chosen specialty. If an applicant has work experience in a given specialty and it was not acquired aimlessly, this will inevitably show up in the examination results.[49]

Changes in admissions rules in 1965 had reduced somewhat the opportunities for vuz entry of youths with work experience by providing that henceforth the number of applicants admitted with and without work experience should be in proportion to the number of applicants from these two groups. This was expected to increase admissions opportunities primarily for intelligentsia youths who were more likely than working-class and peasant children to apply for higher education directly upon graduation from secondary school. The group of Sverdlovsk sociologists whom we have identified with the "meritocratic" response welcomed this measure and sought to minimize its probable impact in further reducing the share of manual strata among the student body. After all, as one of Rutkevich's colleagues argued, "the intelligentsia is also part of the public, of the working people."[50]

It would be a mistake, however, to regard this position as implying an open abandonment of the goal of an increasingly egalitarian society. In fact, this group's justification for existing social inequalities in access to higher education was precisely that these represent "the path to the realization of full equality" in the future.[51] The latter requires above all the continued rapid growth of the "productive forces," a process best served by acceptance into vuzy of those best prepared to absorb advanced technical training. Rutkevich acknowledged that inequalities in youngsters' earlier education and in families' material and cultural circumstances affected the outcome of entrance examinations, but this was one of those "contradictions" that could only be fully resolved when the advance of science and technology permitted the transition from "socialist equality to communist equality." This was a traditional mode of argument in Soviet circumstances (for example, highly differentiated rewards in the present would create the conditions for payment "in accordance with needs" in the future), and it could be expected to receive a favorable hearing by Party and state authorities. Hence Rutkevich's access to the pages of Izvestia in 1967, where he urged that all remaining "privileges" based on prior work experience (as against examination performance) be discarded in selecting students for vuz admission.[52]

However, this did not close the issue. Rutkevich's approach was directly challenged in an effective presentation of the "egalitarian" position by a group of sociologists at Gorki State University in 1970. That some measure of social inequality was unavoidable under socialism was not the issue. The more important question was "the degree of inequality." A society making the transition from socialism to communism must be characterized by an extension of social equality, not its contraction.[53] Yet their study of the social composition of students at Gorki State University showed that youngsters of working-class origins were declining as a proportion of the student population in recent years. Their findings — and, they insisted, Rutkevich's as well — revealed an unmistakable tendency toward the "self-reproduction" of the intelligentsia. This was dangerous on two counts. First, it implied that the economic and scientific development of society was being impeded by the underutilization of talents which were equally distributed among all social classes:

Although natural gifts and talents are distributed highly unevenly among individuals or small groups, they are equally distributed among such large aggregates (mnogomillionnykh sovokupnostei) as workers, peasants, and intelligentsia.[54]

Second, the unrepresentative nature of the student body signified an "obvious injustice" for sections of working-class and rural youth. Thus it fostered a skeptical attitude toward equality as a value of Soviet society and bred "arrogance and self-conceit" among part of the student body. The Gorki sociologists also extended their criticism to "specialized schools" for talented youth, which, they argued, served to establish inequality among children, "the most unjust kind of inequality."[55] The policy recommendation flowing from this discussion called for the establishment of "definite guarantees" for the admission to vuzy of youth from all strata — an obvious appeal for quotas to raise the representation of working-class and peasant youngsters in higher educational institutions.

Once again we cannot be certain how closely political and educational authorities have followed these discussions and their conflicting prescriptions for the "social regulation" of opportunities for a higher education. The divergent views expressed in these discussions, as well as the conflicting interests which they represent, have undoubtedly had their counterparts in disagreements among the political leadership. If this were not the case, the discussion reviewed above would not have occurred. Although there have been no abrupt and decisive moves recently either in the direction of more "meritocratic" or more "egalitarian" policies, the evidence is clear that political authorities have leaned cautiously toward the latter. The principal criterion for vuz admission remains test scores on competitive entrance examinations. But the "proportionality" rule, providing separate "lines" of entry for youngsters with and without work experience in proportion to the number of them applying for admission, has also been retained. Thus the proposal to eliminate this procedure by some of the more extreme proponents of "meritocratic" policies has apparently been rejected. Most significant, however, has been the creation since 1969 of special "preparatory departments" at vuzy whose function is to provide tutoring and other instructional assistance to working-class and peasant youths aspiring to a higher education — a kind of "socialized coaching" service that may partially offset the greater access of more advantaged youths to private tutors. Youngsters who perform adequately in these "preparatory departments" may then enter a vuz directly without taking the regular entrance examinations.[56] Confining these departments to working-class and peasant youth is obviously designed to increase these groups' share of the total student body. There is also some evidence of a preferential admissions policy for rural youths (not necessarily peasant youths) to vuz departments training students for specialities required in rural areas (teachers, agricultural technicians).[57]

Thus to the extent that recent Soviet policy in the area of "social regulation" of student composition has been affected by the discussions reviewed above, it has moved cautiously in the direction of gradually increasing the share of lower-strata youths in institutions training the future intelligentsia. The social composition of vuz students in the mid-1970s was almost certainly somewhat more "representative" — even if not significantly so — than at the end of the preceding decade. But there can be little doubt that such students continued to be disproportionately recruited from non-manual families. The deliberate gradualism of the current policy of increasing the share of students of working-class and peasant background, as well as the continuing underrepresentation of these groups, is apparent in the slowly changing composition of first-year students at Leningrad vuzy: between 1969 and 1975 the proportion of working-class and peasant youths among entering students increased from 48% to 53%.[58]

The avoidance of hasty changes in selection procedures (competitive entrance examinations are still the principal mode of access to a vuz and the failure to act more decisively to eliminate class advantages in access to advanced education are not merely the result of bureaucratic inertia or of the conscious efforts of the privileged to transmit their advantages. They reflect a genuine dilemma, or "contradiction" as Soviet writers prefer to put it. The selection of the "best prepared" for advanced schooling will amost inevitably mean the selection of disproportionate numbers of youngsters from families of professional strata. Adherents of such a policy are fully aware that it "sanctions"[59] a type of inequality that is often not rooted in superior abilities ("talents," "capacities," "potential") but in the economic, cultural, and motivational advantages of children reared in intelligentsia families. Hence the readiness of some Soviet participants in this discussion to admit that a considerable degree of self-recruitment of the intelligentsia is a "normal phenomenon."[60] But its "normalcy" reflects a society in which the existence of a distinct stratum specializing in "intellectual work" (or "spiritual production" as some put it) — and receiving commensurate rewards, both material and nonmaterial — is regarded as required by the social division of labor. The latter, in turn, finds its justification in the need for continuing rapid economic and cultural growth.[61] As long as the legitimacy of the intelligentsia as a distinct professional stratum remains unquestioned, and the family unit functions as a major socializing institution, the problem of social inequalities in access to advanced schooling will remain an unresolved issue in the Soviet Union, whether accessible to open debate or not.

Below the surface of these discussions and deliberate policy shifts we may discern the competing claims of distinct social groups to advanced schooling and the privileges associated with it, as well as the problems of a ruling Party that must ensure not only the technical competence of its future intelligentsia but also its political and ideological reliability.

Notes

1. Frank Parkin, Class Inequality and Political Order (New York: Praeger Publishers, 1971), p. 14. We have relied heavily here on Parkin's formulation of this issue.

2. For an explicit expression of this philosophy, see M. Rutkevich, "Competitive Selection," Izvestia, December 10, 1967.

3. Soviet educators and sociologists explicitly recognize that "the family mediates the connection between the child and the social structure." See Akademiia nauk SSSR, Sem'ia kak ob"ekt filosofskogo i sotsiologicheskogo issledovaniia, Leningrad, 1974, p. 86.

4. V. Ia. El'meev, Problemy sotsial'nogo planirovaniia, Leningrad, 1973, pp. 101-2.

5. Iu. V. Sharov, "Types of Current Senior Class Pupils," in V. T. Lisovskii ed., Molodezh' i obrazovanie, Moscow, 1972, p. 70.

6. V. Ia. El'meev, p. 103.

7. V. N. Stoletov in Molodezh' i obrazovanie, p. 12.

8. Narodnoe obrazovanie, 1973, no. 10, p. 20; L. G. Zemtsov, "Some Social Aspects of Universal Secondary Education," in R. G. Gurova ed., Sotsiologicheskie problemy obrazovaniia i vospitaniia, Moscow, 1973, p. 16.

9. The "lower-level" is our designation, not the Soviet.

10. D. I. Valentei ed., Obrazovatel'naia i sotsial'no-professional'naia struktura naseleniia SSSR, Moscow, 1975, p. 21.

11. N. Aitov, "Social Aspects of Education in the USSR," in Akademiia nauk SSSR, Sotsial'nye issledovaniia, no. 2, Moscow, 1968, p. 190; E. K. Vasil'eva, Sotsial'no-professional'nyi uroven' gorodskoi molodezhi, Leningrad, 1973, p. 27.

12. It should also be recalled that increasing numbers of vocational schools (proftekhuchilishcha) are awarding secondary school graduation certificates.

13. This was the situation in the major Soviet republic, the Russian Federa-

tion. M. N. Rutkevich and F. R. Filippov, Sotsial'nye peremeshcheniia, Moscow, 1970, p. 217.

14. E. K. Vasil'eva, Sotsial'no-professional'nyi uroven', p. 46; M. Yanowitch and N. Dodge, "Social Class and Education: Soviet Findings and Reactions," Comparative Education Review, October 1968, p. 254.

15. M. N. Rutkevich and F. R. Filippov, p. 157; N. B. Lebedeva et al., Partiinaia organizatsiia i rabochie Leningrada, Leningrad, 1974, p. 413; L. Margolin, "The Social Composition of Students in Secondary Specialized Institutions and Their Career Plans," in Ministerstvo prosveshcheniia RSFSR, Voprosy sotsial'noi i professional'noi orientatsii molodezhi, Sverdlovsk, 1972, pp. 25-26.

16. L. Margolin, p. 29.

17. Iu. P. Petrov and F. R. Filippov in Filosofskie nauki, 1972, no. 6, p. 119, cite a figure of 87.5% as the share of workers' children in the vocational schools in Nizhnyi Tagil which simultaneously offer a secondary education and training in workers' skills. They note that the share of nonmanual strata in these schools is somewhat higher than in those that do not offer a secondary education.

18. T. R. Zarikhta and I. N. Nazimov, Ratsional'noe ispol'zovanie resursov moledezhi, Moscow, 1970, pp. 113-14.

19. E. K. Vasil'eva, Sotsial'no-professional'nyi uroven', p. 21.

20. Ibid., pp. 22-23.

21. Molodezh' i obrazovanie, p. 100.

22. V. Vialias, "Estonian Schools on a New Upswing," Narodnoe obrazovanie, 1975, no. 3, pp. 7-8.

23. N. Aitov, "Education and Life," Oktiabr', 1966, no. 7, p. 174.

24. Ibid., p. 176.

25. Narodnoe obrazovanie, 1967, no. 8, p. 4.

26. N. Novoselov, "The Path of Our Schools," Oktiabr', 1967, no. 7, p. 157.

27. L. Kogan, "Necessity or Luxury," Ural, 1968, no. 6, p. 148.

28. Molodezh' i obrazovanie, pp. 77-78.

29. Ibid., p. 17; V. P. Korchagin and S. G. Kosiachenko, Sotsial'no-kul'turnaia programma piatiletki, Moscow, 1971, p. 23.

30. This section draws on the following sources: V. D. Kobetskii ed., Obshchestvo i molodezh', Moscow, 1973, pp. 13-15; V. N. Turchenko, Nauchnotekhnicheskaia revoliutsiia i revoliutsiia v obrazovanii, Moscow, 1973, pp. 108-11; G. I. Antonova, "Social Aspects of the Creation of Specialized Schools," in Molodezh', obrazovanie i nauchno-tekhnicheskii progress, Novosibirsk, 1971, pp. 142-45; N. A. Aitov ed., Nekotorye problemy sotsial'nykh peremeshchenii v SSSR, Ufa, 1971, pp. 103-4.

31. G. I. Antonova, p. 144.

32. Or, to be more precise, for 60% of the entering students "both parents have no higher than a secondary education" (V. N. Turchenko, p. 109).

33. N. A. Aitov ed., pp. 103-4. The case cited in this source concerns the foreign language schools in the city of Ufa in the late 1960s. See also F. R. Filippov, "Sociological Problems of Education in the USSR, Sotsiologicheskie issledovaniia, 1974, no. 2, p. 20.

34. Compare Obshchestvo i molodezh', p. 14, and V. M. Lukin, "On the Cultural Aspect of the Formation of a Socially Homogeneous Society," in Uchenye zapiski obshchestvennykh nauk vuzov Leningrada, Problemy nauchnogo kommunizma, Issue VI, Leningrad, 1972, p. 70.

35. V. N. Turchenko, p. 110.

36. Ibid., p. 109.

37. David W. Carey, "Developments in Soviet Education," in Soviet Economic Prospects for the Seventies, Joint Economic Committee, Congress of the United States, U. S. Government Printing Office, Washington, 1973, p. 612.

38. Calculated from data in ibid., p. 603; S. L. Seniavskii and V. B. Tel'pukhovskii, Rabochii klass SSSR, Moscow, 1971, p. 153; Tsentral'noe statisticheskoe upravlenie, Narodnoe khoziaistvo SSSR v 1973, Moscow, 1974, p. 704; Akademiia nauk SSSR, Institut istorii SSSR, Rabochii klass SSSR, Moscow, 1969, p. 91.

39. Figures for all forms of vuz schooling (full-time, evening, and correspondence) would show higher ratios of admissions to secondary school graduations, particularly in the early 1960s, but the declining proportion of graduates admitted over the period as a whole would be apparent here as well.

40. L. F. Liss, "On the Stability of Characteristics and Specific Features of the Social Origins of University Applicants," from Institut istorii, filologii i filosofii SO AN SSSR, Sotsial'noe prognozirovanie v oblasti obrazovaniia, Novosibirsk, 1969, p. 34; G. A. Zhuravleva and Z. V. Sikevich, "Social Conditioning of the Preparedness of Vuz Applicants," in Chelovek i obshchestvo, Issue VI, Leningrad, 1969, p. 56. The Leningrad study on which we rely here sampled applicants to three departments of the university: mathematics and mechanics, geology, and philosophy.

41. K. N. Minkina, M. G. Sizova, and A. A. Terent'ev, "The Social Characteristics of First-year University Students," in Gor'kovskii gosudarstvennyi universitet im. N. I. Lobachevskogo, Sotsiologiia i vysshaia shkola, Uchenye zapiski, Issue 100, Gorki, 1970, p. 23.

42. F. Parkin, p. 111.

43. M. N. Rutkevich, in Sotsiologicheskie issledovaniia, 1975, no. 1, p. 72.

44. The figures for Novosibirsk in Table 3.9 probably overstate the share of manual strata and understate the share of intelligentsia youths in the student body since they refer to applications rather than admissions.

45. Soviet sources have cited 39% as the share of "workers and workers' children" in the total vuz day-time student body in 1968. This almost certainly exaggerates the proportion of students of working-class social origin since it includes as "workers" those students who were of nonmanual origins but were briefly employed in a worker's occupation before admission to a vuz. The same sources cite the share of "peasants and peasants' children" as 16-19%. This is significantly in excess of the proportion of students of peasant social origin in all individual vuzy for which data are available to us, except for agricultural institutes. See N. F. Krasnov, "A Worthy Addition to the Higher School," Vestnik vysshei shkoly, 1969, no. 4, p. 3; and I. Changli, Trud, Moscow, 1973, p. 245.

46. F. Parkin, p. 110, shows the student body of working-class origin in the universities of eight noncommunist European countries as ranging from 5% (in West Germany and the Netherlands) to 25% (in Great Britain and Norway). Any meaningful comparison with the Soviet figures, of course, must consider the relative shares of the various occupational groups in the total populations of these countries and the Soviet Union.

47. V. N. Shubkin, "On Some Social-Economic Problems of Youth," in Novosibirskii gosudarstvennyi universitet, Nauchnye trudy, seriia ekonomicheskaia, Issue 6, Novosibirsk, 1965, p. 279.

48. Ibid., p. 280.

49. M. N. Rutkevich ed., Zhiznennye plany molodezhi, Sverdlovsk, 1966, p. 36.

50. Ibid., p. 225.

51. M. N. Rutkevich in Voprosy filosofii, 1967, no. 6, p. 18.

52. Izvestia, December 10, 1967. He also urged increased outlays of educational resources for rural schools, vuz-preparatory courses for youth residing outside large cities, and "specialized classes" in the upper grades (or "specialized schools," where possible) which would concentrate in the areas of (a) physics and mathematics, (b) biology and medicine, and (c) the humanities.

53. Gor'kovskii gosudarstvennyi universitet im. N. I. Lobachevskogo, p. 15.

54. Ibid., p. 12.

55. Ibid., p. 16. This characterization of "specialized schools" is cited with approval by the authors of the Gorki study from an article by E. Il'enkova in Literaturnaia gazeta, 1968, no. 9, p. 12.

56. Soviet sources are contradictory on the conditions under which students in these "preparatory departments" may enter a vuz. A. P. Solov'ev, Pravila vybora professii, Leningrad, 1975, p. 115, states that youngsters who pass the final examinations given by these departments are exempt from the normal entrance examinations required of other applicants to higher education. F. R. Filippov, on the other hand (in Sotsiologicheskie issledovaniia, 1974, no. 2, p. 22), states that these departments are intended to "equalize" youngsters' chances to pass "entrance examinations." For other material on the "preparatory departments," see M. N. Rutkevich and F. R. Filippov, p. 147, and N. A. Aitov ed., p. 135.

57. M. N. Rutkevich and F. R. Filippov, pp. 145-46.

58. A. S. Pashkov, Kompleksnye sotsial'nye issledovaniia, Leningrad, 1976, p. 207. A somewhat more rapid "proletarianization" of students in Sverdlovsk is indicated by F. R. Filippov in Sotsiologicheskie issledovaniia, 1974, no. 2, p. 23.

59. M. N. Rutkevich and F. R. Filippov, p. 141.

60. V. M. Lukin in Problemy nauchnogo kommunizma, p. 70.

61. Ibid., pp. 69-70.

4 SOME ASPECTS OF SOCIAL MOBILITY

Our discussion of education obviously tells us something about social inequalities in access to a highly prized value in Soviet society as well as in access to privileged occupational status. But the extent of the "openness" of this society can also be studied more directly and in a way that encompasses a whole range of "upward" and "downward" shifts in social position. We propose to do this by examining the available evidence on social mobility in Soviet society. More specifically, our concerns in this chapter are with the fluidity of this society as reflected in: (a) the social sources of recruitment to various occupational positions; (b) the extent of occupational changes between parents and children (intergenerational mobility); (c) the extent to which individuals are able to shift from one level of the occupational hierarchy to another within the course of their work careers (intragenerational mobility). Although the available evidence on these matters is sometimes fragmentary, our effort to grapple with these issues reflects our attempt to examine Soviet society as a process in movement as well as a fixed structure of socio-occupational positions.

The Assimilation of the Concept of "Social Mobility" into Soviet Marxism

Writing in 1964, the Soviet sociologist V. N. Shubkin noted that up to that time there had been no empirical studies of "the shift of part of the peasantry into the ranks of the working class, and of workers and peasants into the ranks of the intelligentsia."[1] The very concept of "social mobility," to the extent that it was recognized at all, was dismissed as "a concept of bourgeois sociology" linked to the theory of social stratification and as inapplicable to Soviet society.[2] Although the state of stagnation which prevailed in most areas of social science up to this point is hardly a revelation (it has been widely acknowledged by Soviet as well as non-Soviet scholars), there is nonetheless something especially striking about the failure to investigate the variety of processes normally associated with the concept of social mobility. Given the profound changes in occupational structure accompanying rapid industrialization, the considerable Soviet achievement in expanding educational opportunities for manual strata, the pride with which the "simple" social origins of a new intelligentsia were publicly proclaimed, what could be more natural than the encouragement of serious studies of social mobility? The egalitarian ethos fostered by the frequent reiteration of the theme that "all paths are open"[3] for working-class and peasant youths seemed to invite such studies. Whether clothed in a "bourgeois" or "Marxist" conceptual apparatus, the systematic investigation of opportunities for lower-strata youth to transcend the occupational status of their parents could be expected — at least at first glance — to compare favorably with similar indicators for most capitalist societies. In this situation there is something almost paradoxical about the official ideology's rejection of the very concept of social mobility until 1964-65. It also provides additional evidence, if any were needed, of the problems confronting Soviet scholars interested in seriously investigating some of the most obvious features of their own social structure, even when these promise to yield a "positive" picture.

Thus little more than a decade has passed since Soviet sociologists were able to begin their studies in this area, and all the materials we draw on below are the product of this period. Before turning to these materials, however, the process of assimilation of the concept of social mobility into Soviet Marxism deserves our attention. In its own way this process is no less interesting than the findings of Soviet empirical studies of mobility which we examine below. It illustrates the way in which old positions are abandoned and new ones adopted that permit Soviet scholars to characterize their society in terms that would have been inconceivable a few years earlier. It thus reveals the liberating potential contained in the legitimation of sociological research under Soviet circumstances.

When Soviet sociologists initiated their studies of social mobility in the mid-1960s, the justifications offered for such studies were that the frequency and ease of movement from one occupational position to another would reveal the increasing "social homogeneity" of Soviet society, that these movements had to be studied if social mobility was to be a "consciously directed" process (V. N. Shubkin), and that these studies would reveal "incomparably higher" rates of mobility than in capitalist societies (M. N. Rutkevich).[4] But some of those who urged such studies had difficulty in accepting an essential part of the conceptual apparatus which must underlie any investigation of vertical social mobility — the need to rank groups of occupations into "higher" and "lower" categories so that some meaning can be attached to the notion of "upward" and "downward" shifts of individuals and groups in the social structure. The study of mobility almost necessarily conjures up an image of society as a social hierarchy of unequally advantaged groups. Such an image certainly permeates the Western literature on the subject. Consider some typical definitions in this literature, those of Bernard Barber and S. M. Lipset. For Barber social mobility refers to:

...movement either upward or downward, between higher and lower social classes; or more precisely, movement between one relatively fulltime, functionally significant social role and another that is evaluated as either higher or lower.[5]

For S. M. Lipset:

The term "social mobility" refers to the process by which individuals move from one position to another in society — positions which by general consent have been given specific hierarchical values. When we study social mobility we analyze the movement of individuals from positions possessing a certain rank to positions either higher or lower in the social system.[6]

For some of the more cautious Soviet sociologists who were beginning to work in the area of social mobility in the mid-1960s, such formulations were a completely uncongenial and unacceptable mode of conceptualizing the issue. Perhaps the clearest example of the attempt to separate the study of mobility from its traditional association with the concept of hierarchical structures may be found in the early writings of M. N. Rutkevich:

Concepts of "lower" and "higher" classes or social strata are inapplicable, in principle, to Soviet socialist society. In the USSR there are no "higher" and "lower" classes and strata. As for opportunities to shift from some...classes and social groups of our society to others, including from the working class and peasantry to the intelligentsia, they are incomparably greater than in any capitalist country.[7]

But if concepts of "higher" and "lower" could be applied neither to classes nor strata, what was the particular advantage inherent in the "incomparably greater" opportunities which Soviet society allegedly offered for moving from manual to intelligentsia status? The very mode of denying the relevance of hierarchical structures in Soviet society implicitly affirmed their existence. It is significant that in none of his more recent writings has Rutkevich repeated the formulation cited above. In his most important work on social mobility, published in 1970, he retreats, at least implicitly, from that formulation. The "unequal complexity" of various types of labor makes for "vertical gradations" in the social structure and for the applicability of the concept of "vertical mobility" to Soviet society. Without using the language of hierarchy, Rutkevich now proposed the use of "complexity of labor" to rank occupations for purposes of studying "upward mobility."[8] Obviously this is a far cry from his earlier positions that concepts of "higher" and "lower" strata are inapplicable "in principle" to Soviet society.

A striking feature of the Soviet assimilation of the concept of social mobility is not the difficulty but rather the ease with which most Soviet sociologists adopted the conceptual framework of Western mobility analysis, particularly the need for some form of ranking of occupational strata. For some (V. N. Shubkin) the unequal "scope for creativity" was an appropriate criterion for determining occupational rank.[9] For others (R. V. Ryvkina) prestige ratings of occupations could serve this purpose.[10] Still others (Iu. V. Arutiunian) derived occupational rankings based on composite indices of earnings, education, and "influence on the solution of vital questions in the collective" (unfortunately for rural occupations only).[11] The applicability of the concept of hierarchical structures to Soviet society was also explicitly affirmed:

In our sociological literature the view has been expressed that "concepts of 'lower' and 'higher' classes or social strata are inapplicable, in principle, to Soviet socialist society...." However, we cannot ignore the fact that...there are jobs (occupational positions) of different rank connected with the performance of labor of different quality. Because of differences in responsibility, and thus in rights and obligations associated with different positions, the latter form a multiplicity of hierarchies both within individual enterprises and at the level of sectors.[12]

Thus the incorporation of the essential features of the conceptual framework of traditional mobility analysis has met relatively little resistance among Soviet sociologists. There are clearly defined limits, however, which all Soviet mobility studies have observed. The circulation of individuals within the social structure is seen as movement between the "nonantagonistic," officially recognized components of this structure — essentially peasants, · workers, and various nonmanual strata. It hardly needs to be said that we will seek in vain for Soviet studies of movement into or out of a "ruling class," a "bureaucratic elite," a group of "controllers," or an "underclass." But in this respect, too, Soviet mobility studies have followed in the tradition of those Western studies which have seen the division between manual and nonmanual occupations as the principal social boundary whose crossing signifies upward or downward mobility. [13]

There is an element of irony in the spectacle of Soviet sociologists readily adopting, in their own mobility studies, models of occupational stratification essentially similar (with an exception to be noted below) to those used in Western studies. The principal criticism which Soviet writers, as well as non-Soviet Marxists, have made of Western mobility studies [14] is that the implicit model of social structure on which they rely — the focus on the manual-nonmanual division — serves to obscure a more significant social division, that between classes in the Marxian sense. The principal "break" in the distribution of power and privilege between "direct producers," on the one hand, and those whose decisions control the production process and the utilization of society's economic surplus, on the other, is thereby concealed. It has not yet been possible for Soviet sociologists to raise the question whether the occupational gradations utilized in Soviet mobility studies serve a similar function.

The Meaning of Upward Mobility in the Soviet Setting

The problem of where to set the boundary between occupational groupings for purposes of studying social mobility is no small matter. What is certain is that a simple manual-nonmanual dichotomy is inappropriate under Soviet circumstances. Any reasonable method of ranking Soviet occupations would show some of the major components of the nonmanual category ranking above and others below the manual workers' category. We have already seen (Chapter 2) that the average earnings of manual workers typically exceed those of lower-level nonmanual employees. Indeed, in at least some sectors the latter's wages are below those of unskilled manual workers (see our discussion of Leningrad machinery plants in Chapter 2). Soviet studies of occupational prestige reinforce the impression that the movement of individuals from manual workers' jobs to what in Western societies would be considered the more routine "white-collar" positions cannot legitimately be regarded as upward mobility. In Table 4.1 we have compressed the results of four Soviet occupational prestige studies by showing the occupations which were ranked at the two extremes of the prestige hierarchy. The occupations enjoying highest public esteem (the five with highest prestige scores in these studies) were typically drawn from the sciences, medicine, engineering, the academic world, and the arts. Among occupations at the bottom of the prestige hierarchy (the five lowest rated) were sales personnel, clerks, bookkeepers and accountants, and farm workers. It is also striking that managerial personnel of retail stores and service establishments (dining halls) were ranked close to the bottom in the one study in which they appeared. The unpopularity of sales and service jobs apparently "spills over" to supervisory positions in these areas. The principal groups of occupations falling in the intermediate ranges of the prestige rankings (these occupations are not shown in Table 4.1) were manual workers' and engineering positions in various sectors of the economy. The distinctive occupation of professional Party official was apparently too "sacred" to be included anywhere in these rankings.

We are not suggesting that these prestige studies can provide an unambiguous and precise criterion of vertical mobility. At the very least, however, they make it clear that we must distinguish between nonspecialist employees and specialists (roughly speaking, lower and higher nonmanual strata, respectively), and that movement out of manual workers' occupations may be regarded as upward mobility only if it ultimately involves a shift to specialists' status.

The problem of ranking Soviet occupational groups for purposes of mobility research does not end here. The manual worker-nonmanual specialist division is itself not invariably a boundary between "lower" and "higher" occupational groups. Thus the earnings of the more highly skilled manual workers often exceed the earnings of engineering-technical personnel within a given economic sector. Moreover, as we noted in Chapter 2, the average earnings of manual workers in some high-priority sectors exceed those of engineering-technical specialists in less favored industries. This has its counterpart in the prestige ranking of occupations. The prestige scores of steelworkers, chemical workers,

Table 4.1

Highest- and Lowest-Ranking Occupations in Four Soviet Prestige Studies

Area and Year	rank		rank
Novosibirsk Region, 1963* — no. of occupations ranked = 74			
5 highest-ranking occupations:		5 lowest-ranking occupations:	
physicist	1	logger	70
radio technician	2	sales personnel	71
medical scientist	3	accountant, bookkeeper	72
radio engineer	4	municipal services personnel	73
mathematician	5	clerk	74
Leningrad, 1965† — no. of occupations ranked = 40			
5 highest-ranking occupations:		5 lowest-ranking occupations:	
mathematician	1	livestock raising personnel	36
medical scientist	2	painter (in construction)	37
physicist	3	sales personnel	38
personnel in literature and art	4	clerk	39
pilot	5	municipal services personnel	40
Lvov, 1968‡ — no. of occupations ranked = 23			
5 highest-ranking occupations:		5 lowest-ranking occupations:	
chief engineer of enterprise	1	manager of retail store	19
artist, painter	2	lecturer	20
rector of institute	3	personnel in trade enterprise	21
secondary school teacher	4	manager of dining hall	22
army officer	5	cashier	23
Estonian Republic, 1969§ — no. of occupations ranked = 29			
5 highest-ranking occupations:		5 lowest-ranking occupations:	
scientist (uchenyi)	1	livestock specialist	25
physician	2	construction worker	26
physicist	3	bookkeeper, accountant	27
electronics engineer	4	sales personnel	28
"creative intelligentsia"	5	agricultural worker	29

Sources: Novosibirsk: Murray Yanowitch and Norton T. Dodge, "The Social Evaluation of Occupations in the Soviet Union," Slavic Review, December 1969, pp. 642-43. Leningrad: V. V. Vodzinskaia, "Orientation to Occupations," in V. A. Iadov ed., Molodezh' i trud, pp. 85-86. Lvov: S. T. Gurianov and V. V. Sekretariuk, Prizvanie i professiia, p. 30. Estonian Republic: Tartuskii gosu-darstvennyi universitet, Sotsial'no-professional'naia orientatsiia molodezhi, p. 253.

* Applies to urban areas of this region. Respondents included males and females in secondary school graduating classes.

† Respondents were males in secondary school graduating classes.

‡ Respondents were males and females in secondary school graduating classes.

§ Respondents were entering students in higher educational institutions of the Estonian Republic.

and coal miners (in the Novosibirsk studies of the early 1960s) exceeded those of engineers in the clothing, textile, and food industries.[15] The same is true of the prestige ratings of skilled workers relative to those of managers of retail stores (in the Lvov studies of the late 1960s).[16] There is no satisfactory way of translating all these complexities of occupational rankings into simple criteria of vertical mobility. Hence when we rely on the manual worker-nonmanual specialist dichotomy, we do so in full recognition of the fact that this division can serve only as a typical but clearly not universally applicable guide to vertical mobility in Soviet circumstances.

The very difficulty which we confront here reveals an essential aspect of the Soviet reward structure, whether in terms of money earnings or public esteem. Inequalities based on sector of employment interact with inequalities based, at least roughly, on degree of skill. The reward hierarchy thus bears the marks of Soviet economic development strategy: preferential treatment for heavy industry over light industry, for industry generally over sales and service sectors, and for factory occupations over office occupations — or at least the more routine type of the latter. These economic priorities and the rewards associated with them have their counterpart in Soviet literature and in popular perceptions of "higher" and "lower" occupations. The "worker-hero," perhaps studying to become an engineer, appears to be a more familiar and honored figure in Soviet literature than the sales clerk, the accountant, and the office employee.

Finally, how shall we regard the movement of individuals born into families of peasant laborers on collective farms who attain the status of manual workers in factory jobs, especially when the latter involve skilled workers' occupations? Certainly in terms of earnings, popular esteem, and access to material and cultural amenities, such occupational shifts signify "upward" mobility. Once again we are confronted with the limited applicability of the conventional manual-nonmanual occupational division as the principal indicator of vertical mobility. If, in our analysis of Soviet mobility patterns below, we confine the concept of "upward" movements in the occupational hierarchy largely to the inflow of individuals into the nonmanual specialists' stratum, this is done with full recognition of the somewhat arbitrary nature of such a practice. Our principal concern here is to record and analyze the opportunities for movement between distinct socio-occupational groups in Soviet society. The precise specification of all such groups as "higher" and "lower" (and gradations in between) does not seem vital for this purpose, and is in any case probably unrealizable.

Occupational Position and Social Origins

What are the social sources of recruitment to the principal occupational strata, and especially to the more privileged occupational positions in Soviet society? We have already indicated (see Chapter 3) how this question bears on the issue of whether, and to what extent, Soviet society may be characterized as a class system. But there are additional reasons for asking this question. A system which recruits its relatively privileged social groups by drawing extensively on the offspring of lower strata fosters perceptions of occupational opportunity which promote acceptance of the system. High rates of upward mobility are likely to be, on balance, if not invariably, a source of social stability. On the other hand, a narrow base of recruitment to privileged occupational positions and low mobility rates may generate serious social tensions, particularly in a society whose socializing institutions and official spokesmen continually celebrate opportunities for occupational and social promotion ("all paths are open"). Thus our concern here with the general issue of the "openness" of Soviet social structure and with inequalities in access to privileged positions also bears on a process which may be either a source of strength and support or of weakness and disaffection in the system.

We may begin with the most broadly defined components of urban social structure: manual workers, lower-level nonmanual employees, and specialists. Since we shall treat movement into the latter category as implying the attainment of relatively privileged occupational status, let us recall how this stratum is defined: individuals engaged "in complex mental labor of high skills requiring...as a rule higher or specialized secondary education."[17] The social origins of individuals (in terms of father's occupational position) may be conceived as including any of the above three groups as well as the collective farm peasantry. We may initially ignore those Soviet studies of social origins of employed personnel which are confined to individual plants and focus our attention on citywide samples (we know of no studies based on national samples). Table 4.2 brings together, in comparable form, the results of Soviet studies of the social origins of incumbents of the principal occupational positions in the cities of Leningrad, Kazan, and Ufa at the end of the 1960s.

Table 4.2

Social Origins of Incumbents of Various Occupational Positions
in Three Soviet Cities

Current occupational position †	Occupational position of father (in %)*					
	peasant	worker	lower nonmanual employee	specialist	no answer	total
Kazan, 1967						
workers	31.9	49.0	4.8	6.9	7.4	100.0
lower-level nonmanual						
employees	24.3	49.7	7.9	11.2	6.9	100.0
specialists	11.7	29.6	14.9	37.5	6.2	99.9
Ufa, 1970						
workers	33.0	44.6	8.0	7.2	7.2	100.0
lower-level nonmanual						
employees	21.7	35.1	9.3	18.6	15.3	100.0
specialists	17.8	28.1	14.5	32.8	4.8	98.0
Leningrad, 1970						
workers	14.5	54.7	6.7	14.5	9.6	100.0
lower-level nonmanual						
employees	8.4	55.4	8.9	16.4	10.9	100.0
specialists	6.2	42.4	13.6	31.3	6.4	99.9

Sources: Ufa: From N. A. Aitov ed., Nekotorye problemy, pp. 35-36. Kazan: Computed from O. I. Shkaratan, Problemy sotsial'noi struktury, p. 433. Leningrad: Computed from ibid., p. 392, and N. B. Lebedeva et al., pp. 409-10. The figures shown in the latter source for 1970 for individual groups of specialists are combined to derive average figures, using as weights the number of respondents in each group in a similar 1965 study (the first of the above sources).

*The figures for Kazan and Leningrad refer to "head of family"; the figures for Ufa are specified for "father." In all cases occupational position of family head or father applies to the period of initial labor-market entry of current respondents.

† In Kazan and Ufa the respondents were drawn from the city's economy as a whole; in Leningrad, from personnel employed in that city's machinery industry. In Ufa the respondents were above the age of 25. No age restrictions applied in the other cities.

These studies reveal considerable recruitment from "below" to specialists' positions. In all three cities the proportion of specialists recruited from working-class and peasant families combined (40-50%) exceeded that drawn from specialists' families. When recruitment to the specialists' stratum from lower-level nonmanual families is added to the inflow from working-class and peasant families, the emerging picture is one in which a distinct majority of currently employed specialists were recruited from outside their own stratum. In no case did the children of specialists constitute as much as 40% of the current incumbents of specialists' positions. Access to the specialists' stratum is obviously not the restricted prerogative of a socially exclusive group.

Studies of the social origins of specialists in rural areas (by Iu. V. Arutiunian) reinforce the impression of extensive reliance on the offspring of manual strata to recruit managerial and technical staffs. No more than 20-30% of the persons employed in such positions on collective and state farms and in rural industrial enterprises in Arutiunian's studies of 1967 were of intelligentsia social origins.[18]

As we shall see below, the large-scale recruitment of individuals of manual social origins to fill higher-level nonmanual positions does not reflect any significant downward mobility among the offspring of intelligentsia families. Even if all specialists' children were to become specialists, which they do not, the rapid increase in such positions in recent years would require that the supply be replenished by drawing on the offspring of working-class and peasant families. Between 1960 and 1973 the number of specialists' jobs more than doubled, and this occupational stratum increased from 10% to 16% of the total work force. During the same period the share of manual strata — collective farm peasants and workers combined — fell from 80% to 74% of the work force (the decline in the share of the peasantry more than offsetting the rise in the working class), while the share of lower-level nonmanual employees remained essentially constant (see Table 4.3).

Although we are concerned here chiefly with social sources of recruitment to higher nonmanual positions, i.e., specialists, there are some aspects of the social origins of other urban social groups that deserve attention. Unlike the situation prevailing in the early five-year plans, the Soviet working class — at least in cities like Leningrad, Kazan, and Ufa — is no longer predominantly recruited from peasant families uprooted from rural life. In all these cities the current generation of manual workers is more likely to have inherited this social position than to be in transition from peasant to working-class status. As for lower-level nonmanual employees, although they are also more frequently recruited from the children of working-class families than from any other social group, the inflow of children of intelligentsia social origins to lower nonmanual occupations is not unusual. In the cities shown in Table 4.2, some 11-19% of the incumbents of lower-level nonmanual positions were of intelligentsia social origins. Despite the relatively low economic and social status of such position, those children of intelligentsia families who cannot readily reproduce their parents' occupational status apparently often prefer employment in lower-level nonmanual jobs to working-class occupations. We shall see below, however, that employment in routine nonmanual jobs is occasionally a temporary step on the way "upward" to specialist's status.

Table 4.3

Principal Social Groups in the Soviet Work Force

Social groups	1950*		1960		1970		1973	
	in millions	in %	in millions	in %	in millions	in %	in millions	in %
Manual workers	28.7	42.2	45.9	54.4	64.3	60.0	68.8	60.5
Collective farmers	27.6	40.6	21.9	26.0	16.3	15.2	15.3	13.5
Total in manual labor	56.3	82.8	67.8	80.4	80.6	75.2	84.1	74.0
Specialists	{ 11.7	{ 17.2	8.3	9.9	15.2	14.2	18.2	16.0
Lower-level non-manual employees			8.2	9.7	11.4	10.6	11.3	10.0
Total in nonmanual work	11.7	17.2	16.5	19.6	26.6	24.8	29.5	26.0
Total	68.0	100.0	84.3	100.0	107.2	100.0	113.6	100.0

Sources: 1950: Computed from figures in TsSU, SSSR, Narodnoe khoziaistvo SSSR, 1922-1972, p. 345; Joint Committee Print, Soviet Economic Prospects for the Seventies, pp. 514, 520-21. 1960, 1970, 1973: M. N. Rutkevich, "Tendencies of Change in the Social Structure of Soviet Society," Sotsiologicheskie issledovaniia, 1975, no. 1, p. 72.

*Unlike the figures for other years, specialists and nonmanual employees working on collective farms were included among "collective farmers."

Perhaps the most striking aspect of all this material is the evidence of very substantial shifting of social position between generations among all groups. A distinct majority of both specialists and lower-level nonmanual employees are recruited from outside their parents' social group. Even in the case of workers, the group exhibiting the highest degree of self-recruitment, in cities like Ufa and Kazan some one-third are of peasant social origins.

Thus far we have treated each of the three principal components of urban social structure as essentially homogeneous groups. Such a procedure obscures some important differences in the social origins of distinct strata within these broad groups. To take an obvious example: Where unskilled workers can be distinguished as a separate stratum (in the Leningrad and Kazan studies), it is clear that they are predominantly of peasant and farm-worker social origins. Thus peasant youth in Soviet urban labor markets — at least insofar as their entry jobs are concerned — appear to have performed a function broadly similar to that of earlier waves of European immigrants and more recent flows of Latin American immigrants and racial minorities in the American labor market. Soviet skilled workers, on the other hand, have been recruited in recent years mainly from "hereditary" urban workers' families.[19]

But what about the social origins of the incumbents of "higher" and "lower" positions within the broadly defined specialists' (intelligentsia) group? We have already seen (in Chapter 3) that students at specialized secondary schools training individuals for the lower positions in the specialists' stratum are drawn largely from manual strata, while the latter supply a minority, albeit a large one, of the students at higher educational institutions. But this does not bear directly on the issue of the social origins of current incumbents of various types of specialists' positions. Unfortunately the specialists in the Leningrad, Ufa, and Kazan studies whose social origins are shown in Table 4.2 are not broken down in a manner that would permit us to clearly distinguish between "higher" and "lower" levels within the specialists' category.[20] Suppose we accept these studies as revealing the "typical" social origins of incumbents of the broad specialists' stratum as a whole. One way of answering the question we have posed here is to reveal the social origins of individuals in certain "elite" occupational groups not singled out in the studies examined thus far. We use the term "elite" here to correspond, at least roughly, to some of the highest ranking positions in the prestige hierarchy discussed earlier. The social origins of individuals in some of these "elite" groups are shown in Table 4.4 (in some cases we are forced to rely on the social origins of students over an extended period as a proxy for the social background of current incumbents of these professional positions).

The family background of these "elite" groups (samples of scientists, university faculty, future physicians, engineers with a vuz diploma, and the "artistic intelligentsia") may be compared with

Table 4.4

Social Origins of Selected "Elite" Occupational Groups

No.	"Elite" groups	Social origins: parents' occupational position (in %)			
		workers	peasants	nonmanual employees (specialists and nonspecialists)	total
1.	University faculty, Kharkov State University, 1969	24.4	15.5	59.0	98.9
2.	Graduate students of science, Academy of Sciences, Leningrad branch				
	1963	8	4	88	100
	1968	15	13	72	100
3.	Engineers with higher education at scientific institutes and enterprises, Leningrad, 1965*	24.7	4.2	71.1	100
4.	Students at medical and pharmaceutical institutes, RSFSR Ministry of Health				
	1964†	29.7	12.1	58.2	100
	1970	30.7	7.4	61.9	100
5.	"Artistic intelligentsia," Belorussian SSSR, 1970‡				
	architects	19	12	69	100
	composers	13	10	77	100
	artists	27	21	47	95§
	writers	20	58	22	100

Sources: 1. N. I. Sazonov ed., Kritika antimarksistskikh vzgliadov po voprosam sotsial'no-politicheskogo razvitiia sovetskogo obshchestva, pp. 81-82.
2. Akademiia nauk SSSR, Nauchnye kadry Leningrada, pp. 82-83. 3. S. A. Kugel and O. M. Nikandrov, Molodye inzhenery, p. 171. The figures are based on a sample study of "about" 3,000 specialists. 4. Special issue on "Medical School in the USSR," Soviet Education, May-June 1975, p. 31. 5. Akademiia nauk Belorusskoi SSR, Struktura sovetskoi intelligentsii, p. 104.
*These figures apply to "young engineers" (those with up to five years of work experience). Social origins in this case refers explicitly to father's occupation.
†The figures for social origins apply to "workers and workers' children," "peasants and peasants' children," and "employees and employees' children."
‡These figures apply to the membership of the various artistic "unions" in the Belorussian republic.
§The sources do not explain the discrepancy between the "total" and 100%.

the "typical" (undifferentiated) specialists' groups whose social origins were examined earlier (in Table 4.2). The social base of recruitment to our version of "elite" occupational status is clearly more restricted than to the specialists' stratum as a whole. With few exceptions,[21] individuals of nonmanual social origins predominate among the incumbents of our group of "elite" occupations. Among scientists (and what appears to be an unusually select group of engineers[22]) the share of nonmanual strata is more than 70%; among university faculty and future physicians, approximately 60%. Recruits from nonmanual families typically provided a more modest share of the undifferentiated groups of specialists in the studies summarized in Table 4.2 (in two cities less than one-half of the incumbents of specialists' positions were drawn from nonmanual strata, and in one city, slightly more than one-half).

As we noted earlier, the Soviet intelligentsia — in its official Soviet definition as "specialists" — is obviously a highly diverse group. The bottom layers of this stratum (technicians, lower and middle management staff, teachers, individuals holding engineering jobs without engineering diplomas) overlap with workers, especially skilled workers, in earnings and social standing. The considerable influx of the offspring of manual workers to the specialists' stratum undoubtedly occurs largely at the margin between these two groups. Recruitment to the more privileged and prestigious layers of the specialists' stratum — whether adequately represented by our sample of "elite" groups — is more heavily concentrated among the offspring of intelligentsia families. But even among the incumbents of these "elite" occupational positions, the share of individuals of manual social origins is usually close to one-third or more. Moreover, the intelligentsia families whose children staff many of these "elite" positions are themselves, in large part, a newly created rather than a "hereditary" stratum. Many of the new entrants to those occupations officially designated as having specialists' status who are not the children of workers or peasants must be their grandchildren.[23] On the whole the material examined thus far suggests a relatively "open" social structure in the special sense of extensive reliance on individuals of manual social origins to staff nonmanual specialists' positions.

Intergenerational Mobility

The study of social sources of recruitment focuses on one particular aspect of mobility processes. It yields estimates of the proportion of individuals in a stratum whose social origin (usually father's occupation) was outside (or within) that stratum. But it does not tell us anything about the proportion of individuals born in a stratum who "rise" out of, "fall" below, or remain within that stratum. The material we have just reviewed permits us to say, for example, that approximately 40% of the individuals employed in nonmanual specialists' positions in Leningrad machinery plants in 1970 (see Table 4.2) had fathers who were manual workers, but it does not tell us what proportion of the children of manual work- ers attained specialists' positions, nor how this proportion com- pares with the proportion of intelligentsia children who retained their fathers' occupational status. This distinction is, of course, an obvious but highly significant one. The degree to which the so- cial structure is perceived as open and mobility rates as high will depend partly on the location of the observer. From the standpoint of individuals in the intelligentsia stratum (especially its lower level), many of whom have recently risen from manual social backgrounds, Soviet social and occupational divisions may well appear as highly permeable. But how rigid or open will these boundaries appear to the bulk of youngsters reared in working- class and peasant families? We cannot answer this question di- rectly, but we can examine some of the available evidence bearing on it.

The procedures followed in the principal Western studies of in- tergenerational social mobility in the 1950s and 1960s were essen- tially based on deriving "for each occupational grouping (stratum) of fathers...the percentage distribution of their sons into the vari- ous occupational strata."[24] These are the kinds of studies which have begun to appear in recent years in the Soviet Union. Such studies normally distinguish between lower and higher layers of the nonmanual grouping and, unlike many Western studies, focus on "fathers (or family heads)-to-children" rather than on "fathers- to-sons" mobility. Since Soviet mobility studies of this kind are at any early stage, we must be prepared to rely on a small number of citywide and plantwide samples. Our objective is not so much the precise quantitative estimation of mobility rates as the delin- eation of the broad features of Soviet mobility patterns and the ap- proximate extent of social inequalities in occupational opportuni- ties. We shall seek to avoid cluttering our discussion with the many methodological and data problems normally involved in the study of social mobility. As elsewhere in this volume we rely on those Soviet studies which appear to have been guided chiefly by scientific considerations and whose findings appear "reasonable" in the light of a whole complex of related characteristics of Soviet social structure. There is no alternative for the outside observer who seeks to derive a picture of mobility patterns from Soviet published materials.

Some of the more commonly observed features of such mobility patterns are revealed in Table 4.5. Based on a sample of the employed population of a single city in 1970 — Ufa (total population of 771,000) — this table shows the occupational distribution of the children of fathers in distinct occupational groupings. The respondents in this sample were currently employed persons who were asked to specify their father's occupational position at the time of their (the currently employed) initial entry into the work force. What do we find? A distinct majority of intelligentsia children (approximately three-quarters) had themselves attained the occupational status of nonmanual specialists. Most children of working-class fathers, on the other hand, were employed in manual workers' occupations. The same was true of an even larger majority of peasants' children (migrants to the city). If we confine the concept of upward mobility to cases in which individuals of manual social origins attain the status of nonmanual specialists, the results for this city show that some one-fourth to one-third of peasants' and workers' children were upwardly mobile. Movement into the intelligentsia stratum was a more common experience among children of lower-level nonmanual employees than among workers' and peasants' children (approximately one-half of the former group attained intelligentsia status). If we confine the concept of downward mobility to movement out of the intelligentsia stratum, some one-fourth of specialists' children appear to have "skidded."

There are no solid grounds for accepting the precise mobility rates revealed in this one city as "typical" of such rates in other Soviet urban communities.[25] But there are good reasons for stressing certain common features of the mobility pattern here which reappear in other studies. One such feature is the fact that the proportion of intelligentsia children attaining specialists' occupational status is some two to three times the comparable proportion among workers' children. Most intelligentsia parents are able to transmit their occupational status to their children, while the majority of peasant and working-class parents — whatever their aspirations for their children — cannot reasonably expect to see them rise out of manual occupations. The opportunities for such children to attain intelligentsia status are also less than those of children of lower-level nonmanual employees. These are

the broad features of Soviet mobility patterns which appear in the
Ufa study and which recur in whatever other studies are available
to us.

Table 4.5

Relationship between Occupations of Fathers and
Their Children: Ufa, 1970

Occupations of fathers	Current (1970) occupations of children,* in %				
	intelligentsia	worker	lower nonmanual	no answer	total
Intelligentsia	72.5	14.6	11.0	1.9	100
Worker	31.4	59.1	8.6	0.9	100
Lower-level nonmanual employee	55.2	36.2	7.8	0.8	100
Collective farmer	28.5	62.4	7.6	1.5	100

Source: N. A. Aitov ed., Nekotorye problemy, p. 36.

*The "children" were 2,000 residents of Ufa above the age of 25. The source
used states they were selected in proportion to the share of the various occupational groups in the city's adult population.

But what is not revealed by the material examined thus far is
the range and complexity of intergenerational shifts in social position. Some of these become apparent when the manual workers'
and intelligentsia groupings are each subdivided into distinct components. The differing mobility patterns of distinct strata within
the broad manual labor category are particularly illuminating and
raise some interesting questions. The issues involved here may
be illustrated by reference to Table 4.6, which summarizes the
results of a mobility study based on a sample of Leningrad machine-building employees.[26] Rates of movement from manual
social origins to specialists' positions were considerably lower
than in the Ufa study (approximately 20% for urban workers and
7% for collective farm peasant migrants), although the common
features of mobility patterns described earlier may be observed.
More revealing, however, are the results of singling out distinct
strata of the working class. Barely any of the children of urban
skilled workers (less than 3%) were employed in unskilled manual
jobs, but among the children of farm workers almost one-fourth
held such jobs in this sample. The greater mobility opportunities
of the children of urban workers than of rural workers, and of
skilled than of unskilled workers, are apparently a common feature of Soviet mobility patterns. Although the differences between these groups in access to intelligentsia positions are fairly

Social and Economic Inequality

Table 4.6

Relationship between Occupations of Fathers and Their Children:
Krasnaia Zaria Machinery Combine, Leningrad, 1967

Occupations of fathers*	Current (1967) occupations of children,[†] in %					
	unskilled worker	skilled worker	highly skilled worker	lower nonmanual employee	specialist[‡]	total
Collective farmer	12.3	63.3	6.1	10.7	6.6	100
Worker in agriculture	23.2	42.2	11.5	9.2	13.9	100
Unskilled worker in city	5.0	53.9	9.0	13.1	18.9	100
Skilled worker in city	2.7	54.7	11.2	9.3	22.1	100
Lower nonmanual employee	1.4	43.0	3.8	15.5	36.3	100
Specialist with secondary specialized education	1.7	22.2	11.1	7.7	57.3	100
Specialist with higher education	1.6	20.6	4.1	10.8	62.9	100

Source: Institut sotsiologicheskikh issledovanii AN SSSR, Problemy effektivno-go ispol'zovaniia rabochikh kadrov no promyshlennom predpriiatii, p. 95.

*The source used does not indicate the time period to which fathers' occupations apply.

[†] The "children" were approximately 1,500 employees at the chief plant of the Krasnaia Zaria Combine in Leningrad.

[‡] These figures are the sums shown in the source for "personnel in skilled mental work" and "managerial personnel."

small in Table 4.6, they are clearly in favor of the offspring of urban over rural workers, and of skilled over unskilled workers. Similarly, when the specialists in the parents' generation are subdivided into higher and lower categories (based on educational attainment), the children of the former are favored in the competition for intelligentsia positions over the children of the latter.

The nature of downward mobility among the children of intelligentsia parents is also illuminated when the single working-class category is divided into skilled and unskilled groupings. When the children of intelligentsia parents are downwardly mobile, they apparently do not "skid" very far: less than 2% of this group were employed in unskilled workers' jobs in the Leningrad machinery plant study shown in Table 4.6. Those who had not yet attained intelligentsia status were either skilled workers or lower-level nonmanual employees.

The recognition of the obvious fact that the Soviet working class is itself a highly differentiated social grouping poses an important issue in the study of upward mobility in Soviet circumstances.

Thus far we have treated upward mobility as essentially the movement of manual and lower nonmanual groups into the specialists'
stratum. Although we have already placed a rather heavy "load"
on the study of the mobility patterns of employees in a single machinery enterprise (Table 4.6), the same study illustrates the limitations of our conception of upward mobility. Why should the latter
term apply to the urban worker's son or daughter who becomes an
engineer or plant manager but not to the farm worker's or peasant's children who become urban skilled workers? Under Soviet
circumstances the latter type of intergenerational movement is no
less a form of occupational and social "promotion" than the former,
perhaps even more so. Since our primary concern is not the precise quantitative determination of aggregate mobility rates but the
delineation of the range and complexity of mobility patterns, and
thus of the factors affecting Soviet perceptions of the opportunity
structure, it is sufficient at this point to stress that intergenerational shifts from lower to higher strata within a wide range of
manual occupations are a significant feature of Soviet life.

Obviously, most children of peasants and farm workers do not
become skilled industrial workers, although this is not uncommon
among those who have moved to the city. When intergenerational
occupational mobility is examined exclusively within an urban context — so that both the parents' and children's generations are
represented by current urban residents — a distinct sequence of
occupational shifts may be observed. The majority of children of
unskilled manual workers move out of the occupational stratum of
their fathers, but their social ascent is likely to be a "one step at
a time" advance: they are more likely to shift to skilled workers'
occupations than to specialists' positions. For the children of
skilled workers, movement out of the occupational stratum of their
fathers usually means the attainment of specialists' status, although
only a minority of such children reach this level. Finally, most
children of specialists "inherit" their fathers' intelligentsia status;
those who fail to do so typically do not fall very far. The advantages of having been born to a father in an intelligentsia rather
than a worker's occupation, whether skilled or unskilled, are in
any case unambiguous. These are the patterns which emerge
when the occupational positions of a sample of current (1970)
Leningrad employees in the city's machinery industry are compared with the positions attained by their adult children (see
Table 4.7). The relatively favorable mobility opportunities of
workers' children in this study (some 30-40% attained higher non-

manual positions) undoubtedly reflect the special advantages of being raised in a city like Leningrad, although the broad pattern observed here is probably not unusual.

Table 4.7

Relationship between Current Occupations of Fathers and Status of Their Children: Leningrad Machinery Enterprises, 1970

Current (1970) occupations of fathers*	Current (1970) status of children,† in %					
	unskilled worker	skilled worker	lower nonmanual employee	specialist or full-time student at vuz or tekhnikum	housewife	total
Unskilled worker	12.6	42.3	11.5	31.4	2.2	100
Skilled worker‡	13.5	37.8	5.1	43.6	—	100
Lower nonmanual employee	6.9	27.1	12.2	49.5	4.3	100
Intelligentsia: personnel in skilled mental work	7.7	12.7	9.8	69.8	—	100
highly skilled scientific-technical personnel	8.3	14.8	12.4	62.9	1.6	100
managerial personnel	2.5	17.0	2.5	78.0	—	100

Source: N. B. Lebedeva et al., p. 415.

*These were drawn from a sample of approximately 3,500 employees of the principal machine-building enterprises of Leningrad.

†These are the "adult" children of the machine-building employees cited in the previous footnote.

‡The source used cites three categories of skilled workers. We show the category skilled workers "employed on machinery and mechanisms."

There is one important limitation of the kind of mobility data we have been examining, quite apart from the small number of studies at our disposal and the relatively narrow range of population groups they encompass. It is a limitation inherent in the mobility tables (Tables 4.5-4.7) as such. Although these may reveal broad relationships between parents' and children's occupational positions at a given time, they tell us nothing about the process of attainment of occupational status which produces the situation portrayed in mobility tables. Hence it seems useful at this point to briefly recall some of our earlier discussion of social inequalities in education and to introduce one additional matter bearing on the occupational opportunities of different strata.

We noted in Chapter 3 that the children of manual strata tend
to leave school earlier than the children of intelligentsia parents,
that the former are more likely to attend workers' vocational
schools than the latter, and that their access to higher education
upon graduation from secondary school is less frequent than
among specialists' children. The impact of these inequalities in
educational attainment on the initial jobs available to youngsters
of different class backgrounds is obvious. But even for youngsters
with identical schooling in a given locality, entry jobs often differ
in a manner that is systematically related to the occupational position of parents. Youngsters who enter the labor market upon
graduation from secondary school are apparently more successful
in obtaining nonmanual positions (lower-level engineering-technical
jobs or "nonspecialist" employees' positions) if their parents are
nonmanual specialists rather than workers or lower nonmanual
employees. Vasil'eva's Leningrad study[27] showed that most secondary school graduates whose parents were workers or lower
nonmanual employees were employed in manual workers' jobs
one year after graduation. Where at least one parent held a specialist's job, most youngsters were in nonmanual jobs; and where
both parents were employed in intelligentsia positions, only one-
fourth of their children (with a secondary education only) were
employed as manual workers. The desirability of employment in
nonmanual positions at this early stage in a work career obviously
does not lie in any immediate advantages of income or public esteem they offer. But such positions may make it less burdensome
to pursue part-time higher education and in some cases involve
the kind of "servicing" of engineering and technical staff functions
that is useful for the ultimate attainment of higher-level specialists' positions. In both of these respects nonmanual jobs are stepping stones to ultimate intelligentsia status. Thus even when children of intelligentsia parents lack superior educational qualifications, their higher social origins may serve as a "resource" in
securing access to preferred entry jobs. The greater accessibility of
such entry jobs to these youngsters is one phase in a status attainment
process whose results are reflected in the mobility tables. Other
phases are associated with the educational inequalities just reviewed.

A Note on Mobility in the Countryside

All of the mobility processes discussed thus far occur essentially in an urban environment, i.e., they concern either native urban residents or rural migrants to the city. The overwhelming majority of peasants' and farm workers' children who move to the city enter workers' occupations. In the competition for higher nonmanual jobs in the city, they are typically less successful than native urban residents — whether of manual or nonmanual social origins — and rural migrants of nonmanual origins. But what about those who remain in the rural work force? The Soviet rural community also embraces a hierarchy of socio-occupational strata, and processes of occupational inheritance and mobility may be observed there as well as in the city. Although these processes have probably been studied more systematically in rural than in urban areas — thanks chiefly to the work of Iu. Arutiunian — we may focus chiefly on a few essential similarities and differences.

The entry jobs of rural children depend heavily on the occupational positions of their fathers. In Arutiunian's 1967 study of the Tatar Republic, for example, only 8% of the children of fathers in the lowest and most numerous rural stratum — common laborers — began their work careers in professional and managerial jobs. Among the children of rural higher-level specialists in the same region, approximately one-half entered the labor market in such jobs (see Table 4.8). The access to intelligentsia positions among the offspring of other rural strata fell between these two extremes. Although the superior occupational opportunities of children of the rural intelligentsia as a whole are clear-cut, there is an interesting distinction within this group. The most privileged children, in terms of initial job opportunities, are not the offspring of "managers" but of "technical specialists." The higher income and power over production of the higher-level manager (chairman of a collective farm, director of a state farm or other rural economic enterprise) are apparently less of an asset to the career opportunities of children than the superior educational attainment of a higher-level specialist (a vuz-educated agronomist, engineer, teacher).[28]

The advantages of intelligentsia social origins for entry jobs are apparently retained as the work careers of the various rural strata unfold. When Arutiunian compared the current (1967) occupational positions of individuals of differing social origins with the occupational categories of their fathers, the results were broadly similar to the mobility patterns we observed in urban mobility studies. The majority of manual strata children remained in the occupational grouping of their fathers (see Table 4.9). Social ascent for the children of common laborers and other rural manual workers

Table 4.8

Father's Occupation and Children's Opportunity to Start Work Career
in Managerial or Specialist's Occupation: Rural Areas of Tatar Republic, 1967

Father's occupation	Rank of father's occupation according to index of socio-economic status*	% of children[†] starting work career in managerial or specialist's occupation
Manager or technical specialist:		
higher-level manager	1	26.2
higher-level specialist	2	51.6
middle-level specialist	3	42.8
middle-level manager	4	27.6
Lower-level nonmanual employee	5	24.4
Machinery operator	6	13.7
Manual worker:		
manual worker in construction	7	10.8
low-skilled manual worker (on permanent staff)	8	16.7
common laborer	9	8.3

Source: Computed from material in Iu. V. Arutiunian, Sotsial'naia struktura, pp. 323, 354-55.

*The index was derived by Iu. V. Arutiunian by combining indicators of earnings, education, and "influence on...major decisions of the collective."

†The "children" constituted a sample of currently (1967) employed persons in rural occupations.

was more likely to mean short-distance movement to a tractor operator's job (a principal component of the broader "machine operator's" category) than the leap to rural intelligentsia status. If we accept Arutiunian's ranking of the socioeconomic status of the four principal rural occupational groups (1. intelligentsia, 2. lower nonmanual employees, 3. machinery operators, 4. common laborers and other manual workers[29]), the access of children to intelligentsia occupations varied directly with the standing of father's occupation.

The small minority of manual strata children who move into specialists' occupations (15%) suggests a lower rate of manual-to-intelligentsia mobility in the countryside than we observed in the available studies of urban strata. This low rate of mobility, however, is compatible with the predominantly manual social origins of the rural intelligentsia. The small proportion of peasants' and farm workers' children who move into specialists' occupations comprise a majority of the rural intelligentsia. The evidence for this is no less convincing than the evidence of the substantial

Table 4.9

Relationship between Occupations of Fathers and Their Children:
Rural Areas of Tatar Republic, 1967

Occupations of fathers*	Current (1967) occupations of children,† in %				
	manager, specialist	lower nonmanual employee	machine operator	manual worker	total
Manual worker	14.9	8.1	20.6	56.3	99.9
Machine operator	17.9	17.9	35.9	23.1	94.8‡
Lower nonmanual employee	38.8	16.5	14.1	30.6	100.0
Manager, nonmanual specialist	47.3	14.7	17.8	20.2	100.0

Source: Derived from diagrams in Iu. V. Arutiunian ed., Sotsial'noe i natsio-nal'noe, p. 72.

*The source used does not indicate the time period to which fathers' occupations apply.

† The "children" were a sample of 1,361 persons employed in rural occupations in the Tatar Republic in 1967.

‡ The source used provides no explanation for the discrepancy between this figure and 100.

share of individuals of manual social origins among the urban intelligentsia.[30] In neither case, however, does this demonstrate an approximation to "equality of opportunity."

Intragenerational Mobility ("Career Mobility")

Our discussion thus far has been based on the kinds of studies which have compared the current or initial occupational status of samples of respondents with the main occupational positions of their fathers. We now turn to the issue of prospects for social ascent (or descent) within the course of individuals' own work careers. More particularly, to what extent do individuals who enter the labor market as manual workers or lower nonmanual employees rise to positions generally regarded as significantly "higher" than their entry jobs? As is always the case in such discussions, the amount of mobility we discern depends partly on the number of distinct occupational levels we distinguish. We shall observe the procedure followed earlier. Movement into (or out of) higher nonmanual positions (specialists, intelligentsia) will be accepted as a clear indicator of vertical social mobility. Occupational movements of "shorter" distance (within manual occupations, for example) will be considered to the extent that our principal criterion of vertical mobility appears inadequate to encompass significant changes in social position.

A certain type of occupational life-history has often been celebrated in Soviet publications. In its more modest form it frequently projects the image of the "leading worker" studying at an evening vuz to become an engineer. In its more ambitious and complete version it is perhaps best symbolized by the plant director who began his work career as a peasant or manual laborer, earned an engineering degree after years of work experience, and then, by virtue of his outstanding "organizing ability," "political maturity," and prolonged apprenticeship on the shop floor, was promoted to the important post in which he ended his work career. Whether the final position corresponded to plant director or another similarly honored high-status position, the public recounting of such careers typically stressed the long distance traveled between manual entry jobs and final occupational status. The career history, of course, was never presented in a "rags to riches" context but in a manner which stressed the value of early experience in a worker's occupation for effective performance in higher-level positions. Although such life-histories were probably more frequently publicized in the earlier years of industrialization than in the more recent past, the glorification of a work background in manual labor continues to appear in current publications. The remarks of a plant director published in 1971 may serve as an illustration:

I cannot conceive of a genuine economic manager, an enterprise director, who was not a worker in his youth. Even if for a short period, it is absolutely necessary to work with one's hand, to personally create material values.... Everyone must go through the school of being a worker, not only to obtain production skills but to think like the leading class of our society, to breathe in the same rhythm.... The academician, the military officer, teacher, poet — all individuals in our society are proud if they have passed through...the school of the working class.[31]

Whatever the mythology it has fostered, the celebration of the humble origins of individuals in high status positions is rooted in the reality of Soviet economic history. The great majority of Soviet plant directors in the midst of the turbulent period of the prewar five-year plans had been employed in workers' occupations prior to their assumption of managerial positions.[32] Even in the early 1970s Soviet sources could claim that "about 70% of government ministers" and "more than one-half of the directors of the country's largest industrial enterprises" were former manual workers.[33] There is little doubt, however, that the passage of time has seen a decline in the proportion of managerial personnel and technical specialists who begin their work careers in manual positions or, if they do begin there, spend any appreciable time in such positions. Engineers are increasingly recruited from individuals who move directly from secondary school to a higher educational institution.[34] Higher managerial positions are also increasingly staffed by specialists with higher or secondary specialized education received prior to labor market entry rather than by "praktiki" (individuals with no more than a general secondary education who hold managerial positions by virtue of their "practical" experience).[35] Moreover, enrollment in part-time study at vuzy and secondary specialized schools has declined as a proportion of total postsecondary enrollment in recent years.[36] All of these factors, together with the current stress on the "professionalization of management," suggest that the traditionally celebrated occupational life-history of the Soviet manager, engineer, and technician is increasingly obsolete. The entry jobs of individuals who reach these and similar positions today are certainly several notches higher than those of their predecessors of a more "heroic" period. But the echoes of the past continue to foster an ethos which stresses opportunities for significant occupational ascent within a work career.

Whatever the historical changes in the career paths of those who have reached the higher levels of the occupational hierarchy, recent sociological studies have explicitly confirmed what must always have been true of most individuals beginning their work careers in manual jobs: "It must be said that if a person begins his work activity as a worker, it is most probable (vsego veroiatnee) that he will remain such throughout his life."[37] But how frequent is mobility from initial manual and lower nonmanual jobs to upper nonmanual positions?

Ideally, the answer to this question would require data on the complete occupational life-histories of samples of individuals entering the labor market in such jobs. The principal Soviet studies of intragenerational mobility permit us to compare entry jobs and "current" (at the time of the survey) positions of several occupational groups. The findings of three such studies are brought together in Table 4.10. They all reveal what can only be characterized as relatively modest rates of career mobility from manual entry jobs to intelligentsia positions. Among samples of currently employed persons in Leningrad (1970), Kazan (1967), and

Table 4.10

Initial and Current Occupational Positions of Employed Personnel in Leningrad (1970), Kazan (1967), and Al'met'evsk (1967)

Initial occupational position (entry job)	Current (1967-1970) occupational position (in %)						
	unskilled worker	skilled worker*	highly skilled worker	worker, total	lower nonmanual employee	nonmanual specialist†	total
Leningrad:							
collective farmer, agricultural worker	23.4	52.9	5.2	81.5	5.2	13.3	100
unskilled worker	7.1	65.4	3.3	75.8	9.1	15.1	100
skilled worker	4.2	64.0	4.1	72.3	9.3	18.4	100
lower nonmanual employee	3.2	20.1	3.0	26.3	26.5	47.2	100
Kazan:							
unskilled worker	27.4	55.0	0.5	82.9	7.1	10.0‡	100
skilled worker	7.4	69.4	1.0	77.8	9.7	12.5	100
Al'met'evsk:							
unskilled worker	25.2	51.4	1.8	78.4	8.6	13.0§	100
skilled worker	7.4	62.0	2.2	71.6	5.4	23.0	100

Source: Computed from Iu. G. Chulanov, Izmeneniia v sostave i v urovne tvorcheskoi aktivnosti rabochego klassa SSSR, 1959-1970, pp. 34-35.

*Derived as the sum of "skilled workers in...hand work" and "skilled workers...on machines and mechanisms."

†Derived as the sum of "personnel in skilled mental work," "personnel in highly skilled scientific-technical work," and "managerial personnel."

‡Cited in the source as "about 10."

§Cited in the source as "about 13."

Al'met'evsk (1967) whose initial jobs were in rural or urban manual occupations, the rate of movement into nonmanual specialists' jobs was on the order of 10-20%, with the typical figure being closer to the lower than the upper portion of this range. Some three-fourths to four-fifths of those whose entry jobs were in manual occupations remained manual workers. Although opportunities to move into managerial and professional positions were more favorable for those who entered the work world as skilled rather than unskilled manual workers (and were least favorable for those who began as peasants and farm workers), the more striking feature of these studies is the generally low rate of movement out of manual occupations for those whose work careers began there.

Additional evidence pointing in the same direction is provided by Aitov's studies in Ufa and Orenburg. Aitov found that among those of his respondents (in a 1965 study) who had been manual workers in 1950, some 91% remained in this occupational category fifteen years later. Over a period of twenty years (1950-70) approximately 88% of those who had been manual workers at the beginning of the period (and were still employed in 1970) were manual workers at the end of it. After accounting for those who had moved into lower nonmanual occupations, mobility from manual to higher nonmanual occupations appears to have been on the order of 3-10% over a 15-20-year period.[38]

The relatively low rates of career mobility revealed in Aitov's studies and in those summarized in Table 4.10 reflect current practices in recruitment to managerial and other higher-level nonmanual positions. As noted earlier, access to such positions is increasingly restricted to individuals with prolonged formal schooling. This is the essential significance of repeated Soviet efforts to reduce the proportion of "praktiki" (see above) in these positions. The success of these efforts has limited the career opportunities of upwardly mobile manual workers who obviously find it more difficult to complete the requisite higher or specialized secondary education than secondary school graduates who are able to continue full-time schooling. Aitov's studies provide interesting confirmation of this. The same survey (in Ufa and Orenburg) which showed only 3% of workers moving into higher nonmanual jobs in the period 1950-70 revealed considerable downward mobility among the initial incumbents of intelligentsia occupations (only 76% of the original group retained intelligentsia status in 1965). A principal explanation for this occupational demotion is

that many specialists' positions among managerial staffs had to be
filled by "praktiki" in the early postwar years. As shortages of
educated specialists were overcome, the "praktiki" were demoted
to manual workers' and lower nonmanual jobs.[39] But this type of
occupational descent among some groups of managerial and technical personnel obviously did not provide many promotion opportunities for manual workers. The decisive role of the worker's
entry job in limiting his opportunities for ascent to intelligentsia
status is tersely but unambiguously acknowledged by Aitov in his
comments on his own findings:

As a rule an individual begins work with a certain specialty and educational
level, the acquisition of which required a considerable expenditure of energy,
and the exceeding of which (to achieve social mobility) is quite difficult.[40]

A work career begun in a lower nonmanual job seems to provide
more frequent access to eventual intelligentsia status than manual
workers' entry jobs. Although normal mobility rates from lower
to higher nonmanual occupations can hardly be at the level indicated
for Leningrad in Table 4.10 (close to 50%), the advantages of lower
nonmanual over manual workers in this respect are confirmed by
other studies.[41] There is something surprising about this. We
have already indicated that from the standpoint of earnings and
public esteem, lower nonmanual positions are frequently less desirable than manual workers' jobs, particularly when the latter
are in skilled occupations. Why, then, the greater opportunities
for social ascent through the nonspecialist employee (sluzhashchii)
job category? On occasion such entry jobs may provide access to
executive positions in stores and offices. But there is another explanation that has as much to do with the nature of the incumbents
of such jobs as with the characteristics of the jobs themselves.
Secondary school graduates who fail to gain admission to full-time
vuz enrollment (particularly the children of intelligentsia) frequently accept lower nonmanual positions, regarding them as
"temporary," pending their ultimate acceptance for full-time
study. As noted earlier, such jobs may also make it easier to
combine full-time employment with part-time study at an evening
vuz than the more physically demanding manual occupations. In
both of these cases the incumbents of lower nonmanual positions
are "passing through" these jobs, as it were, rather than working
their way up a strictly defined job ladder within an organization,
one of whose steps requires service in a sales, office, or clerical
occupation. Our reasoning here is admittedly speculative, how-

ever, and the need to reconcile the low status and relatively high mobility opportunities offered by such jobs in the Soviet setting remains a task for the future.

Finally, we return to an important issue initially raised in our discussion of intergenerational mobility. The relatively limited opportunities to move from manual workers' to nonmanual specialists' positions within the course of a work career should be seen in the light of the substantial "social distance" frequently covered by movement within manual occupations. The change in income, social standing, and access to cultural amenities associated with an occupational life-history that begins with a job as farm worker, collective farmer, or unskilled industrial worker and ends with a job as skilled industrial worker may be no less significant for the perception of opportunities for social advancement than similar changes associated with skilled worker-to-nonmanual specialist mobility. Quantitative precision is impossible here, but the former type of movement is obviously more frequent than the latter. One difficulty in the analysis is that Soviet mobility studies do not distinguish the category of semiskilled workers: workers are only "unskilled," "skilled," or "highly skilled." Relying on these classification and the data assembled in Table 4.10 would suggest that in recent years something on the order of one-half to two-thirds of those who begin their work careers in unskilled urban or rural jobs (and then migrate to the city) attain skilled manual occupations (or at least move out of the lowest-skilled occupations) in the course of their work careers. It is certainly possible that these figures may exaggerate somewhat the "typical" rates of mobility within manual occupational strata, particularly in small towns and among rural migrants whose first urban jobs are normally in low-skilled construction or industrial occupations.[42] But it hardly seems appropriate to accept Soviet sources when they provide evidence of low manual worker-to-intelligentsia mobility and to ignore the same sources when they point to substantial rates of career mobility within manual occupations. We take it as established that the latter type of mobility is a frequent experience among Soviet urban workers. For those who enter the work force in low-skilled manual jobs and do not set their sights on higher-level nonmanual occupations there may be strong grounds for "optimistic" perceptions of the opportunity structure. For those who aspire to intelligentsia status, postsecondary schooling prior to entry into the labor market has become increasingly necessary.

Although the image of the worker-to-engineer or even the worker-to-plant director sequence has certainly not disappeared from the occupational literature, the latter now often stresses a less ambitious sequence, one that is more readily realizable:

> How was the "growth" of a worker usually publicized (in the past — M. Y.)? We wrote that as soon as he becomes a leading worker he necessarily studies at an evening higher educational institution and becomes an engineer.... But it is obvious that the functions of a worker and engineer are fundamentally different, and genuine growth consists in the mastery of one's skill rather than movement up the occupational ladder.[43]

These remarks point to a serious social problem — the need to moderate the overambitious occupational aspirations of the increasing number of Soviet youngsters who complete a secondary education. Countless sociological studies have demonstrated that the great majority of such youngsters aspire to advanced schooling and to intelligentsia occupational status. Obviously, most are destined to be disappointed, to remain workers. Hence the increased concern for tempering youngsters' unrealistic occupational ambitions, glorifying "workers' dynasties" (families in which successive generations have been workers), and stressing opportunities for short-range mobility — mobility within working-class occupations. But the difficult process of adapting relatively highly educated youth to manual occupational roles has also created pressures for changes in managerial style and has contributed to posing the issue of "participation" at the work place. These are matters to which we now turn.

Notes

1. V. N. Shubkin, "The Utilization of Quantitative Methods in the Empirical Sociological Study of Problems of Job Placement and Occupational Choice," in A. G. Aganbegian ed., Kolichestvennye metody v sotsiologicheskikh issledovaniiakh, Novosibirsk, 1964, p. 168.

2. Filosofskii slovar', Moscow, 1963, p. 277, cited in M. N. Rutkevich, "Processes of Social Shifting and the Concept of 'Social Mobility,'" Filosofskie nauki, 1970, no. 5, p. 21.

3. M. N. Rutkevich, "The Intelligentsia as a Social Group of Socialist Society and Its Increasing Similarity to the Working Class of the USSR," in M. N. Rutkevich ed., Izmenenie sotsial'noi struktury sotsialisticheskogo obshchestva, Sverdlovsk, 1965, p. 30.

4. Ibid., p. 26; V. N. Shubkin in Kolichestvennye metody, p. 169.

5. Bernard Barber, Social Stratification (New York: Harcourt, Brace and World, Inc., 1957), p. 356.

6. S. M. Lipset and R. Bendix, Social Mobility in Industrial Society (Berkeley and Los Angeles: University of California Press, 1962), pp. 1-2.

7. M. N. Rutkevich, "Changes in the Social Structure of Soviet Society and the Intelligentsia," in G. V. Osipov ed., Sotsiologiia v SSSR, Vol. I, Moscow, 1965, p. 410.

8. M. N. Rutkevich and F. R. Filippov, Sotsial'nye peremeshcheniia, Moscow, 1970, pp. 41-42. See also F. R. Filippov's formulation in "Social Mobility as a Factor in the Establishment of Social Homogeneity," in M. N. Rutkevich ed., Protsessy izmeneniia sotsial'noi struktury v sovetskom obshchestve, Sverdlovsk, 1967, pp. 97-98: "'Vertical' social mobility signifies the shift to another social stratum. In this process the movement 'upward' is a shift to a stratum characterized by more complex and responsible character of labor...."

9. V. N. Shubkin in Kolichestvennye metody, p. 173.

10. R. V. Ryvkina, "The Study of Social-Psychological Aspects of Labor Mobility," in T. I. Zaslavskaia and R. V. Ryvkina, Metodologicheskie problemy sotsiologicheskogo issledovaniia mobil'nosti trudovykh resursov, Novosibirsk, 1974, p. 100.

11. Iu. V. Arutiunian, Sotsial'naia struktura, pp. 353-55.

12. R. V. Ryvkina, p. 99.

13. The work of S. M. Lipset and R. Bendix cited in Note 6 is a major example. For a more recent illustration of this tradition, see Stephan Thernstrom, The Other Bostonians (Cambridge: Harvard University Press, 1973).

14. M. N. Rutkevich in Filosofskie nauki, 1970, no. 5, p. 18; Daniel Bertaux, "Two and a Half Models of Social Structure," in Walter Muller and Karl Ulrich Mayer, Social Stratification and Career Mobility (Paris and the Hague: Mouton, 1974), pp. 117-51.

15. V. N. Shubkin in Kolichestvennye metody, pp. 258-61.

16. S. T. Gur'ianov and V. V. Sekretariuk, Prizvanie i professiia, Moscow, 1974, p. 30.

17. M. N. Rutkevich in Sotsiologicheskie issledovaniia, 1975, no. 1, p. 67.

18. Iu. V. Arutiunian, Sotsial'naia struktura, p. 314.

19. N. B. Lebedeva et al., p. 409.

20. For example, the Leningrad study whose results are given in Table 4.2 showed that specialists' children constituted the following proportions of current (1970) incumbents of specialists' positions: among persons in "skilled mental work" — 30%; among persons in "highly skilled scientific-technical work" — 42%; and among managerial personnel — 21%. Roughly similar results were found in the Kazan study cited in Table 4.2. In the latter study, however, the share of intelligentsia children was highest among persons in "creative occupations" (49%).

21. The anomalous exceptions include writers and artists. The high share of individuals of manual social origins shown in Table 4.4 for these groups may reflect the special circumstances of the Belorussian Republic or a loose definition of writers and artists.

22. Other studies of engineers show a distinctly larger proportion recruited from working-class and peasant families. See Irkutskii gosudarstvennii universitet imeni A. A. Zhdanova, Sotsial'nye problemy novykh gorodov vostochnoi Sibirii, Irkutsk, 1971, p. 99.

23. Indirect evidence of this is provided in the Kazan study. Among individuals beginning their work careers in specialists' positions prior to 1942, less than 20% were the children of specialists. In the 1960s, among those beginning their work careers in specialists' positions close to 40% were the children of

specialists. See Iu. V. Arutiunian ed., Sotsial'noe i natsional'noe, pp. 46-47.

24. S. M. Miller, "Comparative Social Mobility," Current Sociology, vol. IX, 1960, no. 1, p. 7.

25. The occupational distribution of the respondents (the "children's" generation) almost certainly overstated the inflow into specialists' occupations. Respondents were distributed as follows: 41% — intelligentsia; 50% — workers; 9% — lower nonmanual employees.

26. The composition of the sample (the "children's" generation) was: workers — 70.5%; engineering-technical personnel — 21.5%; lower nonmanual employees — 8%.

27. E. K. Vasil'eva, Sotsial'no-professional'nyi uroven', p. 49.

28. However, the greater opportunities of technical specialists' children may reflect the situation prevailing in an earlier period (the 1940s and 1950s). The "parents'" generation in Arutiunian's study refers to the fathers of the currently employed. If the schooling gap between managers and technicians has narrowed since, the situation described here may no longer prevail.

29. Unlike the situation prevailing in urban areas, it seems reasonable to rank lower-level nonmanual employees above most or all manual strata in the countryside.

30. Arutiunian found that between one-half and two-thirds of managerial personnel and technical specialists in rural areas of the Tatar Republic, Krasnodar Territory, and Kalinin Region were the children of common laborers and other manual strata. Iu. V. Arutiunian, Sotsial'naia struktura, p. 314.

31. N. B. Lebedeva et al., pp. 412-13.

32. G. Kh. Popov and G. A. Dzhavadova, Upravlenie i problema kadrov, Moscow, 1972, p. 162.

33. Tsentral'noe upravlenie narodno-khoziaistvennogo ucheta gosplana SSSR, Trud v SSSR, Moscow, 1936, pp. 308, 312, 316.

34. Approximately two-thirds of a sample of "young" Leningrad engineers in the late 1960s had moved directly from graduation from secondary school to admission to a higher educational institution. Only 10% of those who were in the work force prior to admission to a vuz had more than two years of work experience. S. A. Kugel' and O. M. Nikandrov, Molodye inzhenery, Moscow, 1971, p. 173.

35. V. G. Afanas'ev ed., Nauchnoe upravlenie obshchestvom, Issue 7, Moscow, 1973, p. 235.

36. TsSU, Narodnoe khoziaistvo SSSR v 1973, p. 711.

37. N. A. Aitov ed., Nekotorye problemy sotsial'nykh peremeshchenii v SSSR, p. 30.

38. N. Aitov, Tekhnicheskii progress i dvizhenie rabochikh kadrov, Moscow, 1972, pp. 32-33; N. Aitov, "Social Mobility in the USSR," in Institut sotsiologicheskikh issledovanii, Akademii nauk SSSR, Institut filosofii i sotsiologii Pol'skoi Akademii nauk, Problemy razvitiia sotsial'noi struktury obshchestva v Sovetskom soiuze i Pol'she, Moscow and Warsaw, 1974, pp. 314-15. The 1965 study applied to Ufa and Orenburg; the 1970 study, to Ufa only.

39. N. Aitov, Tekhnicheskii progress, p. 33.

40. N. Aitov, "Social Mobility," p. 315.

41. N. Aitov, Tekhnicheskii progress, p. 32.

42. I. I. Zaslavskaia and V. A. Kalmyk eds., Sotsial'no-ekonomicheskoe razvitie sela i migratsiia naseleniia, Novosibirsk, 1972, pp. 76-77.

43. G. M. Kochetov, "Occupational Inclinations and Job Placement of Secondary School Graduates," Shkola i proizvodstvo, 1968, no. 7, p. 25.

5 HIERARCHY AT THE WORK PLACE AND "PARTICIPATION IN MANAGEMENT"

Thus far our examination of some aspects of Soviet social inequality has centered on the distribution of income, schooling, mobility opportunities, and — somewhat incidentally — prestige. We have had nothing to say explicitly about the distribution of power. In this chapter we approach the issue of power, albeit in a "microsocial" context. Our focus here is on the distribution of authority and control over the work situation in the individual enterprise. This may appear to be a narrow and limited context in which to examine the issue of power in Soviet society. But it is one of the few contexts in which this issue has been at least on occasion explicitly and seriously discussed in the Soviet literature. We refer to some of the literature on enterprise management and industrial (and rural) sociology which has been concerned with the structure of decision-making at the plant (or farm), the relations between "superiors" and "subordinates," and the empirical study of workers' participation (or the lack of it) in management. In short, Soviet material bearing on inequality of authority and control is available in relative abundance at the level of the individual enterprise. Although a review of this material seems justified in its own right, especially in a study of Soviet social inequality, our discussion will also seek to show its bearing on the broader question of power in the society at large.

But our principal justification for focusing on the management of the individual economic unit is to disclose an aspect of Soviet life that has not received the attention it deserves: the recent emergence of pressures for broadening participation in decision-making at the work place, for the democratization of the work place. Unfortunately, our review will also be a chronicle of the failure of these efforts.

Managerial Ideology and the Formal
Structure of Authority

Recent years have witnessed the emergence of a heightened interest in the "science of management" in the Soviet Union. The management literature which has accompanied this interest embodies a philosophy of management, a set of presuppositions concerning the functional requirements of "relations of management," which may serve as a useful introduction to our examination of the structure of authority in the Soviet enterprise. What follows is our attempt to convey the essence of these presuppositions as they appear in some of the more authoritative management literature. As illustrations of the latter we rely chiefly on the work of V. G. Afanas'ev and Iu. E. Volkov.[1]

Although all memebers of the socialist society are simultaneously "managers" and "managed," the effective functioning of any subsystem of this society — such as an economic enterprise — requires the clear delineation of "relations of subordination." These relations prevail between those who "direct" (or "manage") the organization and those who "execute" the directives of the former. This separation of functions between "the managers and the managed" (or the "subjects" and "objects" of management) is personified in the factory in the relations between ordinary workers, on the one hand, and the foreman, shop superintendent, and factory director, on the other. Relations among the latter groups, as well as between them and workers, may be characterized as relations of subordination. Thus the formal organization of the Soviet enterprise, as of the production system as a whole, is explicitly recognized as a hierarchical structure in which successively higher positions in the organization correspond to "functions ... which are increasingly purely managerial."[2] Such functions are essentially those of planning, coordination, and control.

Although the Soviet management literature acknowledges the "surface similarity" between the general approach outlined here and traditional management philosophy in capitalist societies, it also stresses certain differences. The management function is not performed on behalf of a class of private owners of capital whose interests dominate the production process but on behalf of "society as a whole."[3] Moreover, the need to concentrate managerial functions in the hands of a special stratum of "professional managers" presumably does not conflict with steadily increasing opportunities for workers to influence and participate in manage-

ment activity.[4] We shall examine this latter claim in some detail
below but present it here merely as a frequently reiterated theme
in Soviet management literature.

When we turn to the details of management organization and the
authority structure in the enterprise, the language of Soviet organization theory is often supplemented or replaced by the more
traditional "Leninist principles of management." While some of
these are drawn from the political lexicon of Party history and
may seem more rhetorical than substantive, they are as much
part of the "tone" of Soviet management philosophy as the more
"scientific" organization theory briefly reviewed above. Indeed,
at least on the surface, there seems to be a striking similarity
between the latter (with its explicit acceptance of hierarchy, relations of subordination, the dichotomy between managers and managed) and some of the "Leninist principles of management." What
are these principles and what bearing do they have on the distribution of authority in the enterprise?

1. The principle of "unity of political and economic leadership."
This is essentially a way of affirming that the production program
and economic measures that are to be implemented by any level
of management have their source in the economic policy of the
Communist Party. This follows from the Party's leading role in
directing Soviet economic development. Hence the manager must
be guided by "general state interests," not by "narrow departmen-
tal, local interests." To perform his functions effectively,

...the manager must know the policy of the Party, master Marxist-Leninist theory, have a broad political orientation, and be able to correctly combine current
economic work with political activity....[5]

The implementation of this principle requires close and continuing contact between managerial personnel and the Party organization at the enterprise. The latter serves simultaneously as
a resource that management draws on in meeting plan assignments
and as a "monitor" of management's performance. The discussions of the Party organization's role in the enterprise that appear
in the management literature, however, stress that in no case does
the Party assume the operational functions of managerial personnel, that it never becomes a "substitute" for management.[6] This
point is related to principle 3 below.

2. The principle of "democratic centralism." This is a principle of Party organization which, in its application to enterprise
management, is reducible to the idea that the "organizing and

directing role" of management staffs must be combined with the encouragement of initiative "from below" and must take account of the peculiarities of particular enterprises and localities.[7] It is typically stated in such broad terms that it is difficult to see how it can be anything but a very general guide to managerial behavior. However, it is precisely its nonspecific and all-inclusive character that has made it possible to appeal to this principle to justify arguments for broadening the base of participation in decision-making at the enterprise.

3. The principle of "one-man management" (edinonachalie). This deserves more careful examination than the above two principles, partly because it moves us into the operational details of the authority structure at the enterprise, and partly because of the danger of too facile an interpretation based on the authoritarian image conveyed by the concept. That Soviet management has had a markedly authoritarian character can hardly be doubted, but the principle of one-man management is not reducible to the absolute rule of the factory director. Let us see how this principle is formulated in the management literature and applied in managerial practice.

The principle of one-man management in the management of production consists in the following: the leadership of each production unit (enterprise, shop, section) is assigned to a single executive who is endowed by the state with the necessary rights to manage, and who bears full responsibility for the work of the given unit. All individuals working in the unit are obligated to fulfill the instructions of the executive.

To correctly implement the principle of one-man management it is of great importance that there be a clear demarcation of obligations, rights, and responsibilities.... Every employee must be subordinate to only one individual, from whom he receives an assignment and to whom he is accountable.

In actual practice the principle of one-man management in industry is implemented as follows: the director of the enterprise is appointed by the ministry and directs the enterprise in the interests of the people on the basis of one-man management, answering to the ministry for the activity of the enterprise which he heads. The director of the plant is the highest one-man manager at the enterprise. On his instructions the superintendents of shops and departments, foremen, and other (managerial — M. Y.) personnel...are appointed and relieved of employment. His instructions must be fulfilled by all personnel at the plant without question.

The shop superintendent is the one-man manager for all individuals working in the shop. The senior foreman, correspondingly, is the one-man manager at his section; the shift foreman — on his shift.[8]

What appears initially as a single "principle of management" is translated into an integrated set of organizational rules. A number of important features emerge from this lengthy quotation. Perhaps the most obvious point is that every level of the organization, not only the enterprise as a whole, has its own one-man manager. The authority of the foreman relative to the workers under his supervision appears to be of the same order (absolute) as that of the shop superintendent relative to his direct subordinates. Not only is authority individualized in one-man management but responsibility is as well. Indeed, the stress on fixing individual responsibility for the performance of a particular unit of the enterprise is no less than the emphasis on individual authority. This is symbolized by frequent warnings against obezlichka — the evasion of personal responsibility for a unit's performance. One-man management fixed this responsibility on the single source of authority in the unit. Reliance on "unity of command" (every employee must be directly subordinate to only one superior) is expressly designed to avoid both conflicting orders and the evasion of personal responsibility. Furthermore, accountability is always structured "upward," i.e., managerial personnel are always accountable to their superiors, never to those whom they manage, just as they are always appointed to their posts by a "higher" level of management (the ministry in the case of the director, the director in the case of the shop superintendent, etc.).

There is one qualification that must be introduced at this point. Our discussion thus far has been modeled on the industrial plant. There are no significant departures from this model of formal organization in the case of the state farm. In the case of the collective farm, however, the formal process of selection of top management differs from that in the industrial plant. The chairman and managing board of the collective farm are "elected" by the "highest organ" of the farm, the general membership meeting of collective farm members.[9] We will return later to the question of how much difference this makes for the distribution of effective power over the farm's affairs. For the present the point worth stressing is that, aside from the formal management selection process, the principle of one-man management is also acknowledged to be the guilding principle of farm administration, with emphasis on "the strict administrative subordination of the primary production units (brigades — M. Y.) to the leaders of the various farm subdivisions, and the latter to the collective farm chairman."[10]

It is apparent that, whatever the form of enterprise to which it

is applied, one-man management is essentially a means of specifying the "relations of subordination" which in the Soviet view (although obviously not only in the Soviet view) are inherent in the
effective management of all organizations. The stress on clearly
defined areas of responsibility and lines of authority is all directed
to one objective: "...the fulfillment of the production program,
since under all conditions management must take as its point of
departure the priority of production requirements as the first and
principal task of the enterprise."[11] The plant's production program itself, following its ratification — at least in its broad features — by the appropriate "superior" agency (ministry or combine), is transmitted from the director downward through the various one-man managers corresponding to each "level" of the organization. The number of such "levels" differs, of course, depending on the size and technological characteristics of the organization, but a typical Soviet organization chart for the "basic
production" activity of the enterprise (excluding staff and auxiliary
positions) will show the line of authority moving downward from
plant director to shop superintendent to section foreman to brigade
leaders to production workers.[12]

Seen in this light, as a specification of "relations of subordination," we may be surprised initially to learn that one-man management is compatible with "collegiality" in management. Although
the notion of collegiality is typically not accorded the status of a
"principle of management," it is frequently treated as a necessary
supplement to one-man management. What meaning, if any, can
we attach to this coupling of what, on the surface, appear to be
diverse concepts? Although the notion of collegiality readily lends
itself to empty rhetoric, the essential idea is that management is
encouraged to involve all personnel of the enterprise "in the discussion of the most important problems of the operation of the
enterprise, shop, and section."[13] In its more extreme formulations the concept of collegiality is reflected in the claim that "At
the present time it is difficult to find any important problem which
is decided by enterprise management exclusively on its own
(edinolichno) without first ascertaining collective opinion."[14] The
latter is normally interpreted to mean the views of the factory
trade union organization, the Party, and Komsomol units and the
resolutions adopted at production conferences. In its more concrete form the principle of collegiality in management may be
illustrated by the expectation that in appointing and releasing a

139

shop superintendent the plant director will "consider" the views of the factory union committee. [15]

We are not concerned for the moment with ascertaining the degree to which these prescriptions are realized in managerial practice or the sector of "collective opinion" which receives closest attention. What should be obvious from this brief review of the uses of the collegiality concept, however, is that the latter is certainly compatible with, and indeed may facilitate, one-man management. The function of collegiality is to help the manager make the "best" decision. But his authority to make the decision and the expectation that it will be followed "without question" remain unaffected. The point is simply that the recommendations made in the name of collegiality — at least those not emanating from the Party organization — are of a "consultative" rather than "binding" character.

Our preliminary examination of Soviet managerial philosophy and formal organizational structure is intended mainly to set the stage for our discussion of the issue of participation in decision-making at the enterprise. What has already become apparent, however, is that despite its distinctive terminology (embodied in the Leninist principles of management), Soviet managerial ideology is not strikingly distinctive in content. In fact, it does not seem to depart significantly from some versions of what, in the West, has been labeled as the "classical theory of organization." It was not V. I. Lenin but H. Fayol, one of the founding fathers of classical theory, who, in reviewing some of the principles of management "which I have most frequently had to apply," formulated one of them as follows:

Subordination of individual interest to general interest. This principle calls to mind the fact that in a business the interest of one employee or group of employees should not prevail over that of the concern, that the interests of the home should come before that of its members, and that the interest of the State should have pride of place over that of one citizen or group of citizens. [16]

It seems clear that Soviet management ideology has had little difficulty assimilating some early examples of Western "classical" principles of management. It is not only Fayol's general formulation cited above that Soviet management philosophy would find congenial; his concepts of unity of command, unity of direction, and scalar chain, among others, have become part of the common parlance of Soviet management philosophy — sometimes under the general rubric of one-man management.

The "Humanization" of Soviet Management

It is important to realize that most of the ideas we have just discussed, including one-man management, were originally enshrined as "principles of management" during a historically unique period, that of the prewar five-year plans. Although these principles remain an integral part of current management philosophy, they are rooted in a work situation which obviously differed in important respects from the present. The stress on the clearcut delineation of lines of authority and responsibility, the expectation of unquestioning obedience to the instructions of superiors, the high degree of concentration of decision-making power combined with often perfunctory appeals for "initiative from below," all suggest an authoritarian style of management behavior which must have seemed especially appropriate for the early planning years. It is well to recall that this was a period in which the bulk of new entrants to the industrial work force consisted of unskilled, uprooted peasants or their children, unfamiliar with both the technology and work discipline of their new work sites. The enormous task of rapidly adapting this new labor force to the disciplined work routines of the factory seemed to require the strict ordering of formal authority relationships which is so much a part of one-man management. The apparent absence (beginning in 1931-32) of significant unemployment compounded the problem of maintaining effective work discipline. Nor were the turbulent years of war and postwar reconstruction which followed conducive to an easing of the "command" style of enterprise management.

A striking feature of more recent years is that, without the explicit abandonment of the Leninist principles of management or significant alterations in the formal structure of authority within the enterprise, a new theme has begun to permeate Soviet management literature. This theme stresses that the effective performance of managerial functions has become increasingly complex, not only because of more advanced technology but because of changes in the "human factor." The result has been the emergence of a Soviet version of the "human relations" approach to management. This has been accompanied by the acknowledgement that Western human relations' literature — just as the earlier writings on scientific management by Frederick Taylor — contain "rational elements" which must be "assimilated, interpreted in a Marxist methodological framework, and be applied in practice."[17] Human relations in industry are not a peculiarity of capitalist

society, and there is no reason for Marxist sociology to permit
their study to become "a monopoly of bourgeois sociology."[18]
Thus, as we shall see below, concepts drawn from or inspired by
Western human relations literature are in the process of becoming
incorporated into Soviet managerial theory.

The legitimation of the theme of human relations signals the
need for a modification of the traditional authoritarian management
style. It reflects the recognition that the effective economic
performance of an enterprise depends significantly on "the solidarity
of the collective, the degree of confidence of the collective
in its leadership, the quality of interpersonal relations, the attitude
(nastroenie) of the workers...."[19] It is not only the perfection
of a formal structure of authority that counts but an "improvement
in the psychological climate of the collective" through methods of
supervision that stress dignified treatment of subordinates and increased
reliance on methods of "self-regulation" rather than
purely external controls. Even the manager's presumed duty to
"fulfill the plan at any price" is no longer an excuse for ignoring
the interests of the members of the collective. Moreover, managerial
personnel must recognize that many jobs continue to be
"uninteresting, arduous, dirty, monotonous..." and that workers
must be imbued with a sense of the social significance of such
work if it is to be performed adequately. This requires a "benevolent,
comradely atmosphere" and supportive attitudes of managerial
personnel.[20]

However moderate or even trivial some of these strictures
may appear, they must be seen as part of a new "tone" in Soviet
management philosophy, and they undoubtedly have had
some impact on managerial behavior. Before turning to some
elaborations and illustrations of the human relations approach
under Soviet circumstances, let us ask why it should have appeared
at all.

Perhaps the most obvious explanation lies in the changed composition
of the work force. Young people now entering the urban
labor market are less likely to be displaced peasants or their
children. They are mainly the offspring of urban workers and
have been reared under the "looser" controls of urban life. They
are substantially more educated than their predecessors of the
prewar industrialization period. As late as 1939 less than 10% of
industrial workers had received seven years or more of schooling;
by the late 1960s in excess of one-half had attained this level.[21]
Crude and authoritarian methods of supervision at the work
place — symbolized by the "peremptory command"[22] — which

seemed appropriate in the past are less so now. In the words of two Soviet industrial sociologists:

> While in the past people were capable of tolerating the 'inconvenience' of rude interpersonal relations and even ignoring them — since they were under the pressure of material need — now, under changed circumstances, they are just as sensitive to rudeness, coarseness, bureaucratism as they were in the past to need and deprivation.[23]

But the problem is not simply that the extended schooling and urban upbringing of workers require a more "cultured" style of supervision at the work place. One of the principal findings of Soviet industrial sociology has been that the extension of education has created aspirations for a "creative" job content that the existing structure of job opportunities frequently cannot satisfy.[24] The result has been a "surplus" of educated workers in the special sense that their formal schooling is in excess of that required for effective performance of the many routine, manual, or assembly-line types of jobs that must be filled. Much of the recent Soviet concern with job dissatisfaction is explicitly centered on this issue of the apparent "disproportion" between the level of formal schooling and limited opportunities for intellectually rewarding work. The perennial problem of excessive labor turnover is no longer interpreted simplistically as largely reflecting the search for the "long ruble" or irrationalities in the wage structure but is seen as significantly affected by workers' aspirations for a "richer" job content.[25] The acknowledgement of substantial work dissatisfaction has posed the issue of how to "compensate" workers for the gap between their limited work content and the aspirations fostered by extended schooling. One means of offsetting this dissatisfaction, according to the sociologist whose work has probably contributed most to the discussion of this issue, is the

> development of all types of participation of workers in the management of production. The highly educated worker now coming to the factory is prepared to assume greater responsibility for the affairs of production and the organization of labor. It is perfectly obvious that much more must be done to develop all forms of initiative in the sphere of management than we have done up to now....[26]

Given the context of this statement, it should not be interpreted as a merely perfunctory appeal for "collegiality" in management, although the failure to spell out the form that worker participation in management might take obviously weakens its force. It is, in any case, a proposal directed to meeting a serious problem. What must be stressed here is that under conditions in which the scope for genuine worker participation in managerial decisions is insignificant or nonexistent, this proposal becomes a persuasive argument for a more participatory, less authoritarian style of leadership at the plant. And it is primarily with matters of managerial style, rather than with the substance of decision-making power, that the Soviet human relations approach is concerned. In this sense Soviet sociologists' studies of work attitudes and the linking of work dissatisfaction to extended education have helped to legitimate a human relations approach to management.

We have seen that this approach stresses the importance of a solidaristic psychological climate and a higher "culture" of interpersonal relations at the enterprise. But these are rather broadly stated prescriptions. What are their more specific implications for managerial behavior? One illustration is provided by the "Recommendations to Managers" issued at large plants and designed to improve the work of supervision by equipping managerial staffs with "social-psychological knowledge." A Soviet volume on industrial sociology which urges the assimilation of human relations' techniques cites with obvious approval the following rules at a Dnepropetrovsk steel plant:

A good manager must not only think of the technology of production but also be a "guardian" of his subordinates; he must be aware of their frame of mind.

An inseparable feature of the style of leadership is courtesy, friendliness, and tact. Instructions issued in a firm but courteous manner always lead to better results than those issued rudely.

Do not wait for a subordinate to be the first to show friendship and affability, but take the initiative yourself. Even if the subordinate does not immediately respond, your affability will ultimately be worthwhile.

The subordinates of a poor manager live in a world of rumors, conjectures.... A good manager keeps his subordinates informed about the general state of affairs....

Do not "throw yourself" on someone who has made a mistake. Even when you are about to reprimand someone, it is better to begin with praise....[27]

Another illustration of the attempt to affect specific norms of managerial behavior is the suggestion that managers recognize and cultivate "informal relations" (and groups) at the enterprise. Exclusive reliance on the formal structures and instruments of authority generates a superfluous flow of official directives, instructions, written orders. Increased reliance on "informal" modes of communication can help to overcome the sense of "alienation" between managers and subordinates, make for frankness in their discussions of production problems — apparently something that is often not present — and improve the quality of information received by managers. Finally, in what must be regarded as a somewhat rhetorical flourish by the Soviet writers on whose work we rely here, "informal relations promote...the democratization of management."[28]

Despite the apparently trivial and obvious nature of some of these recommendations and guidelines, their significance should not be dismissed. They are part of a relatively recent theme in Soviet management literature and a response to new problems. All of them have this in common: they point to an effort to inculcate a more "humane," looser, less rigid style of supervision in the enterprise while leaving the Leninist principles of management — and one-man management in particular — essentially undisturbed. We may take this as a hallmark of what might be called Soviet human relations theory. A nonauthoritarian style of management is encouraged, while the substance of managerial power — the exclusion of workers from significant decision-making — remains intact. Nowhere is this more clearly expressed than in a Soviet writer's (I. P. Volkov) recent attempt to elaborate a typology of management styles, specifying their various advantages and disadvantages. No single style, according to Volkov, is appropriate for all circumstances. A "directive" (authoritarian) style may be appropriate for wartime or other emergency situations, but under normal conditions it stifles initiative. A "permissive" style may be required in research institutes or where work is highly individualized. However, the "norm" should be ("is," according to Volkov) a collegial style of management. A collegial manager's subordinates "participate actively" in the decision-making process, but the manager "leaves to himself the right of final decision." Perhaps the most significant quality of this ideal type of Soviet manager is that "his art consists of the ability to use power without appealing to it."[29]

We can hardly judge from our review of the literature how frequently the various recommendations and models offered under the rubrics of human relations or collegiality are applied in managerial practice. There is some evidence of considerable resistance by managerial staffs to their implementation.[30] But their very emergence in the management literature testifies to the search for management methods more appropriate to the changing composition of the current Soviet work force and its aspirations. This search has gone beyond the issue of management style and has touched, sometimes hesitantly, on the more sensitive issue of the structure of power in the enterprise.

Beyond "Humanization":
The Issue of Participation in Management

The fog of rhetoric surrounding the theme of "democratization of management" is an obstacle to the analysis of an important issue in Soviet society: the search for more effective modes of organization in economic enterprises. The problem is, in part, that worker participation in management is regarded as something that has already been substantially attained and to which homage is constantly paid. Moreover, the further extension of such participation is an officially approved value. This often makes it difficult to distinguish between ritualistic celebrations of an alleged "achievement" and serious attempts to pose the problem. The latter almost invariably contain elements of the former. Concrete proposals for changing the distribution of managerial authority are typically presented as improvements in a system which is already highly participatory — when it obviously is not.

Nonetheless there is unmistakable evidence that recent years have witnessed an upsurge of efforts to broaden the social base of participation in management functions. These efforts appear to have been largely unsuccessful thus far. But the discussions which ensued were accompanied by specific proposals for the redistribution of managerial authority, revealing studies of the limited extent of worker (and peasant) participation in decision-making, and a remarkable but short-lived experiment in the democratization of management. What follows is a review of the limited but distinct forms recently assumed by the issue of "production democracy" in the Soviet Union.

The economic reforms of 1965 provided the setting in which serious public discussion of the democratization of management began to emerge. Among their other features, the reforms were intended to increase the autonomy of individual enterprises by reducing the number of centrally fixed plan assignments and increasing the share of profits that could be retained and allocated at the enterprise. They did not directly provide for changes in the structure of authority within enterprises. In this sense they appeared to offer promise of "decentralization" rather than "democratization" of management. But the Party resolutions which accompanied the reforms stressed that they "provide the economic prerequisites for wider participation by the masses in the running of production." A. N. Kosygin's speech at the time made the same point: "Better management is impossible unless it becomes more democratic and unless the participation of the masses is considerably extended.... Every worker should be made to feel that he is one of the owners of the factory."[31]

Indeed, there was a certain logic to linking the opportunities offered by the reform to the issue of the structure of authority in the plant. Under conditions in which the scope for autonomy by the enterprise was severely limited by a myriad of assignments and instructions from higher agencies (whether these were regional economic councils or industrial ministries), the possibility of effectively broadening the social base of participation in management could hardly be taken seriously. Worker participation could mean little more than conscientious performance of job tasks assigned by managerial personnel. The reform, by appearing to enlarge the scope of decisions that could be made at the enterprise (particularly by permitting increases in decentralized investment and premium payments out of retained profits), provided a kind of "platform" for reopening the issue of the structure of managerial authority at the enterprise.

One of the first questions to be raised in the years immediately following the reforms was the need to limit the applicability of one-man management. As one of the participants in this discussion put it, the increased involvement of workers in management required that "a clear line of demarcation be established between the rights and obligations of the one-man manager and the collective organs of management at enterprises."[32] In this context such "collective organs" included the factory trade union and production conferences through which the principles of "collegiality" and "democratic centralism" were formally implemented. The need for more clearly defining (i.e., restricting) the rights of management officials arose from the "considerable discrepancy" which had developed between the theory of participation by the masses in management and actual managerial practice. This was a heritage of the prereform period, when management would frequently ignore "rational" proposals of the collective organs and thereby even generate "hostility" among workers toward the factory administration. But the reforms would not automatically force management to cease ignoring "the will of the collective." What was required was a specification of those decisions which should fall within the authority of the collective organs and whose implementation would become "juridically obligatory" for the plant director.[33] The distribution of premiums was offered as one example of such a decision. The writer who offered this illustration hastened to add that it would not conflict with the principle of one-man management. The latter would continue to apply to all "operational" or "technical" decisions at the enterprise. The allocation of premiums was to be regarded as an aspect of "social management" falling within the competence of the plant's collective organs.

The point to be stressed here is not the specific, relatively modest proposal concerning the authority to allocate premium funds, but the fact that a much larger issue could now be treated as an open question:

...which elements of managerial activity should be implemented solely by management, which through the obligatory participation of the collective, and which exclusively by the collective.[34]

Some of the literature urging the "democratization of management" in the years immediately following the economic reforms of 1965 exhibited an unprecedented boldness in criticizing prevailing interpretations of the Leninist principles of management. As an illustration we may consider a volume of essays by members of the philosophy faculty of Moscow State University edited by V. A. Fomin. One of the contributors noted that the concept of democratic centralism had been reduced by some to the idea of "initiative from below and leadership from above"; in other cases it was treated simply as the need to subordinate one level of an organization to another. This had unduly narrowed a concept whose real intent was to provide for "participation in management by every worker"[35] (emphasis in the original — M. Y.). The result was that democratic centralism had often been transformed into "bureaucratic centralism," causing "harm which we cannot yet fully estimate."[36] Perhaps the most challenging aspect of such criticisms was directed against the simplistic identification of "democracy" with the existence of socialized property. The latter, however, was only a necessary condition for democratic management, not identical with it.[37] The very concept of property was typically viewed — mistakenly — from a "juridical" aspect only, i.e., from the standpoint of its legal form of ownership. In this view the greater the amount of socialized property and the more centralized its management, the "higher" the form of property. But for Marxists the juridical aspect of property is only an "external cover" for "real economic relations." The analysis of property systems in their broader, nonjuridical aspects must encompass "the totality of relations of production, exchange, and distribution."[38] The distinction made here (in a 1967 publication reporting on a 1966 conference) between the "juridical" and "real" aspects of property was to become a hallmark of the literature urging the democratization of management (pages 151 and 159 below). "Real" socialization implied not only some form of public (state or cooperative) "possession" (vladenie) of property but collective control over the utilization and "disposal" (rasporia-zhenie) of property.

The very manner of posing the issue of evolving a more partici-patory mode of management in the postreform period suggests a seriousness of intent that was absent in earlier years. Some of the formulations of this issue in the work of Iu. E. Volkov may serve as an additional illustration. Writing in 1970, Volkov stressed that involving workers in management functions cannot mean simply providing opportunities for them to assist mana-gerial personnel in the latter's efforts to strengthen work disci-pline, locate "production reserves," and generally to "improve production." While all this is necessary it is not enough, for the main feature of management is decision-making in the enterprise. Those who make decisions

possess the highest rights of management. And if we are to speak of democracy in management, its highest manifestation consists in the fact that decisions are made with the participation of the masses and are implemented under their con-trol.[39]

This was not the usual participatory rhetoric, for Volkov was pointing out that to conceive of worker participation as exclusively an aid to managerial staffs in the performance of the latter's func-tions was to "stand things upside down." Workers must themselves assume managerial functions because in a socialist society "they are the masters" of the production process (Volkov's readers would understand that "are" meant "should be").[40] Volkov also called for sociological studies of the effectiveness of existing forms of participation and the working out of "specific recommendations" designed to extend them.

Although our discussion thus far has focused on the emergence of the theme of worker participation in management in an industrial setting, suffice it to note for the present that it also appeared in agriculture. The search for more effective modes of work organi-zation was, if anything, more pressing there than in industry.[41]

It is all too easy to dismiss the increased attention paid in Soviet public discourse to the issue of "production democracy" as empty phrase-making or as a facade used by the Party to reinforce its authority over management at the plant and farm. But too much has occurred in this area during the postreform period that can-not be encompassed by such a facile explanation. This should be-come apparent from our examination of the studies, policy pro-posals, and experiments bearing on participation in management.

Sociological studies. Soviet empirical studies of decision-

Social and Economic Inequality

making in economic enterprises are of interest not only for what
they reveal about the distribution of power in the producing unit
but also because they have served as vehicles for an argument:
the need for more participatory forms of economic organization.
They obviously have also served as signals of themes which political authorities (or some faction among them) deem "legitimate"
for public discussion.

Perhaps the most illuminating studies of this type have been
conducted by Iu. V. Arutiunian in rural areas. Although the latter
feature limits the applicability of his findings, Arutiunian included
rural industrial enterprises as well as collective and state farms
in his studies. He sought to determine the "distribution of rights
and power within the collective" among six socio-occupational
groups, ranging from common laborers at one extreme to higher-
level managers and specialists at the other. Arutiunian's respondents were asked to indicate whether, in their judgment, they
"exercised an influence in deciding major questions of the collective." Thus what emerged were subjective perceptions of influence in the enterprise, differentiated by occupational status of
respondents. We show Arutiunian's findings in one of the three
investigated regions in Table 5.1 (the results in the other two were
essentially the same).

Table 5.1

Percentage of Individuals Having No Influence on Major Decisions
at the Work Place, Rural Areas, Tatar Republic, 1967
(by socio-occupational group)

Socio-occupational groups	Percentage without influence on major decisions			
	on collec-tive farms	on state farms	in other enterprises	total
Higher-level managerial per-sonnel and specialists	13		20	12
Middle-level managerial per-sonnel and specialists	17	36		20
Nonmanual employees	33	48	37	38
Machine operators	54	45	45	50
Skilled manual workers	64	51	58	58
Low-skilled and unskilled manual workers	69	72	68	69
Total	63	55	50	56

Source: Iu. V. Arutiunian, Sotsial'naia struktura, p. 108.

All forms of rural economic organization were obviously hier-

150

archical in the sense that the frequency of perceived influence declined markedly as we move from the highest-ranking occupations to low-skilled and unskilled peasants and workers. Some two-thirds to three-fourths of the latter group — the most numerous rural stratum — perceived itself as without influence over important decisions in farms and other rural enterprises. Moreover, the majority of all respondents combined felt themselves to be without influence. Perhaps the most striking result was that the type of organization which in a strictly formal sense was the most participatory exhibited the lowest sense of participation among its members. The collective farm, it will be recalled, was presumably a cooperative that elected its own top management and held regular meetings of its members through which "control" over its operations was to be exercised. But the employees of state farms and rural industrial enterprises (in which "state" as distinct from "cooperative" property prevailed) experienced their roles as providing greater scope for participation in management than did collective farm members.[42]

Arutiunian did not hesitate to draw the obvious conclusion that differences in the legal form of property ownership in the Soviet setting had little impact on the distribution of control over the use of property.[43] Whatever the form of ownership, the typical worker or peasant could hardly feel himself "a master" of the production process. In a manner that departed from the typically simplistic definition of socialism, Arutiunian distinguished between "juridical" socialization (the elimination of private ownership) and "real" socialization (measured by the "degree to which the producers themselves perform the functions of management").[44] His findings clearly seemed to demonstrate that the latter kind of socialization was a long way from being achieved. In this context his formulation of the "task" ahead, although stated in general terms, flowed naturally from his research findings and illustrates the seriousness with which the issue of "production democracy" was regarded in some quarters: "The social task standing on the order of the day points to the necessity for the further democratization of the functions of control over property."[45]

None of the recent studies of urban industrial enterprises of which we are aware has replicated Arutiunian's design. But several provide additional illustrations of the kind of empirical research whose findings — at least implicitly — served to buttress Arutiunian's conclusion cited above. Each points in its own way to the limited influence of workers outside their regular (non-managerial) job functions. One study of the sources of directives issued by plant management (in a Sverdlovsk machinery plant) over the course of a year sheds a revealing light on the limited nature of "collegiality" in decision-making. Some 90% of such directives were initiated by the management staff alone, less than 1% were based on proposals submitted by individual workers, and the remainder were based on the recommendations of the "collective organs." But of the latter the vast majority concerned safety regulations. It was hardly surprising that the author concluded that one-man management was not being adequately combined with "collegiality."[46]

Another recent study of an individual plant (a tractor factor in Kishinev) is of interest chiefly because it specifies the meaning that can be attached to the concept of "worker participation in deciding important problems of the collective" within the framework of centralized planning and existing legal procedures. Such "important problems" were identified as the revision of output norms, the distribution of premiums, the preparation of drafts of production plans, the distribution of housing facilities, and the selection of new lower-level managerial staff (foreman, brigade leader). The rate of participation by workers in such decisions was typically on the order of 30%, which the author of the study characterized as "relatively low."[47]

There is no need and no basis on which to accept such findings for individual plants as typical of a broader range of industrial enterprises. If anything, they probably overstate the typical rate of worker participation in managerial decisions. Their significance, like that of Arutiunian's work, lies elsewhere. They are part of a current in the management and sociological literature which recognizes that the traditional distribution of authority and influence in the enterprise is an obstacle to effective work performance. The same is true of those Soviet studies which have found that opportunities for participation in decisions on the organization of the work process and the distribution of its rewards have important psychological correlates: they increase work satisfaction and promote a feeling of "being a master of the work place" (chuvstvo khoziaina).[48]

But are there any conceivable changes in decision-making power and work organization at enterprises that could stimulate this feeling and simultaneously be politically and economically acceptable?

Specific proposals for "democratization" of management. One of the proposals which emerged during the late 1960s called for selected categories of managerial personnel in industry to be "elected" by their subordinates rather than appointed by their superiors. When the idea was raised in 1965 (prior to the economic reform announced in September of that year) by Iu. Volkov, it was presented as something that could not be implemented "today" but would mark the "completion" of self-management in the communist society of the future.[49] By 1968, however, one of the most authoritative Soviet spokesmen for "scientific management," V. G. Afanas'ev, proposed that the time had come to introduce such elections on an experimental basis as part of the search for more participatory forms of management. Afanas'ev couched his proposal in the following terms:

> The election of enterprise managers can become one of the forms of participation in management....
> The fate of the manager is essentially in the hands of higher-level organs rather than in those of the collective which he manages. Hence the tactics adopted by some managers of orienting themselves not to those "below" them, not to gain the respect and confidence of the collective, but to those "above" them. It is not the respect of the collective which is important to them but primarily the good will of their superiors. This creates bureaucrats and zealous administrators, some of whom unfortunately have not yet been removed. This situation would be fundamentally changed if the masses had the right to elect enterprise managers....
> Elections would be an effective form of direct participation of the masses in management of enterprises.[50]

At first glance there are obvious grounds for doubting the seriousness of this proposal. What meaning could be attached to elections of either plant directors or lower managerial staffs by a working population long unaccustomed to freely choosing its leadership at any level of economic or social organization? Could such elections be anything but a facade behind which the plant's Party organization would make its selections? Moreover, Arutiunian was shortly to show (his work was published in 1971) that the perception of influence on the enterprise was no more widespread in rural economic units in which management was formally elected than in those in which it was appointed. The proposal should not be dismissed as an empty gesture, however, for it was made at a time when even more far-reaching experiments were under consideration.

In any case the ensuing discussion of this proposal revealed considerable support for some new kind of mechanism which would give a plant's employees a direct role in selection or retention of managerial staffs. Even without formal "elections," factory trade union and Party organizations could appeal to the appropriate ministry to remove a factory director; but such appeals were apparently often ineffective. Cases were cited in which tyrannical directors had caused the firing, exclusion from the Party, and even imprisonment of workers criticizing managerial behavior. Such instances were cited to justify the desirability of giving employees the right to "independently" replace factory managers.[51] Support for the idea of electing lower-level management staffs (foremen, brigade leaders, shop superintendents) was expressed by some who thought that employee selection of plant directors was "premature."[52] A scattering of sociological surveys sought to elicit the responses of different occupational groups to the proposal. Not surprisingly, the reactions were related to the social positions of the respondents. A Kiev study, published in 1968, showed that more than 70% of a sample of factory directors, chief engineers, chairmen of trade union committees, and Party secretaries opposed the principle of elections to managerial positions.[53] A study of a Cheliabinsk factory issued in 1970 revealed almost two-thirds of the workers holding the view that "the collective itself should choose its leader," while the comparable figure among foremen was only 13%. Apparently the proper mix of "democracy" and "centralism" in democratic centralism was interpreted differently by workers and managerial personnel. The authors of the latter study concluded that "workers hold more radical views on democracy than managers."[54] The implication here that attitudes toward forms of organization differed markedly, depending on class position, was a rather remarkable feature of the brief discussion that followed Afanas'ev's proposal. It may even help to explain why the issue of "election" rather than appointment of managers largely evaporated by the early 1970s. To the extent that it reappeared at all, it was raised in the context of the "future society" rather than current experiments.[55]

Another illustration of the search for more participatory organizational forms appears in proposals to enhance the authority of trade unions and production conferences at the enterprise. Until 1965 the collective agreements between factory administrations and trade unions did little more than spell out the assignments embodied in the state plan for the given enterprise and some details of labor law applicable to it (rules governing overtime work, safety measures, etc.). As a recent Soviet commentary puts it, "It (the collective agreement — M. Y.) only reproduced the norms established for the given enterprise from 'above.'..."[56] Since the 1965 reform the increased availability of retained profits has provided some scope for at-plant decisions on the uses of various "incentive funds" drawn from these profits. Such funds may be used as wage supplements (about 5% of average earnings of workers in industry were drawn from these funds in 1973) or as sources of financing improvements in recreational and housing facilities. Collective agreements now incorporate provisions governing projected uses of such funds and specify that their precise allocation will be decided by management "jointly with" or "in agreement with" the factory trade union. This means that in a formal sense unions are regarded as having "parity rights," along with factory management, on questions of the allocation of such funds.[57] It is also clear, however, that violations of collective agreements by management often go unpunished, and that it is not difficult for management to obtain the agreement of the union committee's chairman to the former's views on the proper forms of expenditure of incentive funds.[58] Nonetheless at least the principle of joint decision-making is recognized as appropriate here, and examples of management obtaining union "permission" for specific uses of incentive funds have been publicized as models of "collective management."[59]

The case is quite different, however, with respect to other forms of union "participation." In the drafting of production plans, capital investment plans, and in the choice of new technology, the union has only a "consultative" role. Its proposals are in no sense binding on management, and there is no pretense of joint decision-making.[60] The same is true of any recommendations made by the plant's production conferences, most of whose participants are manual workers. The purely "consultative" or "advisory" status of their recommendations in these areas means that their influence on managerial decisions hardly adds up to effective participation in management. This is readily admitted in the more serious Soviet literature on the role of unions:

Today our chief weakness in the sphere of participation of the working people in the management of the production affairs of the enterprise is the frequent nonfulfillment of the recommendations of the trade union committee and the production conference.[61]

It is against this background that two recent proposals made in the name of extending "production democracy" assume some significance. One of these calls for extending the principle of "parity rights" of unions to areas in which they have previously exercised only a "consultative" role — in particular to the adoption of plans

for the introduction of new technology and to production plans generally. The other proposal calls for the decisions adopted on these
matters by production conferences of workers and employees to
be treated as "juridically obligatory" for management.

> Since workers and employees at the enterprise have the obligation of fulfilling
> the plan, they should have a deciding voice in formulating it.[62]

There is nothing to indicate that such proposals will soon be
formally implemented, or that if they are the typical worker (as
distinct from the union official) will experience a heightened sense
of involvement in important decisions at the plant. But such proposals (as well as the short-lived proposal for election of managers) imply a readiness to consider restricting the still-sacred
principle of one-man management in favor of more "collegial"
forms. What is most striking here is that the participatory rhetoric (if not the practice of participation) has been extended to a
significant new area — the choice of production technology. The
idea that the choice of technology must be justified "not only on
technical and economic grounds but on social grounds as well,"
and that this requires "joint decisions" of management and the
work collective, is a rather recent one in Soviet discussions.[63]
The Soviet source on which we rely here does not spell out the
"social grounds," but the latter obviously refer to the impact of
new technology on work satisfaction and job skills.[64] The introduction of such ideas into the literature on "production democracy," rather than any tangible changes in the distribution of
decision-making power, is probably the chief consequence thus
far of proposals for extending the role of unions at the enterprise.

Efforts to extend "production democracy" appeared in a very
different guise in agriculture than in industry. They were associated with a movement, which initially emerged in the early 1960s,
to rely increasingly on the small, self-managing work team
(beznariadnoe zveno) as the basic unit of work organization on
the farm rather than on the more traditional large work brigades
of several hundred members requiring close managerial supervision. The work teams were assigned their "own" plot of land and
complement of machinery for more or less extended periods. The
conflict between adherents and opponents of the work-team method
deserves a separate study which we shall not undertake here. The
issue raised was that of "internal" control (by the work group itself) versus "external" control (by farm administrators standing
apart from the "direct producers") over the peasant's work ac-

tivity. Little wonder that some published accounts of the movement reported that it generated a "social struggle" in the countryside. Our examination of a short-lived experiment which not only incorporated the idea of self-managing work teams but also a most unusual form of farm administration and leadership selection should make clear the importance of this issue. Suffice it to say for the moment that this experiment constituted a radical challenge to traditional Soviet management philosophy and organization. It projected the vision of a highly equalitarian and participatory form of economic organization.

The Akchi experiment. This experiment is probably the most important illustration of recent efforts to devise less authoritarian forms of organization in economic enterprises. The precise period covered by the experiment is uncertain, but it is apparent that it was in effect at least during the years 1968-70. Although it directly concerned only a single state grain farm, it embodied a management ideology that departed so drastically from prevailing management principles that it could not have been authorized except by high-ranking levels of political authority. The only materials at our disposal which describe the experiment are a few journalistic accounts in 1969-72 and a brief post-mortem comment in a sociological journal in 1974.[65] The experiment was inspired — or at least explicitly justified — by an aspect of the Leninist heritage that is almost never cited in the voluminous management literature of recent years.[66] We refer to Lenin's remarks in State and Revolution that socialism will create

...an order in which the functions of control and accounting — becoming more and more simple — will be performed by each in turn, will then become a habit, and will finally die out as the special functions of a special stratum of the population....

Under socialism all will govern in turn and will soon become accustomed to no one governing.[67]

There is nothing unusual about a particular industrial plant or farm being singled out in Soviet press reports for achieving levels of economic performance substantially in excess of the norm. This was true in the case of the experimental farm at Akchi in Kazakstan. Its economic performance as measured by the usual indicators of labor productivity, production costs, and profits per worker was reported to be vastly superior to that of the typical farm in its region. What was unusual was that its success apparently had nothing to do with high levels of mechanization, long hours of work, or the high quality of the educational and practical work of the farm's Party organization. In the words of the leader of the experiment, it reflected the ability to create a form of work organization in which "the functions of production and management were not divided" between different occupational strata.

In the brief description of the experiment which follows we are less interested in the details of the farm's organization — these are reported rather sketchily and in somewhat idealized terms in the press accounts — than in the ideas on authority and participation it articulated. The basic structural units were the small work teams referred to earlier, the members of which were paid from the proceeds of the team's "final output" (grain available for delivery to the state). Unlike the system prevailing on most farms, no individual output norms and piece rates were established. No payments were based on tilled or sown area, only on the team's harvest of grain. Work activities of team members were coordinated from "within" by team leaders who worked in the field. The team's income was distributed equally among its members, although there was no separate accounting of the amount of work done by individual members. "Conscience," the pressure of the team's "internal control," was relied on to maintain work discipline.

The most striking aspects of the farm's organization concerned the structure and functions of its management staff. The latter consisted of a "coordinating team" of only two individuals: the farm director and the bookkeeper-economist. The mode of payment, the absence of individual output norms, and the moral authority of the work teams over their members all presumably operated to reduce the need for "external" (managerial) sources of supervision and authority. The functions of the managerial staff were described in unusual terms. Such functions were, in part, "diplomatic" (maintaining "external" relations with the government ministry and supply organizations) and, in part, "educational" (providing instruction in the new mode of work organization). The decision to reduce to a minimum the number of individuals who were not "direct producers" reflected the views of the experiment's organizer that the excessive administrative staffs of most farms created attitudes of "dependence" among workers — a feeling that "the authorities know best" — and simply added unnecessarily to overhead costs.

In the words of the experiment's organizer, "it is important in our methodology that all people should manage in turn." Hence the principle of job rotation was to be applied to the positions of farm director and work-team leaders. The new director would be chosen from among team leaders, and the latter would be drawn from team members. The selections would be made by an "economic council" composed of the coordinating team, work-team leaders, and the farm's "social organizations" (clearly the Party and trade union).

The somewhat idyllic and undoubtedly oversimplified picture of a single farm's operations which emerges in these accounts should not obscure the significance of the Akchi experiment. Nor should the fact that the farm's staff was specially selected for experimental purposes and thus contained a larger proportion of skilled and experienced personnel than was typical on state farms. The decision to initiate the experiment, and perhaps even more important to publicize it, represented a challenge to the most sacred principles of management and to prevailing views concerning the requirements of effective work organization. It was obviously in conflict with the whole spirit of one-man management. It downgraded the need for a large social stratum of professional managers and "specialists." It denied that Soviet technological backwardness was the principal source of poor economic performance in agriculture. It affirmed the compatibility of an equalitarian income distribution (at least within work teams) with efficient work performance. It revived an aspect of the socialist heritage (reflected in the above citation from Lenin) long concealed by selective quotations from Engels on the need for authority and Lenin on the need for "unity of will" and subordination to a single leader. There was good reason for one of the published commentaries on Akchi to invoke the distinction between "juridical" socialization — long in effect — and the "real" change in relations of production which the experiment sought to institutionalize. Perhaps most important — and most threatening — the experiment left unclear just what useful role could be played by the Party organization in an economic enterprise modeled on the Akchi farm. Its "mobilizing" and "monitoring" role (its function of kontrol') hardly seemed necessary here. The only reference to the Party organization in the accounts of the Akchi experiment concerned its participation in selecting the rotating incumbents of managerial positions. But this was hardly a structural requirement of the farm's mode of operation. In short, the Akchi experiment, by moving from the "juridical" socialization of property to its "collective management," projected a form of economic organization that could not help but raise serious questions about the prevailing distribution of power and rewards in the enterprise and in the society at large. This was undoubtedly the principle source of its undoing.

In 1974 a Soviet sociological journal reported that at a conference held the previous year on social and economic problems of the countryside, a number of speakers had argued that the principles of the Akchi experiment represented "the only promising path for the country's agricultural development."[68] The writer then presented what must be interpreted as the "official verdict" on the experiment, a verdict that in effect sealed its fate:

> As for the experiment at Akchi, ... we must see two features of it: on the one hand an attempt to "drag" into being a communal form (artel'nuiu formu) of work collective — clearly in conflict with the collective and state farm forms — known in Russia since prerevolutionary times and representing a rudimentary form of organization of work collectives on democratic principles, and on the other hand a more or less successful form of organization of production utilizing value levers. The first clearly has no prospects for its development, but the second is being used and deserves wider application as an effective means of raising labor productivity in small work groups.[69]

Thus the only acceptable feature of the Akchi experiment was judged to be a system of payment based on a work group's finished product ("value levers"). But its efforts to affirm the principle of collective management, to test the feasibility of rotating incumbents of leadership positions, and to reduce the role in the enterprise of privileged strata who were not "direct producers" were all dismissed as a throwback to "rudimentary" forms of democratic work organization. There is nothing to indicate that the experiment was ended because of poor economic performance. Although we cannot unravel all the elements in the "social struggle" obliquely referred to in the scanty published accounts, it seems much more likely that Akchi was aborted by the threat it posed to the power and privileges of "professional" managers, both in the economic and political spheres. Whatever the experiment's other features, one can readily imagine the resistance that such groups would offer to the apparently serious attempt to test the principle that "all should manage in turn."

Finally, we must not exaggerate the pressures for more participatory forms of organization in the enterprise or oversimplify the obstacles to their implementation. The chronically unsatisfactory performance of agriculture, the reliance on deeply rooted authoritarian methods of enterprise management, and the emergence of a more highly educated urban work force often dissatisfied with the limited content of available jobs are all part of the setting in which the issue of "production democracy" has been raised. But the various studies, proposals, and experiments reviewed here have not yet produced tangible changes in the hierarchical distribution of authority and influence at the factory or farm. Only the Soviet version of "human relations" in management seems to be taking hold. As for the obstacles to worker participation, the whole structure of centralized economic administration continues to limit the scope for at-plant decisions (even on the use of incentive funds) and hence for worker participation in such decisions. But not all such obstacles can be reduced to the "power" considerations of economic and political authorities. The increased stress on the need for expertise in "scientific management" — presumably beyond the capacity of most manual workers — is not only a cover for managerial privileges, although it certainly helps to maintain them. Thus Soviet authorities will undoubtedly find it easier to rely on the less disruptive social mechanism of short-range occupational mobility to mitigate the effects of hierarchy than to institute effective forms of worker participation in enterprise decision-making. Among other problems this would threaten too many entrenched interests, as the Akchi experiment did.

Notes

1. V. G. Afanas'ev, "The Management of Society as a Sociological Problem," in V. G. Afanas'ev ed., Nauchnoe upravlenie obshchestvom, No. 2, Moscow, 1968, pp. 190-97; Iu. E. Volkov, "The System of Management of Society and the Type of Social Structure," in L. A. Volovik ed., Sotsiologiia i ideologiia, Moscow, 1969, pp. 168-71.

2. G. V. Suvorov, "The Problem of Studying the Structure of Management of the Production Collective," in A. S. Pashkov, Chelovek i obshchestvo, Issue VIII, Leningrad, 1971, p. 76.

3. Iu. E. Volkov, pp. 168-69.

4. V. G. Afanas'ev, pp. 190, 192.

5. F. F. Aunapu, Chto takoe upravlenie, Moscow, 1967, p. 14.

6. Ibid., p. 14.

7. Ibid., p. 15; S. Kamenitser et al., Organizatsiia i planirovanie promyshlennykh predpriiatii, Moscow, 1967, p. 45.

8. F. F. Aunapu, pp. 16-17.

9. G. M. Loz, Upravlenie v sovkhozakh i kolkhozakh, Moscow, 1972, pp. 102, 108.

10. Ibid., p. 111.

11. V. G. Podmarkov, Vvedenie v promyshlennuiu sotsiologiiu, Moscow, 1973, p. 157.

12. Ibid., p. 46.

13. F. F. Aunapu, p. 18.

14. V. N. Ermuratskii, Sotsial'naia aktivnost' rabotnikov promyshlennogo predpriiatiia, Kishinev, 1973, p. 26.

15. F. F. Aunapu, p. 75.

16. D. S. Pugh ed., Organization Theory (Baltimore: Penguin Books, 1971), pp. 101, 108.

17. D. P. Kaidalov and E. I. Suimenko, Aktual'nye problemy sotsiologii truda, Moscow, 1974, p. 54.

18. V. G. Podmarkov, p. 31.

19. Iu. V. Kolesnikov, "On the Social Functions of a Leader of a Socialist Production Collective," in V. G. Afanas'ev ed., Nauchnoe upravlenie obshchestvom, No. 6, Moscow, 1972, p. 108.

20. D. P. Kaidalov and E. I. Suimenko, pp. 59-60; Iu. V. Kolesnikov, pp. 103, 119-20, 129.

21. D. P. Kaidalov and E. I. Suimenko, p. 92.

22. Ibid., p. 62.

23. Ibid., p. 56.

24. V. A. Iadov, "Orientation — Creative Work," in G. M. Gusev et al. eds., Obshchestvo i molodezh', Moscow, 1968, pp. 129-44.

25. D. P. Kaidalov and E. I. Suimenko, p. 92.

26. V. A. Iadov, p. 142.

27. D. P. Kaidalov and E. I. Suimenko, pp. 67-68. We include a partial listing of the 16 rules cited in this source.

28. Ibid., pp. 73-74.

29. I. P. Volkov, "The Style of Management in Solving Problems of the Social Development of Enterprise Collectives," in E. S. Kuz'min and A. A. Bodalev eds., Sotsial'naia psikhologiia i sotsial'noe planirovanie, Leningrad, 1973, p. 89.

30. D. P. Kaidalov and E. I. Suimenko, p. 59. A survey of managerial personnel of the Ukrainian Ministry of Ferrous Metallurgy found that about 35% "categorically insist on a hard (zhestkii) style of work with people and complained about excessive democratism which results in a weakening of the work discipline of their subordinates."

31. Cited from Roy A. Medvedev, On Socialist Democracy (New York: Alfred A. Knopf, 1975), p. 247.

32. A. F. Sinel'nikov, "On the Relation between One-Man Management and the Participation of the Masses in the Management of the Production Process," in V. A. Fomin ed., Nekotorye voprosy nauchnogo upravleniia obshchestvom, Moscow, 1967, p. 51.

33. Ibid., pp. 48-50, 54-55.

34. P. M. Panov, "Problems of the Development of Democratic Principles in the Management of Production," in Iu. E. Volkov ed., Sotsiologicheskie problemy upravleniia narodnym khoziaistvom, Sverdlovsk, 1968, pp. 111-12.

35. L. Klepatskii, "On the Question of Forms of Organization and Management of Industry in the USSR," in V. A. Fomin, p. 63.

36. Ibid., p. 64.

37. Ibid., p. 65.

38. A. Tsipko, "On the Economic and Legal Concept of Property," in V. A. Fomin, p. 124.

39. Iu. E. Volkov, "Problems of Development of Democratic Principles in the Management of Socialist Production," in V. G. Afanas'ev ed., Nauchnoe upravlenie obshchestvom, No. 4, Moscow, 1970, pp. 152-53.

40. Ibid., p. 153, 158.

41. See, for example, L. Nechaeva and A. Yanov, "Help the Strong," Molodoi kommunist, 1970, no. 2, pp. 55-63.

42. Other studies of farm management in the more "popular" literature reinforced Arutiunian's findings. Collective farm membership meetings were often dominated by managerial staff, with farm specialists reporting to each other and with ordinary peasants rarely participating in discussions. The principal subject of these discussions was often the problem of work discipline rather than broad issues of economic policy. See the study of the Frunze Collective Farm in ibid., pp. 60-61.

43. Iu. V. Arutiunian, Sotsial'naia struktura, p. 111.

44. Ibid., p. 104.

45. Ibid., p. 109.

46. V. I. Oligin-Nesterov, Ispol'zovanie ekonomicheskikh zakonov sotsializma i upravlenie proizvodstvom, Moscow, 1973, pp. 94, 95.

47. V. N. Ermuratskii, pp. 102, 104.

48. N. I. Alekseev, "The Interaction of Social Factors in Determining the Attitude toward Work," Sotsiologicheskie issledovaniia, 1975, no. 3, pp. 120-21.

49. Iu. E. Volkov, Tak rozhdaetsia kommunisticheskoe samoupravlenie, Moscow, 1965, p. 176.

50. V. G. Afanas'ev, Nauchnoe upravlenie obshchestvom, Moscow, 1968, pp. 259-60. Earlier support for the idea of elections of managers appears in Ia. S. Kapeliush, "Democracy and Centralism," in V. A. Fomin, p. 44.

51. P. M. Panov, p. 114.

52. F. M. Rudich, O sochetanii gosudarstvennykh i obshchestvennykh nachal v upravlenii proizvodstvom, Kiev, 1968, p. 77.

53. Ibid., p. 76.

54. Ia. E. Stul' and I. O. Tishchenko, "Social-Psychological Principles of Management," in V. G. Afanas'ev, Nauchnoe upravlenie obshchestvom, No. 6, 1970, p. 276.

55. G. Kh. Popov and G. A. Dzhavadov, Upravlenie i problema kadrov, Moscow, 1972, p. 17.

56. N. I. Alekseev and I. A. Riazhskikh, "The Highest Organ of the Collective," in V. G. Afanas'ev ed., Nauchnoe upravlenie obshchestvom, No. 6, p. 151.

57. N. I. Alekseev, I. I. Kravchenko, and E. G. Plimak, "The Myth of 'Statism' and Socialism without Myths," Voprosy filosofii, 1971, no. 5, p. 49; S. A. Ivanov, Trudovoe pravo i nauchno-tekhnicheskii progress, Moscow, 1974, pp. 400-1; N. I. Alekseev and I. A. Riazhskikh, pp. 149-50.

58. S. A. Ivanov, p. 398. N. I. Alekseev and I. A. Riazhskikh, p. 150.

59. Ibid., p. 145.

60. S. A. Ivanov, pp. 407-8.

61. Ibid., p. 414.

62. Ibid., pp. 415-17.

63. Ibid., p. 414.

64. A. Yanov in Molodoi kommunist, 1972, no. 2, pp. 64-69, explicitly urged that choices among alternative technologies be guided, at least in part, by the opportunities they created for higher skill levels. Yanov's article, however, was primarily concerned with the functions of the industrial sociologist rather than the trade union at the plant.

65. Iskusstvo kino, 1972, no. 11, pp. 93-96; Literaturnaia gazeta, May 21,

1969; Molodoi kommunist, 1970, no. 2, pp. 62-68; Sotsiologicheskie issledovaniia, 1974, no. 2, pp. 186-87. All quotations in the text concerning the experiment are drawn from these sources. The author is grateful to Alexander Yanov for calling some of these sources to his attention.

66. The only recent reference we have found to Lenin's remarks, cited below, other than in the accounts of the Akchi experiment, appears in Voprosy filosofii, 1971, no. 5, p. 56.

67. The first part of the quotation is given in the translation appearing in V. I. Lenin, Selected Works, Vol. VII (New York: International Publishers, 1943), p. 48. The second part is from V. I. Lenin, The State and Revolution (Peking: Foreign Languages Press, 1973), p. 140. In each case we have selected the translation which seems to us to best fit the original Russian.

68. V. I. Vladimirov, "Problems and Prospects of Socioeconomic Development of the Countryside," Sotsiologicheskie issledovaniia, 1974, no. 1, p. 186.

69. Ibid., p. 187. It appears that the fate of the experiment's organizer has also been sealed. See the article by A. Yanov in the New York Times, December 31, 1975.

One of the principal contexts in which the issue of social inequality has been raised in the Soviet Union has centered on the
economic and social position of women. The bare "facts" concerning women's disadvantaged status are fairly well known and are not
our main concern here. But they will be briefly reviewed chiefly
for the purpose of setting the stage for this chapter's principal objective: to examine some of the ways in which the issue of women's
subordinate position has been posed and discussed in Soviet society.
Of particular interest is the manner in which discussions of the
"woman question" have been a vehicle for raising questions which
transcend inequality between the sexes and touch on broader problems of work and the nature of power.

Aspects of Women's Economic and Social Position

The obvious starting point for any examination of the status of
women in Soviet society is the unusually high rate of female labor
force participation. In the early 1970s some four-fifths of Soviet
women of working age (16-55) were employed outside the household, a proportion recognized by Soviet economists as "close to
the maximum possible."[1] The principal groups outside the work
force were mothers of young children and full-time students. In
the 30-49 age group some 90% of Soviet women were in the work
force. The overall female participation rate was almost double
that of the United States and also exceeded the relatively high
rates (72-74%) of most East European countries.[2]
    The female share of the total labor force had already reached
approximately 40% in the immediate prewar period. Heavy wartime manpower losses and the delayed impact of low wartime

birth rates on the number of new labor force entrants in the early 1960s intensified pressures for high female labor participation throughout most of the postwar period. Similar pressures were generated by chronically ambitious production plans and an ideology which stressed the traditional socialist view that female participation in social production was a necessary condition for attaining equality between the sexes. These are some of the factors contributing to the stabilization of the female share of the total labor force at 50-51% since the late 1960s.[3]

But in addition to the impact of war, rapid industrialization, and an ideology favorable to female labor participation, there is another factor at work here. For most families with dependent children, the average wages of a single earner have not been sufficient to meet Soviet standards of per capita "minimum material needs." Since the late 1960s Soviet estimates of the per capital outlays corresponding to these standards in urban areas have typically assumed a figure on the order of 50 rubles per month.[4] With average monthly earnings of workers and employees ranging from 100 rubles in 1966 to 135 rubles in 1973, it is clear that the presence of dependent children in the household has normally required the employment of both husband and wife. The increase in the age at which youngsters enter the work force (involving an increase in the "cost" of rearing children) has undoubtedly operated in the same direction. It would be a mistake, however, to exaggerate the role of sheer economic necessity — in the sense of the family's need for physical survival — in accounting for the near-universal employment of women. Although there is evidence for some areas that wives whose husbands are in high-income occupations have lower participation rates than women generally, female economic participation is obviously not confined to low-income families.[5] The higher level of schooling of women than of men in younger age groups (at least through the age of 30) undoubtedly creates aspirations for economic participation quite apart from the household's need for additional income. It is true that recent sociological studies of working women have found that the principal motive for female employment is "the need for additional family income."[6] But we cannot simply ignore (or dismiss as improbable) similar studies which have found that a majority of working women would remain in the work force even if family income was unaffected by their departure.[7]

Our point, of course, is not to deny the obvious fact that female employment is typically required to meet family subsistence needs.

But it is worth stressing that economic "necessity" interacts with "opportunity" and with a socialization process that affirms the value of female employment both as a means of self-realization and as a social obligation. In this situation it would be surprising if the roughly 30 years spent in employment outside the home (after accounting for brief interruptions for child rearing) were not regarded as part of the "normal" course of a woman's life. [8]

There is no doubt that the occupational status of employed Soviet women is generally inferior to that of men. Numerous Soviet studies of women's status have yielded abundant evidence on this score. The problem is how best to provide a summary picture of the extent of occupational inequality between the sexes. Most of the Soviet work force (78% of men and 68% of women according to the 1970 census[9]) is employed in manual jobs. A recent study of a "typical industrial center" may be used to compare the differing skill composition of men and women in such jobs. The results are shown in Table 6.1. Fully two-thirds of female manual workers were employed in jobs classified as low skilled, while the comparable figure for males was one-fifth; only 4% of women held highly skilled manual jobs, compared to 30% of men. Although these are the results for a single city, they are reinforced by other studies which similarly document the concentration of women in low-skilled positions and the privileged access of men to the more-skilled manual jobs even where educational attainments of the sexes are essentially the same. Moreover, one of the country's leading labor economists, writing in the early 1970s, relied on the results of the "typical industrial center" study to characterize prevailing inequalities in the skill composition of men and women manual workers. [11] It hardly seems likely, therefore, that the data in Table 6.1 exaggerate the relative skill disadvantages of female manual workers.

When we turn to the nonmanual sector of the work force, the problem becomes somewhat more complex, but once again the data point unmistakably to the advantaged position of males. Women constitute a majority (59% in recent years) of all nonmanual employees as well as of "specialists" (individuals with a secondary specialized or higher education). [12] Within these broad categories, however, the female share of the lower-ranking positions is distinctly higher than of those at the upper end of the occupational spectrum. But while women are clearly underrepresented in some of the highest-ranking intelligentsia occupations, it would be misleading to characterize their work roles as "restricted" — either

Table 6.1

Distribution of Male and Female Manual Workers by Degree of Skill
in "Typical Industrial Center," Late 1960s (in %)*

Skill group	Male workers (in %)	Female workers (in %)
Highly skilled	30	4
Semiskilled	50	30
Low-skilled	20	66
Total	100	100

Source: L. A. Gordon and E. V. Klopov, Chelovek posle raboty, p. 353.
*The figures are based on a survey conducted in 1967-69 in the city of Taganrog.

in an approximate or literal sense — to low-ranking positions in the nonmanual occupational hierarchy. There is little basis for accepting the view expressed in a recent Western study which finds a "virtual absence of women in the highly skilled categories of the labor force...."[13]

Both typical and nontraditional female work roles are apparent in Table 6.2, which shows the female share of selected nonmanual positions. As elsewhere, such traditionally female jobs as telephone operators, typists, and stenographers are almost exclusively filled by Soviet women, and they also hold more than 70% of teaching positions in primary and secondary schools. But in addition to filling almost three-fourths of physician's jobs, women also staff a significant minority of positions (some 30-40%) in such traditionally male occupations as engineers, college teachers, and scientific personnel. It is chiefly among the highest-ranking managerial and scientists' posts that women often have little more than token representation. To the extent that women attain a sizable share of positions with managerial authority, it is likely to be in enterprises with a predominantly female work force.[14] Perhaps one of the more striking examples of Soviet "tokenism" with respect to women in positions of economic authority may be found in agriculture. With women constituting somewhat more than one-half of the total agricultural work force and about one-third of agricultural specialists (agronomists, veterinarians, etc.), only 1.5% of state farm directors and collective farm chairmen in the early 1970s were women. Although the gap between male and female occupational status generally seems less pronounced among intelligentsia groups than among manual workers, there is every reason to accept a Soviet economist's (M. Sonin) summary statement that "among personnel in both mental and manual labor, the share of women in the most highly skilled groups is considerably less than the share of men."[15]

Table 6.2

Proportion of Women in Selected "Nonmanual" Occupational Positions, Early 1970s (in %)

Occupational positions	Women in % of total
Typists and stenographers (1970)	99
Secretaries and clerks (1970)	95
Telephone operators (1970)	96
Teachers in primary and secondary schools (1974)	71
Physicians (1974)	70
Teachers in higher educational institutions (1970)	43
Engineers with higher education (1973)	33
Scientific personnel (1973)	40
Agronomists, veterinarians, zootechnicians with higher education (1973)	38
Foremen in industry (1973)	24
Scientific personnel with doctor of science degree (1973)	13
Deputy directors and chief engineers of industrial enterprises (1973)	10
Directors of industrial enterprises (1973)	9
Directors of state farms and chairmen of collective farms (1972)*	1

Sources: Itogi, Vol. VI, p. 169; Narodnoe khoziaistvo SSSR v 1973 g., pp. 175-76; Tsentral'noe statisticheskoe upravlenie pri sovete ministrov SSSR, Zhenshchiny v SSSR, pp. 78, 80, 84, 86.
*The year to which this figure applies is not certain. It appears in the general context of a discussion of female employment in agriculture in 1972 (Voprosy ekonomiki, 1975, no. 12, pp. 57-58).

Only the roughest estimates can be made of the male-female earnings gap associated with the differing work roles of the sexes. That such a gap exists is acknowledged by Soviet writers and that it may be fairly substantial should be apparent from the brief review above of male-female skill characteristics and occupational positions. The scattered Soviet data available to us have been assembled in Table 6.3. They have been supplemented by our own computed estimates based on the occupational distribution of men and women in three cities and the assumption of identical male-

Table 6.3

Male-Female Monthly Wage Differentials

Area and category of employee	Wages, in rubles per month		Women's wages in % of men's
	men	women	
Direct Soviet data			
Leningrad, 1970:			
workers in machine-building plants, married	149.1	108.1	73
workers in machine-building plants, unmarried	132.6	98.6	74
Kiev, 1970:			
sample of newlyweds	116	87	72
Tatar Republic, rural enterprises, 1967*			
manual workers, under age 35	69	47	68
manual workers, 35 and older	60	37	62
nonmanual personnel, under age 35	109	76	70
nonmanual personnel, 35 and older	104	80	74
Computed Estimates †			
Kazan, 1967, citywide sample of employed	102.5	93.6	91
Al'met'evsk, 1967, citywide sample of employed	109.0	90.1	83
Menzelinsk, 1967, citywide sample of employed	87.1	79.4	91

Sources: E. K. Vasil'eva, Sem'ia i ee funktsii, pp. 124–25; Akademiia nauk Ukrainskoi SSR, Vliianie sotsial'no-ekonomicheskikh faktorov na demograficheskie protsessy, p. 115; Iu. V. Arutiunian, Sotsial'noe i natsional'noe, pp. 168, 189, 323–24.

*These figures apply to persons of Russian ethnic background. The male-female differential is generally somewhat greater for Tatars.

†These figures are computed by applying male and female employment weights to the average wages of eight occupational groups. See Chapter 2 for the occupational groups included.

female wages within occupations. The data given directly in Soviet sources (under "direct Soviet data" in Table 6.3) point to an average female wage on the order of 65-75% of the male wage. The sample of areas covered (Leningrad, Kiev, and rural areas of the Tatar Republic) is obviously too small to justify any broad generalizations, but it is significant that some of the wage comparisons are for groups in roughly similar occupational and age categories. It is also clear that the Soviet earnings gap between the sexes is not only the result of the high concentration of males in highly paid sectors of heavy industry and of women in low-wage sectors of light industry. Where earnings can be compared within given economic sectors, they also disclose a higher wage level for males than for females. Our own estimates (under "computed estimates" in Table 6.3), showing a female-to-male wage ratio on the order of 83-91%, obviously understate the typical wage differential based on sex. They may best be regarded as indicating the upper limit of the female-to-male wage ratio (in a small sample of cities) under conditions in which earnings differences within identical occupational categories are assumed to be nonexistent. The ratio of 65-75% suggested by the scattering of "direct" Soviet data, which we accept as more typical of the female-to-male wage gap, is also roughly similar to estimates of full-time earnings differentials between men and women in some East European countries (Czechoslovakia, Poland, Hungary).[16]

Soviet comparisons of husbands' and wives' earnings provide additional evidence of sex-based wage differentials. Several studies of married couples' earnings in the late 1960s reported that in some 70-75% of the families surveyed the husband's wage exceeded the wife's. The authors of one of these studies also concluded that the category of low-paid workers was recruited largely from "women employed in unskilled and low-skilled work."[17]

Although we do not assay any comparisons with sex-linked wage differentials in the United States — partly because of the scarcity of Soviet data — there is one important factor making for a narrower male-female income gap in the Soviet Union than in the United States. This is quite apart from differences in prevailing attitudes toward female employment and the greater access of Soviet women to traditionally male work roles (engineering, medicine, science). One of the principal explanations often offered for earnings differentials between men and women in the United States in the same age group is that women tend to work intermittently, leaving the work force for extended periods in connection with

171

child-rearing responsibilities and returning when their children begin school, or later. They thereby accumulate less work experience than men in similar occupational categories and are at a disadvantage in "bidding" for promotion to more responsible and higher-paying jobs.[18] This factor is also at work in the Soviet Union. But the extremely high female labor force participation rates in the "prime" working years (85% in the 20-29 and 91% in the 30-39 age groups) and the greater continuity of employment suggest that differences in male-female work experience are considerably less in the Soviet Union than in the United States. That sex-linked earnings inequalities nonetheless remain substantial in the Soviet Union should be obvious from the wage data reviewed above. But our expectation is that they are less pronounced than in the United States. For the present, however, this remains a hypothesis in need of verification.

In contrast to the scanty data available on the male-female earnings gap, there is no aspect of the unequal status of the sexes that has been more amply studied and documented than their unequal burden of responsibility for household chores. It sometimes appears that the limited opportunities to study and discuss the various forms of social inequality in the Soviet Union have been "displaced" to the endless investigation of time budgets. These investigations invariably point in the same direction: despite the high rate of female employment outside the home, the provision of household services (shopping, cooking, cleaning, laundering) and care of children continue to be regarded largely as "women's work." Soviet sociologists admit that in this respect Soviet socialism has failed to produce "a fundamental transformation of household management."[19] Although significant class and strata differences exist in the duration of women's domestic labor (with collective farm women in the most disadvantaged position),[20] employed women's total working time — including paid and domestic labor — exceeds men's in all occupational groups. Soviet women's "double burden" is illustrated in a study conducted in 1966 of eight urban occupational strata (which we have compressed to four in Table 6.4), ranging from unskilled laborers to managerial personnel. Despite marked strata differences in earnings, education, and power at work, there was a striking uniformity within each of the strata in the relationship between male and female total working time: in all groups the female working day was on the order of 11-12 hours, the male — 9-10 hours. Although work schedules have changed since this study was conducted (in connection with the shift from a six- to a five-day workweek in the late 1960s), there is no evidence of a significant closing of the gap between male and female working time in recent years.

Table 6.4

Male-Female Differences in Duration of Housework and Total Working Day, Selected Occupational Strata, Leningrad, 1966*

Occupational strata	Housework, in hours and minutes per working day		Total working day, in hours and minutes	
	men	women	men	women
Unskilled workers	2-28	4-51	9-42	11-56
Skilled workers†	2-07	3-38	9-21	10-59
Personnel in highly skilled mental work	2-22	3-53	9-37	11-04
Managerial personnel	1-43	3-32	10-12	11-40

Source: Computed from I. P. Trufanov, Problemy byta, p. 106. The same source shows figures for nonspecialist employees, personnel in skilled mental work, and highly skilled manual workers which reveal essentially similar patterns of male-female differentials as those shown above.

*The figures are based on a sample of persons employed in eight "large enterprises" and three scientific-research institutes.

†Computed as simple averages of figures for skilled workers on machinery and skilled workers in manual work.

The unequal distribution of household and child-care responsibilities between the sexes obviously contributes to women's disadvantaged position in employment outside the home. Soviet women in even the most "advanced" strata — scientists, for example — are apparently subject to the traditional sexual division of domestic labor.[21] Little wonder, then, that the average length of time between the defense of the candidate's and doctor's dissertation for men is approximately 11.5 years, and for women, 16.5 years.

An additional indicator of women's subordinate status — albeit a "subjective" indicator — is provided by data on the sex of heads of families.[22] Although women's work force participation rates are close to men's, and household chores fall chiefly on women's shoulders, the traditional attitude which identifies the male as the "family head" often remains in force. But this attitude is apparently more widespread among men than among women. A recent study of households in which both husband and wife were present (see Table 6.5) showed a distinct majority of men, especially among lower strata, regarding themselves as family heads.

Table 6.5

Identification of "Head of Family":
Responses of Husbands and Wives, Kazan, 1967

Occupational status	Respondents	"Who is head of family?"		
		husband	wife (in %)	no single head
"Younger" families:				
specialists	husband	66	5	29
	wife	44	17	39
specialists and other occupational groups †	husband	81	1	18
	wife	37	32	31
other occupational groups	husband	88	1	11
	wife	52	19	29
"Older" families:				
specialists*	husband	77	5	18
	wife	51	23	26
specialists and other occupational groups †	husband	88	4	8
	wife	53	22	25
other occupational groups	husband	91	2	7
	wife	50	35	15

Source: E. K. Vasil'eva, Sem'ia i ee funktsii, p. 80.
*Both husband and wife were specialists, i.e., held jobs normally requiring a higher or secondary specialized education.
† One adult was a specialist while the other was not.

Women also accepted their husbands as family heads more often than they accorded themselves this status. But there was an important difference between male and female perceptions of the dominant figure in the family. Women were more likely than men to cite "no single family head." Moreover, although men almost never recognized their wives as family heads, women accorded themselves this position in some one-fifth to one-third of the cases (depending on occupational and age category). The precise meaning that should be attached to such appraisals remains in doubt. But at the very least they suggest a consciousness of "relations of subordination" in many households, less evident among intelligentsia families than among others. We shall return to this theme below when we examine how Soviet sociologists have sought to elaborate the concept of "power in the family."

Our cursory survey of Soviet women's economic and social position has been intended chiefly as an introduction to our principal objective: to examine some of the ways in which Soviet discussions of women's status have provided an opportunity for airing conflicting attitudes toward women's social roles and the problem of power in the family. As elsewhere in this volume we find the attitudes expressed in these discussions no less revealing than the bare "facts" of inequality.

Women's Roles as an Issue in Soviet Discussions

Until the late 1960s there appeared to be no obvious conflict between policies pursued in the name of promoting economic development and policies that could be justified on the grounds of promoting equality of the sexes. The increase in women's work force participation rates (from 63% in 1958 to 79% in 1965[23]) and educational attainments appeared to serve both objectives. However, the decade of the sixties was also marked by a considerable decline in the birth rate (from 24.9 per 1,000 in 1960 to 17.0 in 1969).[24] This posed the threat of a reduction in future additions to the work force and hence in long-run rates of economic expansion. Although the decline in the birth rate could not be attributed exclusively to the rise in women's economic participation, the two phenomena were obviously closely linked. This is the setting in which, in the late 1960s, the need for a "more active" population policy emerged as a principal theme in both the popular and professional (economic and sociological) literature. The ensuing discussions not only revealed conflicting responses to the problem of low birth rates but to the whole issue of sexual inequality.

At the risk of some oversimplification, we may characterize two fairly distinct positions that have emerged in these discussions as "traditionalist" and "feminist," respectively. Reliance on such labels is admittedly somewhat arbitrary, but the differing orientations to which they refer in the Soviet setting will become apparent as we proceed. Although both positions affirm a commitment to reducing inequality between the sexes, they do so in rather different ways. The essential feature of the first approach is a reassertion of the economic and social importance of certain traditional female roles. As an illustration we may briefly consider the responses of some demographers and economists to the problem of low birth rates, taking the views of V. Perevedentsev as representative of this group. Perevedentsev's argument (we rely here on one of his articles published in 1968) was essentially an appeal for the recognition of child rearing in the home as a distinct form of "socially necessary labor," which, like all such labor, should be paid for by society:

It hardly seems necessary to demonstrate — at least to parents — that raising children requires considerable work. And the work is difficult. It is borne chiefly by women. Working in production, a woman with a family actually has two work loads: eight hours at work plus five or six hours at home. . . .

But a profoundly negative attitude toward the domestic labor of women has developed and become rooted in our society. The point has even been reached where some zealous economists have ceased to regard domestic labor as socially useful. . . .

In raising her children the mother creates the main value of society — human beings, working people, those who produce all goods. But this most important labor is just about the only kind of socially necessary labor which is unpaid. . . .

Since the fruits of rearing children are received chiefly by society, the work of rearing children should be paid for as all other socially necessary labor under socialism, according to its quantity and quality.[25]

The proposed payments would offset, at least partially, the normal decline in family income which occurred when women remained out of the work force for an extended period following the birth of a child. Thus, in Perevedentsev's view, they would be an effective means of raising the birth rate. The payments would not go to the "head of the family" (this would simply perpetuate sexual inequality) but to those who perform the "labor" of raising children — in most cases their mothers. "Payments for children would be the wages of those who rear them." Perevedentsev did not specify the duration of the proposed payments (obviously it would exceed the 16 weeks of paid leave provided for in current regulations) but held that it would be "rational" for women to be employed until the birth of the first child and then again when the child was "grown." The interruption in female economic participation would depend on the growth of the service sector which, "as we know, is extremely backward."

This proposal was supported by some economists who sought to demonstrate (through cost-benefit analysis) the economic advantages of wages for child rearing. The payments to mothers, it was claimed, would be less costly than required outlays on the construction and staffing of child-care facilities. Moreover, the temporary withdrawal from employment of women with young children (in one calculation even through the age of seven) would be more than handsomely recouped by future increments in society's labor supply.[26]

Originally raised in the late 1960s, these arguments have continued to receive support in more recent years in spite of a gradual leveling off of the earlier decline in birth rates. Thus in 1975 an economist reiterated the essence of Perevedentsev's earlier proposal by appealing for a shift to "a system in which a woman, having worked for a number of years before marriage and the first child, would then — partially and in some cases wholly — concentrate on family concerns for several years, and when the children are grown would return to her occupation." Once again this was coupled with the suggestion that direct payments to mothers (based on a percentage of earlier salary) would be a more "effective" form of investment in the rearing of the young than outlays on kindergartens. [27]

But what we have termed the traditionalist position in Soviet discussions of women's roles should not be seen simply as an appeal for grants for "breeding" (as a critic was to put it). It is part of a broader interpretation of Soviet women's status which views their domestic activities — child rearing and housework — as part of their total "labor time." In the Marxian terminology used in these discussions, such activities may be regarded as part of the process of "reproducing labor power," not only in the sense of reproducing and socializing the next generation of workers but also in the sense of providing the household services which daily re-create the present generation's ability to work. [28] Given the slow growth of the service sector and the inadequacy of child-care facilities, as well as the persistence of customary male attitudes toward housework, the prospects for significant reductions in women's domestic chores in the near future seem slight. Hence the traditionalist orientation seeks to alleviate the "double burden" of Soviet women — to reduce their total "labor time" — by urging the adoption of policies which will curtail their work load outside the home. The proposal for "wages for child rearing," although originally linked to the problem of low birth rates, is only one expression of this broader strain in Soviet thinking.

Another variant, perhaps a more "moderate" one, of the same underlying approach is embodied in recent proposals for reduced hours on the job and lower production norms for women (without loss of pay). The implementation of such measures would signify public recognition of both the indispensability and "laboring" quality of women's current domestic roles and would not require prolonged interruptions in female work force participation. The social benefits of easing women's work burdens on the job would include closer supervision of children in the home, thereby improving their school performance and reducing their proneness to delinquency. The "traditionalist" element also appears here in the distinctive ways in which proponents of such measures define the "rational employment" of women and men. For women this requires work schedules which permit them to "harmoniously combine occupational and family-household roles." No such strictures apply to the "rational employment" of men. For the latter this means simply the full employment in social production of all able-bodied individuals.[29] Reduced working hours and easier work norms for women, it is argued, would also be a step toward "equal pay for equal work," a principle that is violated by the acceptance of unequal total work burdens for the sexes. Here is how a proponent of reduced hours on the job for women with "family obligations" prefaces his proposal:

> ...the existing system of recording the amount of labor...starts from the assumption that one's labor contribution is made only by participating in social production as a worker, employee, or collective farmer. Thereby women employed in social production are placed in an unequal position compared to men, for the magnitude of their real labor contribution is understated.[30]

Some adherents of this version of the traditionalist stance seem fully aware of a troubling dilemma in their approach to problems of sexual inequality. They accept as axiomatic the need for a more equitable distribution of household obligations and the liberation of women — indeed of the family — from domestic drudgery. But the measures which they propose are intended to reduce women's work activity in social production (whether through reduced participation rates, a shorter working day, or lighter work assignments) on the grounds of their obligation in domestic labor. Is there not a danger, therefore, that such measures would serve to reinforce public acceptance of domestic labor as "women's work," in effect paid for by released time from social production? Moreover, will not reduced working time on the job for women (while men's hours remain unchanged) diminish their opportunities for professional advancement? Indeed, this is precisely what has happened at some industrial enterprises that have introduced shortened work schedules on an experimental basis for previously full-time women employees. All of this is acknowledged by some of those we have classified as traditionalists. But for the present, with the burdens of household duties falling chiefly on women's shoulders, the traditionalist sees a limited reduction in women's labor force roles as promoting equality between the sexes. "As long as household work significantly increases the labor contribution of women, this must somehow be considered in setting work norms for women's professional labor."[31]

What are some of the views which we classify under the rubric of "feminist" in Soviet discussions of women's status? On some occasions this position emerges in direct confrontation with some versions of the traditionalist approach examined above; in other cases the difference between the two approaches is more a matter of emphasis on certain aspects of women's disadvantaged status rather than on others. Perhaps the principal manifestation of the feminist standpoint is opposition to measures which promise to limit women's opportunities for advancement in the work world. Some of the critical responses to proposals for stimulating birth rates and accepting women's abstention from work force roles (such as Perevedentsev's suggestion of wages for child rearing) illustrate this aspect of the Soviet feminist position. We may summarize some of these critical reactions as follows:[32]

1. Low birth rates should not be regarded merely from the economic vantage point of their implications for the future labor supply. They also reflect the aspirations of women for social equality and have contributed to "new, more democratic family relationships." These social advances make any significant reversal in the trend of birth rates unlikely.

2. Demographic problems must be solved without reducing the "economic activity" of women. To the extent that pronatalist policies encourage or pressure women to leave the work force for extended periods, the consequence will be a reinforcement of women's already disadvantaged status in the occupational hierarchy. Pressures will be created to reduce child-care facilities since they will appear to duplicate the functions that nonworking women will perform at home. Public outlays on higher education for women will appear less "profitable" than for men, and this will be reflected in admissions policies. Women's choice between work and child rearing will thus be largely predetermined by the limited opportunities for advanced professional status.[33] (These warnings may sound a somewhat panicky note, but they reflect the fear of a consistently "economic" approach to the profitability of investment in women's schooling and socialized child-care facilities.)

3. There is nothing particularly "humane" about recognizing a certain kind of labor (child rearing and provision of household services, for example) as socially useful and then paying for it. A more "humane" approach would be to transform routine domes-

tic labor by extending the "industrialization of housework" and the availability of communal child-care facilities. Such measures would also help to meet the birth rate problem without requiring women to reduce their work roles outside the home. Moreover, "why do we ignore such a perfectly practicable and just... path as the assumption by men of one-half of the concerns and burdens now borne by women?"[34]

Although some participants in these discussions have sought to combine elements of the traditionalist and feminist perspectives, most of the literature embodies predominantly one or the other of these approaches.[35] The traditionalist position argues for a reduction or easing of women's work force roles on the grounds of their "family obligations" or in the name of a "more active" population policy. The feminist response, on the other hand, invokes the ideal of social equality primarily to assert women's claims to self-realization in the occupational sphere. The obstacles to occupational advancement are usually seen as rooted in women's heavy burdens in domestic labor, and the need to lighten such burdens is a frequent theme in discussions of the "woman question" (see point 3 above). But the feminist perspective also appears in those Soviet studies which stress that the barriers to women's professional advancement emerge even before the onset of women's "double burden." The Leningrad studies of E. K. Vasil'eva, for example, document what is, in effect, discrimination against women in access to advanced schooling and the subordinate position at the work place of women unencumbered by family obligations. Vasil'eva has shown that despite the superior academic performance of female secondary school graduates, a larger proportion of male than of female graduates are accepted for full-time study in higher educational institutions.[36] Similarly, even before the assumption of child rearing and other family-related obligations, women workers' wages and occupational status lag behind those of men in comparable situations.[37]

The very selection of such topics for study, as well as Vasil'eva's documentation of the discrimination confronting women in their pursuit of socially approved professional goals, imply a very different policy orientation to the "woman question" than is stressed in the traditionalist standpoint. In its Soviet version the feminist position thus emerges as a continuing reminder of a classical socialist goal: "... without the full and equal participation of women in social production, their genuine equality with men is inconceivable."[38] The traditionalist position, on the other hand, by accommodating itself to a reduced role for women at the work place, has accepted the postponement of "genuine equality" for the sake of an easing of women's total work burdens. However, all participants in these discussions invoke the ideal of social and economic equality of the sexes in one form or another. That they do so in different ways is not merely a token of the diversity of opinion on social issues which sometimes surfaces in Soviet public discourse but also a reflection of deep social divisions within the female population. Although we cannot gauge the reactions of the mass of Soviet women to the conflicting views in these discussions, it is probable that such reactions would exhibit marked class and strata differentiation. There can be little doubt that the traditionalist proposals would find their greatest support among the many working-class and peasant women for whom work-place roles offer relatively little opportunity for personal growth, creativity, or social recognition, while the feminist orientation expresses the concerns of the growing strata of women in intelligentsia occupations. For the latter groups the prospects for professional advancement require continuity of employment and an ability to assume the same work loads on the job as their male colleagues. The concern expressed by some participants in these discussions that "loss of skills" would be associated with the prolonged interruption of work activity clearly reflects the fears of women in specialists' occupations who have skills to lose, rather than the bulk of women in manual occupations. At the same time, the debate between traditionalists and feminists (again we must stress the somewhat arbitrary use of these labels) also reveals the unresolved tensions associated with the multiple roles expected of almost all Soviet women — in the work force, in domestic labor, and in child rearing.

There is another aspect of Soviet discussions of women's roles and, more broadly, of family relationships that deserves our attention. Such discussions have provided the occasion for conceptualizing issues that are not readily raised in other contexts in the Soviet Union. We refer specifically to the issue of power. Although some of the ways in which problems of power have surfaced in the Soviet sociological literature have already been examined (see Chapters 1 and 4), it is obvious that the scope for the serious analysis of this theme is severely limited. All the more interesting, therefore, that the study of family relationships has provided one of the few opportunities for the explicit consideration of the concept of power.

A study of "power in the family" by the sociologist A. L. Pimenova illustrates the way in which the issue of sexual inequality has served as a vehicle for exploring the delicate problem of power. A brief background note to Pimenova's study will be helpful here. In 1965, in one of the first collections of sociological literature to appear in the Soviet Union, an article by V. I. Selivanov called for special attention to be paid to educational work with "heads of families," whose role in the "leadership of the family collective" was so important in the proper socialization of the young members of the family: "The state is interested in having the head of the family be not only an authoritative but also a socially progressive family member, an educator of his family collective."[39] Such formulations implied that particular individuals — family heads, who were usually males — were to be regarded as responsible to the state for the leadership of their family units.

Pimenova's study, which appeared in 1971, explicitly rejected such an approach. The public identification of particular individuals as family heads would imply a "social sanctioning of their position and would promote the conservation of their privileges." This would signify social approval of glavenstvo — individual domination (or supremacy) in the family. Family domination, which Pimenova formulated as "the question of power in the family," was characterized in the following terms:

Domination (of an individual in the family — M. Y.) assumes that other members of the family are not equal to the family head, either in their opportunities or in their actual role in the family. Thus domination bears the marks of dependence, of subordination, and in its most coarse and open forms, of tyranny (proizvol). Hence it is incompatible with equality in the family.[40]

Glavenstvo implies that the functions of directing or regulating family life are concentrated in a single family member, the family head. Where this prevails, Pimenova suggested, the family is characterized by an "autocratic structure." When power is divided more or less equally between husband and wife, it would be appropriate to characterize its structure as "democratic."[41] As for the prevailing condition of the Soviet family, Pimenova described it as "in a transition stage from an autocratic to a democratic type of internal structure."

One final aspect of Pimenova's discussion is worth noting. How is the dominant position of the family head — glavenstvo — commonly justified? The legitimations normally invoke some combination of the following factors: (a) assigning "special importance" to a particular obligation of a family member, such as the provision of material support for the family; (b) the acceptance of prevailing "public opinion, traditions, customs"; (c) the acceptance of certain "individual or specific" traits of individuals (age, sex, education, occupation) as grounds for their dominant position in the family. But for Pimenova such justifications often "distort" or "exaggerate" the actual role of individual family members. Thus even when the wife's earnings equal or exceed the husband's, the latter's alleged "economic" responsibility may be cited to legitimate his position as family head. Similarly, the wife's responsibilities for organizing the "everyday life" (byt) of the family are not usually accorded the recognition assigned to the breadwinning function as the grounds for individual domination in the family. The usual justifications for such domination thus embody a "peculiar fetishization" of particular family functions and serve to buttress the privileged position of the family head. In families in which glavenstvo is absent, i.e., where power is shared and the functions of both husband and wife are accorded proper recognition, there is no need for a "family cult" to reinforce individual privilege.[42]

Our purpose in presenting this somewhat detailed summary of a Soviet discussion of family relationships should be obvious. "Power in the family" can be taken as a metaphor (hardly unintended, we must assume) for power relationships in the society at large. Claims to power are not necessarily rooted in the real social contribution of the particular individuals who monopolize "regulating" functions. The concentration of all such functions in a single center, the privileges associated with the exercise of control, the semimythical character of the "objective factors" invoked to defend such arrangements — all of these characteristics of Soviet power relationships and their legitimation emerge here in the model of the "autocratic" family. Perhaps when the explicit and serious study of the structure of power at a macrosocial level becomes possible in the Soviet Union, the imagery now used to describe changing family relationships will also be applicable in a broader context: "Authoritarian relationships are being replaced by egalitarian ones, relationships of subordination by relationships of equality."[43]

It is striking that one of the few serious attempts to conceptualize the issue of power, and to do so in the framework of a critical analysis, should have emerged as a by-product of Soviet discussions of sexual inequality.

Notes

1. G. Sergeeva, "The Labor of Women in the USSR," Planovoe khoziaistvo, 1975, no. 11, p. 104. The figures on Soviet female labor participation in this paragraph are drawn from V. Bezrukov and A. Anan'ev, "On the Long-term Interbranch Distribution of Labor Resources," Planovoe khoziaistvo, 1975, no. 11, pp. 46-47.

2. N. Shishkan, "The Participation of Women in Social Production," Ekonomicheskie nauki, 1975, no. 11, p. 32. Only Czechoslovakia had a participation rate (83%) comparable to that of the USSR. The Polish rate (63%) was unusually low for an East European country.

3. TsSU SSSR, Narodnoe khoziaistvo SSSR, 1922-1972, Moscow, 1972, p. 348; Vestnik statistiki, 1975, no. 1, p. 86; M. Fedorova, "The Utilization of Female Labor in Agriculture," Voprosy ekonomiki, 1975, no. 12, p. 55.

4. A. Ia. Kvasha, Problemy ekonomiko-demograficheskogo razvitiia SSSR, Moscow, 1974, p. 150. This source notes (p. 54) that the 50-ruble figure may be an underestimate.

5. I. P. Trufanov, Problemy byta, pp. 95-96. Some 11% of Soviet managers in a Leningrad study of machinery plants were married to "housewives," compared to 3-7% for other occupational groups. A study of coal-mining areas of the Ukraine in the late 1960s showed that the wives of highly paid miners were rarely employed outside the home. But this may have had as much to do with the absence of employment opportunities for women in such areas as with the high earnings of their husbands. See N. A. Sakharova, Optimal'nye vozmozhnosti ispol'zovaniia zhenskogo truda v sfere obshchestvennogo proizvodstva, Kiev, 1973, pp. 29-30.

6. Belorusskii ordena trudovogo krasnogo znameni, gosudarstvennyi universitet im. V. I. Lenina, Proizvodstvennaia deiatel'nost' zhenshchin i sem'ia, Minsk, 1972, p. 20.

7. M. Shishkan, p. 35.

8. This statement obviously does not apply to the Central Asian republics, where female labor participation is significantly lower than in European Russia.

9. TsSU, Itogi vsesoiuznoi perepisi naseleniia 1970 goda, Moscow, 1973, vol. VI, p. 7.

10. M. Shishkan, p. 35. N. V. Cherina, "Some Problems of Investigating the Occupational-Skill Advancement of Workers," Izvestiia sibirskogo otdeleniia Akademii nauk SSSR, Seriia obshchestvennykh nauk, 1974, no. 11, pp. 30-31; Proizvodstvennaia deiatel'nost' zhenshchin i sem'ia, pp. 41-42.

11. M. Ia. Sonin, "Labor Resources as a Factor in Accumulation under Conditions of Scientific-Technical Progress," in A. I. Notkin ed., Sotsialisticheskoe nakoplenie, Moscow, 1973, pp. 140-41.

12. Itogi, vol. VI, p. 167; Narodnoe khoziaistvo SSSR v 1973, p. 591.

13. Gail Warshofsky Lapidus, "USSR Women at Work: Changing Patterns," Industrial Relations, May 1975, p. 192.

14. V. G. Afanas'ev ed., Nauchnoe upravlenie obshchestvom, No. 7, Moscow, 1973, p. 239.

15. M. Ia. Sonin, p. 141. Sonin also adds: "But since the share of female labor in the sphere of primarily mental labor is much higher than in the sphere of manual labor, the average skill level of female labor in the economy as a whole according to approximate calculations is somewhat higher than of male

labor." This is difficult to accept given the very restricted access of women to highly skilled manual jobs.

16. Gail Warshofsky Lapidus, p. 193. This source cites female-to-male earnings ratios of 67.1%, 66.5%, and 73% for these three countries, respectively.

17. N. E. Rabkina and N. M. Rimashevskaia, Osnovy differentsiatsii zarabotnoi platy i dokhodov naseleniia, Moscow, 1972, p. 47; N. A. Sakharova, Optimal'nye, p. 31.

18. L. E. Suter and H. P. Miller, "Income Differences between Men and Career Women," in Joan Huber ed., Changing Women in a Changing Society (Chicago: The University of Chicago Press, 1973), pp. 200-1.

19. V. D. Patrushev, "Socioeconomic Problems of Free Time of the Rural Population," Sotsiologicheskie issledovaniia, 1974, no. 1, p. 92.

20. Ibid., p. 93.

21. Proizvodstvennaia deiatel'nost' zhenshchin i sem'ia, p. 139.

22. Census data on heads of families are not especially useful for our purpose since they exclude the possibility that a household will not have a single family head. Moreover, the relatively large proportion of families headed by women in the 1959 and 1970 census reports (27% and 23%, respectively) reflect chiefly households without adult males. Our interest is in the sex of the family head where both husband and wife are present in the household. See E. K. Vasil'eva, Sem'ia i ee funktsii, Moscow, 1975, pp. 76-77.

23. P. P. Litviakov ed., Demograficheskie problemy zaniatosti, Moscow, 1969, p. 106.

24. Narodnoe khoziaistvo SSSR v 1973 g., p. 44.

25. V. Perevedentsev, "How Many Children to Have," Literaturnaia gazeta, November 20, 1968.

26. K. Vermishchev, "What Is More Profitable for Society?" Literaturnaia gazeta, January 22, 1969.

27. G. Popov, "Paradoxes in Reconnoitering the Future," Literaturnaia gazeta, 1975, no. 22. A step in this direction has been taken in the draft of the five-year plan for 1976-80 which promises to introduce "partially paid" leaves from work for women with children up to one year old.

28. "Housekeeping, in the present state of everyday services, is a necessary link in the process of reproduction of labor power. . . .

"The restoration of the ability to work requires rest, normal nutrition, the satisfaction of many household needs. Labor in the household is necessary for society."

There can be little doubt as to who performs most such labor. The above quotation is from N. A. Sakharova, Optimal'nye, p. 43.

29. Z. A. Iankova, "The Development of the Personality of Women in Soviet Society," Sotsiologicheskie issledovaniia, 1975, no. 4, pp. 44-45; Proizvodstvennaia deiatel'nost' zhenshchin i sem'ia, p. 54.

30. Ibid., p. 51.

31. Z. A. Iankova, p. 44. For another illustration of this position, see E. V. Porokhniuk and M. S. Shepeleva, "On Combining Production and Family Functions by Women Workers," Sotsiologicheskie issledovaniia, 1975, no. 4, pp. 102-8.

32. This summary draws on the following: I. A. Badamian, "Urbanization and Problems of Reproduction of the Population," in Akademiia nauk SSSR, Urbanizatsiia i rabochii klass v usloviiakh nauchno-technicheskoi revoliutsii, Moscow, 1970, pp. 299-312; S. Berezovskaia, "A Windfall on the Way . . . Backward,"

Literaturnaia gazeta, January 22, 1969; V. S. Steshenko and V. P. Piskunov eds., Demograficheskaia politika, Moscow, 1974, pp. 23-27.

33. I. A. Badamian, p. 305.

34. S. Berezovskaia; the immediately preceding point is made by I. A. Badamian, p. 310.

35. The work of M. Sonin combines elements of both perspectives. Sonin rejects the advisability of encouraging women to leave the labor force for extended periods as a means of increasing the birth rate. The basis for his opposition is "the task of equalizing the skills of male and female labor...." However, he recognizes the need to "coordinate the natural-social maternal function of women with their participation in social production" by introducing more flexible work schedules and extending part-time work opportunities for women. See M. Sonin, "Changes in the Occupational-Skill Structure of Female Labor and the Family," a paper prepared for the Twelfth International Seminar on Research on the Family, Moscow, 1972, p. 6.

36. E. K. Vasil'eva, Sotsial'no-professional'nyi uroven', p. 36. Although in recent years women have made up about one-half of the student body at higher educational institutions, their share of graduating classes of secondary schools has consistently exceeded that of males.

37. E. K. Vasil'eva, Sem'ia i ee funktsii, pp. 124-25.

38. Proizvodstvennaia deiatel'nost' zhenshchin i sem'ia, p. 61.

39. V. I. Selivanov, "Primary Rural Collectives and Their Influence on the Formation of the Personality," in Sotsiologiia v SSSR, Moscow, 1965, vol. I, p. 462.

40. A. L. Pimenova, "The New Mode of Life and the Establishment of Equality within the Family," in Akademiia nauk SSSR, Sotsial'nye issledovaniia, No. 7, Moscow, 1971, p. 34.

41. Here Pimenova explicitly relied on a formulation appropriated from "bourgeois sociology" (the work of E. Bogardus) which could properly be applied by Soviet sociologists. Ibid., p. 35.

42. Ibid., pp. 36-37, 44-45.

43. Z. A. Iankova, "Changes in the Structure of Social Roles of Women in the Developed Socialist Society and the Model of the Family," a paper prepared for the Twelfth International Seminar on Research on the Family, Moscow, 1972, p. 12.

BIBLIOGRAPHY

Afanas'ev, V. G. Nauchnoe upravlenie obshchestvom. Moscow, 1968.
_____, ed. Nauchnoe upravlenie obshchestvom, No. 2. Moscow, 1968; No. 4.
Moscow, 1970; No. 6. Moscow, 1972; No. 7. Moscow, 1973.
_____ et al., eds. Problemy nauchnogo kommunizma, No. 9. Moscow, 1975.
Aitov, N. A. "Education and Life." Oktiabr', 7, 1966.
_____, ed. Nekotorye problemy sotsial'nykh peremeshchenii v SSSR. Ufa, 1971.
_____. "Social Aspects of Education in the USSR," in Akademiia nauk SSSR.
Sotsial'nye issledovaniia, No. 2. Moscow, 1968.
_____. "Social Mobility in the USSR," in Institut sotsiologicheskikh issledo-
vanii, Akademii nauk SSSR, Institut filosofii i sotsiologii Pol'skoi Akademii
nauk. Problemy razvitiia sotsial'noi struktury obshchestva v Sovetskom
soiuze i Pol'she. Moscow and Warsaw, 1974.
_____. Tekhnicheskii progress i dvizhenie rabochikh kadrov. Moscow, 1972.
Akademiia nauk Belrusskoi SSR. Struktura sovetskoi intelligentsii. Minsk, 1970.
Akademiia nauk SSSR. Nauchnye kadry Leningrada. Leningrad, 1973.
_____. Sem'ia kak ob"ekt filosofskogo i sotsiologicheskogo issledovaniia.
Leningrad, 1974.
_____. Sotsial'nye issledovaniia, No. 7. Moscow, 1971.
_____, Institut filosofii. Problemy izmeneniia sotsial'noi struktury sovetskogo
obshchestva. Moscow, 1968.
_____, Institut filosofii. Sotsialisticheskoe obshchestvo. Moscow, 1975.
_____, Institut istorii SSSR. Rabochii klass SSSR. Moscow, 1969.
_____, Institut mezhdunarodnogo rabochego dvizheniia. Urbanizatsiia i rabochii
klass v usloviiakh nauchno-tekhnicheskoi revoliutsii. Moscow, 1970.
Akademiia nauk Ukrainskoi SSR. Vliianie sotsial'no-ekonomicheskikh faktorov na
demograficheskie protsessy. Kiev, 1972.
Alekseev, N. I. "The Interaction of Social Factors in Determining the Attitude
toward Work." Sotsiologicheskie issledovaniia, 3, 1975.
_____, Kravchenko, I. I., and Plimak, E. G. "The Myth of 'Statism' and So-
cialism without Myths." Voprosy filosofii, 5, 1971.
Antonova, G. I. "Social Aspects of the Creation of Specialized Schools," in
Molodezh', obrazovanie i nauchno-tekhnicheskii progress. Novosibirsk, 1971.
_____. "Social Mobility of Secondary School Graduates (from Materials of
Novosibirsk Region)," in Tartuskii gosudarstvennyi universitet. Materialy
konferentsii 'kommunisticheskoe vospitanie studenchestva.' Tartu, 1971.
Arutiunian, Iu. V. Opyt sotsiologicheskogo izucheniia sela. Moscow, 1968.
_____. "The Results of a Socioethnic Investigation." Sovetskaia etnografiia,
4, 1968.

Social and Economic Inequality

_____. "Social Structure of the Rural Population." Voprosy filosofii, 5, 1966.
_____. Sotsial'naia struktura sel'skogo naseleniia SSSR. Moscow, 1971.
_____, ed. Sotsial'noe i natsional'noe. Moscow, 1973.
Aunapu, F. F. Chto takoe upravlenie. Moscow, 1967.
Barber, Bernard. Social Stratification. New York: Harcourt, Brace and World, Inc., 1957.
Belorusskii ordena trudovogo krasnogo znameni, gosudarstvennyi universitet im. V. I. Lenina. Proizvodstvennaia deiatel'nost' zhenshchin i sem'ia. Minsk, 1972.
Berezovskaia, S. "Windfall on the Way... Backward." Literaturnaia gazeta, January 22, 1969.
Bertaux, Daniel. "Two and a Half Models of Social Structure," in Walter Muller and Karl Ulrich Mayer, eds. Social Stratification and Career Mobility. Paris and the Hague: Mouton, 1974.
Bezrukov, V. and Anan'ev, A. "On the Long-Term Interbranch Distribution of Labor Resources." Planovoe khoziaistvo, 11, 1975.
Bliakhman, L. S. "Production Interests of Youth," in Obshchestvo i molodezh'. Moscow, 1973.
_____ and Shkaratan, O. I. NTR, rabochii klass, intelligentsia. Moscow, 1973.
Carey, David W. "Developments in Soviet Education," in Soviet Economic Prospects for the Seventies. Joint Economic Committee, Congress of the United States, U. S. Government Printing Office. Washington, 1973.
Changli, I. Trud. Moscow, 1973.
Cherina, N. V. "Some Problems of Investigating the Occupational-Skill Advancement of Workers." Izvestiia sibirskogo otdeleniia Akademii nauk SSSR, Seriia obshchestvennykh nauk, 11, 1974.
Chulanov, Iu. G. Izmeneniia v sostave i v urovne tvorcheskoi aktivnosti rabochego klassa SSSR, 1959-1970. Leningrad, 1974.
"Education and the Personality" (editorial). Narodnoe obrazovanie, 8, 1967.
El'meev, V. Ia. Problemy sotsial'nogo planirovaniia. Leningrad, 1973.
_____, Polozov, V. R., and Riashchenko, B. R. Kommunizm i preodelenie razdeleniia mezhdu umstvennym i fizicheskim trudom. Leningrad, 1965.
Ermuratskii, V. N. Sotsial'naia aktivnost' rabotnikov promyshlennogo predpriiatiia. Kishinev, 1973.
Fainburg, Z. "The Current Stage of the Scientific-Technical Revolution and Social Planning," in Nauchno-tekhnicheskaia revoliutsiia i sotsial'nyi progress. Moscow, 1972.
Fedorova, M. "The Utilization of Female Labor in Agriculture." Voprosy ekonomiki, 12, 1975.
Filippov, F. R. "Changes in the Social Profile and Composition of the Soviet Intelligentsia," in Institut sotsiologicheskikh issledovanii Akademii nauk SSSR, Institut filosofii i sotsiologii Pol'skoi Akademii nauk. Problemy razvitiia sotsial'noi struktury obshchestva v Sovetskom soiuze i Pol'she. Moscow and Warsaw, 1974.
_____. "Sociological Problems of Education in the USSR." Sotsiologicheskie issledovaniia, 2, 1974.
Fomin, V. A., ed. Nekotory voprosy nauchnogo upravleniia obshchestvom. Moscow, 1967.
Glezerman, G. E. Istoricheskii materializm i razvitie sotsialisticheskogo obshchestva. 2nd ed. Moscow, 1973.
Gordon, L. et al. "Developed Socialism: The Well-being of Workers." Rabochii klass i sovremennyi mir, 3, 1974.

Gordon, L. A. and Klopov, E. V. Chelovek posle raboty. Moscow, 1972.
_____. "The Social Development of the Working Class of the USSR." Voprosy filosofii, 2, 1972.
Gur'ianov, S. T. and Sekretariuk, V. V. Prizvanie i professiia. Moscow, 1974.
Gurova, R. G., ed. Sotsiologicheskie problemy obrazovaniia i vospitaniia. Moscow, 1973.
Huber, Joan, ed. Changing Women in a Changing Society. Chicago: The University of Chicago Press, 1973.
Iadov, V. A. "Orientation − Creative Work," in G. M. Gusev et al., eds. Obshchestvo i molodezh'. Moscow, 1968.
Iagodkin, V. N., ed. Ekonomicheskie problemy podgotovki kvalifitsirovannykh rabochikh kadrov v sovremennykh usloviiakh. Moscow, 1967.
Iankova, Z. A. "Changes in the Structure of Social Roles of Women in the Developed Socialist Society and the Model of the Family." A paper prepared for the Twelfth International Seminar on Research on the Family, Moscow, 1972.
_____. "The Development of the Personality of Women in Soviet Society." Sotsiologicheskie issledovaniia, 4, 1975.
Institut sotsiologicheskikh issledovanii AN SSSR. Problemy effektivnogo ispol'-zovaniia rabochikh kadrov na promyshlennom predpriiatii. Moscow, 1973.
Ivanov, S. A. Trudovoe pravo i nauchno-tekhnicheskii progress. Moscow, 1974.
Kaidalov, D. P. and Suimenko, E. I. Aktual'nye problemy sotsiologii truda. Moscow, 1974.
Kamenitser, S. et al. Organizatsiia i planirovanie promyshlennykh predpriiatii. Moscow, 1967.
Kartofianu, M. D. "The Influence of Social Differences on the Everyday Life of the Rural Population," in Akademiia nauk Moldavskoi SSSR. Problemy izmeneniia sotsial'noi struktury sovetskogo obshchestva. Kishinev, 1971.
_____. Novyi byt Moldavskogo sela. Kishinev, 1973.
Kobetskii, V. D., ed. Obshchestvo i molodezh'. Moscow, 1973.
Kochetov, G. M. "Occupational Inclinations and Job Placement of Secondary School Graduates." Shkola i proizvodstvo, 7, 1968.
Kogan, L. "Necessity or Luxury." Ural, 6, 1968.
Kokashinskii, V. "The Experiment at Akchi." Literaturnaia gazeta, May 21, 1969.
_____. "The Power of Collectivism." Molodoi kommunist, 2, 1970.
Komarov, V. E. Ekonomicheskie problemy podgotovki i ispol'zovaniia kadrov spetsialistov. Moscow, 1972.
Korchagin, V. P. and Kosiachenko, S. G. Sotsial'no-kulturnaia programma piatiletki. Moscow, 1971.
Kosolapov, R. I. Sotsializm. Moscow, 1975.
Krasnov, N. F. "A Worthy Addition to the Higher School." Vestnik vysshei shkoly, 4, 1969.
Kugel', S. A. Novoe v izuchenii sotsial'noi struktury obshchestva. Leningrad, 1968.
_____ and Nikandrov, O. M. Molodye inzhenery. Moscow, 1971.
_____ and Shkaratan, O. I. "Some Methodological Problems of Studying the Social Structure of Society." Nauchnye doklady vysshei shkoly, filosofskie nauki, 1, 1965.
Kunel'skii, L. E. Sotsial'no-ekonomicheskie problemy zarabotnoi platy. Moscow, 1972.

_____. Zarplata, dokhody, stimulirovanie. Moscow, 1968.

Kuz'min, E. S. and Bodalev, A. A. Sotsial'naia psikhologiia i sotsial'noe plani-rovanie. Leningrad, 1973.

Kuzminov, I. I., Dunaev, V. S., and Tsakynov, V. V., eds. Ekonomicheskii zakon raspredeleniia po trudu. Moscow, 1975.

Kvasha, A. Ia. Problemy ekonomiko-demograficheskogo razvitiia SSSR. Mos-cow, 1974.

Lapidus, Gail Warshofsky. "USSR Women at Work: Changing Patterns." Indus-trial Relations, May 1975.

Lebedeva, N. B. et al. Partiinaia organizatsiia i rabochie Leningrada. Lenin-grad, 1974.

Lenin, V. I. Selected Works, Vol. VII. New York: International Publishers, 1943.

_____. The State and Revolution. Peking: Foreign Languages Press, 1973.

Leningradskii ordena Lenina i ordena trudovogo krasnogo znameni gosudarst-vennyi universitet imeni A. A. Zhdanova. Khozraschet v sovremennykh usloviiakh upravleniia promyshlennost'iu. Leningrad, 1972.

Levin, B. M. Sotsial'no-ekonomicheskie potrebnosti: zakonomernosti formi-rovaniia i razvitiia. Moscow, 1974.

Liapin, A. Trud pri sotsializme. Moscow, 1951.

Lipset, S. M. and Bendix, R. Social Mobility in Industrial Society. Berkeley and Los Angeles: University of California Press, 1962.

Lisovskii, V. T., ed. Molodezh' i obrazovanie. Moscow, 1972.

Liss, L. F. "On the Stability of Characteristics and Specific Features of the Social Origins of University Applicants," in Institut istorii, filologii i filosofii SO AN SSSR. Sotsial'noe prognozirovanie v oblasti obrazovaniia. Novosi-birsk, 1969.

_____. "The Social Conditioning of Occupational Choice," in Tartuskii gosu-darstvennyi universitet, Materialy konferentsii 'kommunisticheskoe vospi-tanie studenchestva.' Tartu, 1971.

Litviakov, P. P., ed. Demograficheskie problemy zaniatosti. Moscow, 1969.

Loz, G. M. Upravlenie v sovkhozakh i kolkhozakh. Moscow, 1972.

Lukin, V. M. "On the Cultural Aspect of the Formation of a Socially Homoge-neous Society," in Uchenye zapiski obshchestvennykh nauk vuzov Leningrada. Problemy nauchnogo kommunizma, Issue VI. Leningrad, 1972.

Margolin, L. "The Social Composition of Students in Secondary Specialized Institutions and Their Career Plans," in Ministerstvo prosveshcheniia RSFSR. Voprosy sotsial'noi i professional'noi orientatsii molodezhi. Sverdlovsk, 1972.

"Medical School in the USSR." Soviet Education, May-June 1975.

Medvedev, Roy A. On Socialist Democracy. New York: Alfred A. Knopf, 1975.

Miller, S. M. "Comparative Social Mobility." Current Sociology, 1, IX, 1960.

Minkina, K. N. et al. "The Social Characteristics of First-Year University Students," in Gor'kovskii gosudarstvennyi universitet im. N. I. Loba-chevskogo. Sotsiologiia i vysshaia shkola, Uchenye zapiski, Issue 100. Gorki, 1970.

Murniek, E. A. "Intraclass Differentiation of the Collective Farm Peasantry," in Akademiia obshchestvennykh nauk pri TsK KPSS. Problemy nauchnogo kommunizma, No. 6. Moscow, 1972.

Nechaeva, L. and Yanov, A. "Help the Strong." Molodoi kommunist, 2, 1970.

Notkin, A. I., ed. Sotsialisticheskoe nakoplenie. Moscow, 1973.

Novoselev, N. "The Path of Our Schools." Oktiabr', 7, 1967.

Oligin-Nesterov, V. I. Ispol'zovanie ekonomicheskikh zakonov sotsializma i upravlenie proizvodstvom. Moscow, 1973.

Osipov, G. V., ed. Sotsiologiia v SSSR, Vol. I. Moscow, 1965.

Ossowski, Stanislaw. Class Structure in the Social Consciousness. London: Routledge and Kegan Paul, 1967.

Parkin, Frank. Class Inequality and Political Order. New York: Praeger Publishers, 1971.

Paskhaver, B. L. Rentnye problemy v SSSR. Kiev, 1972.

Patrushev, V. D. "Socioeconomic Problems of Free Time of the Rural Population." Sotsiologicheskie issledovaniia, 1, 1974.

Perevedentsev, V. "How Many Children to Have." Literaturnaia gazeta, November 20, 1968.

Petrov, Iu. P. and Filippov, F. R. "The Formation of the Young Replacements of the Soviet Working Class." Nauchnye doklady vysshei shkoly, filosofskie nauki, 6, 1972.

Podmarkov, V. G. Vvedenie v promyshlennuiu sotsiologiiu. Moscow, 1973.

Popov, G. "Paradoxes in Reconnoitering the Future." Literaturnaia gazeta, 22, 1975.

Popov, G. Kh. and Dzhavadov, G. A. Upravlenie i problema kadrov. Moscow, 1972.

Porokhniuk, E. V. and Shepeleva, M. S. "On Combining Production and Family Functions by Women Workers." Sotsiologicheskie issledovaniia, 4, 1975.

Prokof'ev, M. A. "On the Condition of General Secondary Education in the USSR and Measures for Its Further Improvement." Narodnoe obrazovanie, 10, 1973.

Pugh, D. S., ed. Organization Theory. Baltimore: Penguin Books, 1971.

Rabkina, N. E. and Rimashevskaia, N. M. Osnovy differentsiatsii zarabotnoi platy i dokhodov naseleniia. Moscow, 1972.

Rubin, B. and Kolesnikov, Iu. Student glazami sotsiologa. Rostov, 1968.

Rudich, F. M. O sochetanii gosudarstvennykh i obshchestvennykh nachal v upravlenii proizvodstom. Kiev, 1968.

Rutkevich, M. N. "Competitive Selection." Izvestia, December 10, 1967.

_____. "The Concept of the Intelligentsia as a Social Stratum in Socialist Society." Nauchnye doklady vysshei shkoly, filosofskie nauki, 4, 1966.

_____, ed. Izmenenie sotsial'noi struktury sotsialisticheskogo obshchestva. Sverdlovsk, 1965.

_____. "Processes of Social Shifting and the Concept of 'Social Mobility.'" Nauchnye doklady vysshei shkoly, filosofskie nauki, 5, 1970.

_____, ed. Protsessy izmeneniia sotsial'noi struktury v sovetskom obshchestva. Sverdlovsk, 1967.

_____. "Social Sources of Replenishing the Soviet Intelligentsia." Voprosy filosofii, 6, 1967.

_____. "The Social Structure of a Developed Socialist Society." Kommunist, 2, 1974.

_____, ed. Sotsial'nye razlichiia i ikh preodolenie. Sverdlovsk, 1969.

_____. "Trends in Changes in the Social Structure of Soviet Society." Sotsiologicheskie issledovaniia, 1, 1975.

_____, ed. Zhiznennye plany molodezhi. Sverdlovsk, 1966.

_____ and Filippov, F. R. Sotsial'nye peremeshcheniia. Moscow, 1970.

_____ and Sennikova, L. "The Social Conditioning of Motives for Entering a

Higher Educational Institution and the Choice of a Future Occupation," in Motivatsiia zhiznedeiatel'nosti studenta. Kaunas, 1971.

Sakharova, N. A. Optimal'nye vozmozhnosti ispol'zovaniia zhenskogo truda v sfere obshchestvennogo proizvodstva. Kiev, 1973.

Sapil'nikov, E. N. "The Social Structure of the Rural Population and the Path of Its Development." Voprosy filosofii, 11, 1971.

Sarkisian, G. S. Dokhody trudiashchikhsia i sotsial'nye problemy urovnia zhizni naseleniia SSSR. Moscow, 1973.

_____. Uroven', tempy i proportsii rosta real'nykh dokhodov pri sotsializma. Moscow, 1972.

Sazonov, N. I., ed. Kritika antimarksistskikh vzgliadov po voprosam sotsial'no-politicheskogo razvitiia sovetskogo obshchestva. Kharkov, 1972.

Seniavskii, S. L. Izmeneniia v sotsial'noi strukture sovetskogo obshchestva. Moscow, 1973.

_____ and Tel'pukhovskii, V. B. Rabochii klass SSSR. Moscow, 1971.

Sergeeva, G. "The Labor of Women in the USSR." Planovoe khoziaistvo, 11, 1975.

Sharutin, S. V. "Some Problems of Improving the Organization of Wages of Engineering-Technical Personnel," in Uchenye zapiski kafedr obshchestvennykh nauk vuzov Leningrada, politicheskaia ekonomiia, Issue XIV. Raspredelitel'nye otnosheniia sotsializma i ikh ravitie na sovremennom etape. Leningrad, 1973.

Shishkan, N. "The Participation of Women in Social Production." Ekonomicheskie nauki, 11, 1975.

Shkaratan, O. I. "The Ethnosocial Structure of the Urban Population of the Tatar ASSR." Sovetskaia etnografiia, 3, 1970.

_____. "Problems of Social Structure of the Soviet City." Nauchnye doklady vysshei shkoly, filosofskie nauki, 5, 1970.

_____. Problemy sotsial'noi struktury rabochego klassa SSSR. Moscow, 1970.

_____. "The Social Structure of the Soviet Working Class." Voprosy filosofii, 1, 1967.

_____. "The Working Class of Socialist Society in the Epoch of the Scientific-Technical Revolution." Voprosy filosofii, 11, 1968.

_____ and Rukavishnikov, V. I. "The Social Structure of the Population of the Soviet City and Trends in Its Development (Theoretical Propositions)." Sotsiologicheskie issledovaniia, 2, 1974.

Shkurko, S. "New Conditions of Payment of Labor." Voprosy ekonomiki, 10, 1975.

Shubkin, V. N. "On Some Social-Economic Problems of Youth," in Novosibirskii gosudarstvennyi universitet. Nauchnye trudy, seriia ekonomicheskaia, Issue 6. Novosibirsk, 1965.

_____. "The Utilization of Quantitative Methods in the Empirical Sociological Study of Problems of Job Placement and Occupational Choice," in A. G. Aganbegian, ed. Kolichestvennye metody v sotsiologicheskikh issledovaniiakh. Novosibirsk, 1964.

Solov'ev, A. P. Pravila vybora professii. Leningrad, 1975.

Sonin, M. "Changes in the Occupational-Skill Structure of Female Labor and the Family." A paper prepared for the Twelfth International Seminar on Research on the Family, Moscow, 1972.

Steshenko, V. S. and Piskunov, V. P., eds. Demograficheskaia politika. Moscow, 1974.

Sulimov, E. F., ed. XXIV s"ezda KPSS i problemy nauchnogo kommunizma. Moscow, 1973.

Suvorov, G. B. "The Problem of Studying the Structure of Management of the Production Collective," in Chelovek i obshchestvo, Issue 8. Leningrad, 1971.

Tartuskii gosudarstvennyi universitet. Sotsial'no-professional'naia orientatsiia molodezhi. Tartu, 1973.

Thernstrom, Stephan. The Other Bostonians. Cambridge: Harvard University Press, 1973.

Tikhonov, N. M. Neobkhodimyi produkt v usloviiakh razvitogo sotsializma. Leningrad, 1974.

Trufanov, I. P. Problemy byta gorodskogo naseleniia SSSR. Leningrad, 1973.

Tsentral'noe statisticheskoe upravlenie pri Sovete Ministrov SSSR. Itogi vse-soiuznoi perepisi naseleniia 1970 goda, Vol. VI. Moscow, 1973.

_____. Narodnoe khoziaistvo SSSR v 1973 g.. Moscow, 1974.

_____. Trud v SSSR. Moscow, 1968.

_____. Zhenshchiny v SSSR. Moscow, 1975.

Tsentral'noe statisticheskoe upravlenie SSSR. Narodnoe khoziaistvo SSSR, 1922-1972. Moscow, 1972.

Tsentral'noe upravlenie narodnokhoziaistvennogo ucheta gosplana SSSR. Trud v SSSR. Moscow, 1936.

Turchenko, V. N. Nauchno-tekhnicheskaia revoliutsiia i revoliutsiia v obrazo-vanii. Moscow, 1973.

Ural'skii politeknicheskii institut im. S. M. Kirova. Sotsializm i ravenstvo. Sverdlovsk, 1970.

Valentei, D. I., ed. Obrazovatel'naia i sotsial'no-professional'naia struktura na-seleniia SSSR. Moscow, 1975.

Vasil'eva, E. K. Sem'ia i ee funktsii. Moscow, 1975.

_____. Sotsial'no-professional'nyi uroven' gorodskoi molodezhi. Leningrad, 1973.

Vermishchev, K. "What is More Profitable for Society." Literaturnaia gazeta, January 22, 1969.

Vialias, V. "Estonian Schools on a New Upswing." Narodnoe obrazovanie, 3, 1975.

Vladimirov, S. V. "Attitudes toward an Occupation, Depending on the Motives for Its Selection," in Permskii gosudarstvennyi universitet. Trud i lichnost' pri sotsializme, Issue II, Uchenye zapiski, No. 295. Perm, 1973.

Vladimirov, V. I. "Problems and Prospects of Socioeconomic Development of the Countryside." Sotsiologicheskie issledovaniia, 1, 1974.

Vodzinskaia, V. V. "On the Question of the Social Conditioning of Occupational Choice," in Chelovek i obshchestvo, Issue 2. Leningrad, 1967.

_____. "Orientation to Occupations," in V. A. Iadov, ed. Molodezh' i trud. Moscow, 1970.

Volkov, Iu. E., ed. Sotsiologicheskie problemy upravleniia narodnym khoziaist-vom, Sverdlovsk, 1968.

_____. Tak rozhdaetsia kommunisticheskoe samoupravlenie. Moscow, 1965.

Volovik, L. A., ed. Sotsiologiia i ideologiia. Moscow, 1969.

Yanov, A. "The Cinema and the Scientific-Technical Revolution." Iskusstvo kino, 11, 1972.

_____. "What Will the Sociologist Put on the Table." Molodoi kommunist, 2, 1972.

Yanowitch, M. "The Soviet Income Revolution." Slavic Review, December 1963.

_____ and Dodge, N. T. "Social Class and Education: Soviet Findings and Reactions." Comparative Education Review, October 1968.

_____ and Dodge, N. T. "The Social Evaluation of Occupations in the Soviet Union." Slavic Review, December 1969.

_____ and Fisher, W. Social Stratification and Mobility in the USSR. White Plains, N. Y.: International Arts and Sciences Press, 1973.

Zarikhta, T. R. and Nazimov, I. N. Ratsional'noe ispol'zovanie resursov molodezhi. Moscow, 1970.

Zaslavskaia, T. I., ed. Doklady vsesoiuznomu simpoziumu po sotsiologicheskim problemam sela. Novosibirsk, 1968.

_____ and Kalmyk, V. A., eds. Sotsial'no-ekonomicheskoe razvitie sela i migratsiia naseleniia. Novosibirsk, 1972.

_____ and Ryvkina, R. V. Metodologicheskie problemy sotsiologicheskogo issledovaniia mobil'nosti trudovykh resursov. Novosibirsk, 1974.

Zelepukin, A. V. "Formation and Social Functions of the Soviet Intelligentsia," in I. N. Chikhichina, ed. Sotsial'no-klassovaia struktura i politicheskaia organizatsiia sotsialisticheskogo obshchestva. Saratov, 1971.

Zhdanova, A. A. Sotsial'nye problemy novykh gorodov vostochnoi Sibiri. Irkutsk, 1971.

Zhuravleva, G. A. and Sikevich, Z. V. "Social Conditioning of the Preparedness of VUZ Applicants," in Chelovek i obshchestvo, Issue VI. Leningrad, 1969.

INDEX

Index

ABOUT THE AUTHOR

Murray Yanowitch is currently Professor of Economics at Hofstra University. Educated at Columbia University, he has published numerous articles on Soviet affairs and is the co-editor of the journals Problems of Economics and International Journal of Sociology. With Bertram Silverman he co-edited The Worker in "Postindustrial" Capitalism, and with Wesley A. Fisher, Social Stratification and Mobility in the USSR.